Also By the Same Author

Study Guides

Gītā Subodhinī

Īśopanishad Subodhin

Upadeśāmrta Subodhin

Bhakti Rasāmṛta Subodhinī

Caitanya Subodhinī (4 volumes)

Bhāgavata Subodhinī (10 volumes)

The Art of Studying & Teaching Scriptures

Self-Enrichment

Dhruva

From Chaos to Calm

Secrets of Bhakti

Caitanya Pravāha

Bhāgavata Pravāha

Answers to Life's Questions

Disapproved but Not Disowned

Illustrated Children's Books

Mindful Me!

Bhāgavatam Tales (6 volumes)

Gita Wisdom Tales (5 volumes)

Verse Books (Pocket Size)

Gītā Ratnamālā

Gītā Tattvamālā

Caitanya Ratnamālā

Bhāgavata Tattvamālā

Bhāgavata Ratnamālā (2 volumes)

REVELATIONS FROM THE BHAGAVAD GITA

50 VERSES ✺ 100 STORIES

GAURANGA DARSHAN DAS

Om SHAKTI
An Imprint of Om Books International

Reprinted in 2026

Om
SHAKTI An Imprint of Om Books International

Corporate & Editorial Office
A-12, Sector 64, Noida 201 301
Uttar Pradesh, India
Phone: +91 120 477 4100
Email: editorial@ombooks.com
Website: www.ombooksinternational.com

Sales Office
107, Ansari Road, Darya Ganj,
New Delhi 110 002, India
Phone: +91 11 4000 9000
Email: sales@ombooks.com
Website: www.ombooks.com

ISBN: 978-93-6395-367-3

Printed in India

10 9 8 7 6 5 4 3 2

REVELATIONS FROM THE

BHAGAVAD GITA

Gauranga Darshan Das, a disciple of His Holiness Radhanath Swami, is a distinguished educator, prolific speaker, and spiritual author of over forty books. He holds a master's in Systems Science and Automation from the prestigious Indian Institute of Science (IISc), Bangalore, India. His contributions have been recognized with accolades such as the "Visionary Leader: Spirituality" award from Brand Vision Inc. and the "Spiritual Scientist" award from Andhra University.

Before embracing monkhood in 2009, Gauranga Darshan Das had a brief yet impactful corporate career spanning about two years. During this time, he conducted research in esteemed organizations like TCS Innovation Labs, authored over ten technical papers, and filed a provisional patent for his research.

Currently, he serves as the Dean of Bhaktivedanta Vidyapitha at ISKCON Govardhan Ecovillage (GEV), where he leads spiritual education programs both online and in residential settings. Known for his ability to present timeless wisdom in a clear and contemporary manner, he connects with diverse audiences, including children, teens, professionals, and educators. His teaching and speaking engagements have taken him across India, Australia, the United States, the United Kingdom, New Zealand, Singapore and other countries, where he has addressed forums in spiritual organizations, schools, colleges, the corporate sector and platforms like TEDx, ISRO,

DRDO, Hindustan Times and so on. To date, he has lectured for over 8,000 hours and conducted more than fifty online courses (available at www.vidyapitha.in).

As an accomplished author, Gauranga Darshan Das has written over forty books. His works include study guides (such as the *Subodhini* series), storybooks, self-enrichment titles (*From Chaos to Calm*, *Dhruva*, *Disapproved but Not Disowned*, and more), and children's literature (*Mindful Me!*, *Bhagavatam Tales*, and *Gita Wisdom Tales* series). He also runs a monthly e-zine, *Bhagavata Pradipika*, and contributes thought-provoking articles to magazines in both India and internationally.

His dedication to sharing spiritual wisdom has made him a highly respected figure in spiritual, educational, and corporate circles. Learn more about his inspiring work at www.gaurangadarshan.com.

Contents

Author's Note

Among all the scriptures, the Bhagavad Gita holds a special significance. While most of the scriptures in the Vedic library are written by wise sages, the Bhagavad Gita is directly spoken by Lord Sri Krishna.

Even the situation in which the Gita was spoken was quite unique. While all the scriptures were written by sages in their peaceful hermitages in solitary forests after deep contemplation and meditation, Lord Krishna voiced the Gita in an emergency situation just before a fierce war, to motivate a despondent warrior.

On the battlefield of Kurukshetra, Arjuna felt overwhelmed with emotions and became confused in preforming his duty as a warrior. Seeing his dear friend immersed in deep confusion, Krishna tried motivating him. To clear the confusions in Arjuna's mind, Lord Krishna voiced the Bhagavad Gita.

Many times, we also get confused in our lives while performing our duties. This is where the Gita takes us on a journey from confusion to clarity.

Although the Gita was narrated in the context of war, there is little discussion about war in the Gita. Then what does the Gita contain? The Gita presents amazing truths of this world and deep practical wisdom to lead a meaningful life. Through Arjuna, Lord Krishna passed on His divine teachings to humankind. So let us read the beautiful Bhagavad Gita, God's message to all of us.

The Gita is not a storybook. While sharing the Bhagavad Gita with various audiences, I found that explaining the profound concepts of the Gita with suitable stories makes the philosophy more accessible. Whether it a virtue or a concept or a process presented by Krishna in the verses, explaining it with fitting stories makes it more relatable, digestible and actionable. I have therefore attempted to combine the Gita's verses with beautiful stories in this book.

This book is divided, into five sections—Karma (Action), Jnana (Knowledge), Dhyana (meditation), Bhakti (devotion) and Sadguna (virtues)—each presenting ten key verses from the Gita, each verse explained with two stories.

The intriguing anecdotes and examples in this book enrich its flavour and open up a totally new dimension of the Gita for all! These stories have been carefully selected from various scriptures, including the Srimad Bhagavatam, the Ramayana, the Mahabharata, the Puranas, biographies of great people, and even some traditional folklore. These stories are meant to drive away the 'abstractness' from love and showcase love's practical nature.

SECTION I: KARMA–ACTION

Everyone works, but how many know how to work smartly? How can we work in a way that prevents negative consequences? What kinds of work provide lasting benefits? How can we make our work fulfilling for ourselves, beneficial to others, and pleasing to God?

In the Bhagavad Gita, Lord Krishna imparts the wisdom of smart work, known as karma-yoga. This section delves into the art of working without incurring adverse reactions, focusing on how to elevate our quality of life both materially and spiritually. Through karma-yoga, we learn to perform our duties with intelligence and devotion, ensuring that our efforts lead to positive outcomes and personal growth.

1

Freedom in Regulation

Our bodies and minds require rest and moderation to function optimally.

Is constant work without rest the key to success in your professional or academic pursuits? Not necessarily! Maintaining a balanced approach to life is essential for overall well-being. While it might seem tempting to work incessantly or indulge in activities without breaks, it's not sustainable in the long run.

Lord Krishna eloquently conveys this idea through the following verse in the Bhagavad Gita.

yuktāhāra-vihārasya
yukta-ceṣṭasya karmasu
yukta-svapnāvabodhasya
yogo bhavati duḥkha-hā

"One who is regulated in one's habits of eating, recreation, working, and sleeping need not experience unnecessary suffering." (6.17)

Thus, whether it's work, eating, recreation, or any other activity, moderation and self-awareness are essential for a fulfilling and sustainable lifestyle. Taking breaks during work allows rest and rejuvenation, leading to improved focus and efficiency when returning to tasks. Structuring time for meals ensures mindful eating and proper digestion.

Passionate work without rest can lead to burnout, decreased productivity, and negative impacts on physical and mental health. Similarly, irregular eating habits can disrupt digestion and can result in health issues like obesity or digestive disorders. Excessive unrestricted entertainment and gaming can result in eye strain, addiction, and decreased social interaction. Striking a balance tailored to individual needs and priorities is critical for maintaining overall well-being.

Additionally, the ultimate aim of human life is self-realization. So, while doing the needful in one's material pursuits, one must strive to save time for spiritual activities, and thus live a regulated and balanced life. Irregulated habits bind us to their bad consequences, while regulated habits of working, eating, sleeping and recreation give us freedom from such bondage.

The following stories further illuminate the principle of regulating habits, emphasizing the importance of controlling the mind and steering clear of distractions.

Habits Die Hard

In a lavish home, a wealthy man grew increasingly worried as he observed his young son entangled in a web of harmful habits. The boy indulged in junk food at odd hours, stayed up late, used foul language, engaged in negative behaviour with friends, and even dabbled in intoxication. The father realized that their luxurious lifestyle was contributing to these issues, and he was deeply concerned about his son's future. Desperate for help, he turned to a wise sage for guidance.

"Please help me," the father implored. "I fear for my son's future. I want him to become a disciplined, well-educated gentleman." The sage, moved by the father's plea, replied, "Bring your boy to me, and I will speak to him." When the boy arrived, knowing why he was there, he respectfully bowed to the sage. The sage then invited the boy for a walk in the garden, signalling the start of a transformative lesson. As they strolled in silence, the sage suddenly stopped and pointed to a small sapling. "Can you pull out that tender sapling?" he asked. The boy easily uprooted it, and they continued walking. The sage then pointed to progressively larger plants, each time asking the boy to uproot them. The boy managed to pull out each plant, showing his growing strength.

Eventually, they reached a thick bush. The boy struggled but finally managed to uproot it, albeit in several pieces. Then the sage pointed to a massive tree. "Can you uproot this one?" The boy tried but quickly realized it was impossible. He shook his head, admitting defeat. The sage then imparted his wisdom. "Bad habits are like these plants," he explained. "When they are new, like the small saplings, they are easy to remove. But as they grow, they become harder and harder to uproot. If you let them take root for too long, they can consume and ruin your life." He continued, "Understand your father's concern. Avoid bad habits and seek the company of good friends. Stay away from toxic influences."

The boy, moved by the sage's guidance, realized the truth of his words. This moment marked a turning point in his life. The boy's character began to transform with the sage's wisdom and his father's love. From that day on, he made a conscious effort to break free from his harmful habits and surround himself with positive influences.

This story of the boy's transformation serves as a timeless reminder of the importance of addressing bad habits early and the powerful impact of wise guidance and supportive relationships.

We can easily get rid of bad habits, if we detect and address them in their early stages.

Overcoming Distractions

Once a student and his teacher were walking together. The student had a question that had been troubling him for a long time, and he finally gathered the courage to ask. Of late, the student was distracted by everything that he saw, heard, smelt, ate or touched. He was too disturbed by his senses and his mind was restless. He couldn't focus on what the teacher taught him.

He asked his teacher, "What can we do to calm the mind? Most people's minds are restless, and only a few have a calm mind." The teacher smiled and narrated a short story to his restless student. Once a mighty elephant was eating bananas. Suddenly, a small fly came by and started buzzing near the elephant's ear. The elephant drove the fly away with its wide ears. But, after some time, the fly returned. The elephant drove it away once again. But the fly repeatedly came back and buzzed around the elephant's ears. Troubled, the elephant asked the fly, "Why are you so restless and noisy? Why can't you remain calm even for a short while?" The fly was a little surprised at the question and replied, "Somehow, I am attracted to everything that I see, hear or smell. My senses keep pulling me in different directions. I am curious to explore everything that is happening around me. I cannot resist the urge to keep moving from place to place. Dear elephant, what is your secret? How can you remain so calm and composed, at one place?"

The elephant stopped eating and replied, "I can control my mind and body. I can use them the way I want. I focus on whatever work I do. Now that I am eating, my whole attention is focused on this activity. I am enjoying my food and chewing it mindfully. Similarly, when I carry the Lord's deities on my back, I focus on that service. Many dogs bark at me while I walk on the road, but I don't let them distract me. I just focus on my work. Thus, I stay calm, composed, and peaceful."

On hearing the story of the fly and the elephant, the boy's eyes opened wide, and a smile spread across his face. He said, "I have understood that we shouldn't be like the restless fly, otherwise we will never find calm and peace. We must be like the mighty elephant instead, completely focused on the task at hand. I know that my senses will keep distracting me, but I must control my mind and thoughts to regulate my actions. Please bless me, so I may practise this principle."

The guru, pleased with his disciple's new-found insight, blessed him warmly, initiating a journey of gradual transformation within him.

We need to regulate our mind, body, and habits and focus on our goals to achieve success in life.

These stories underscore the importance of cultivating balanced habits in eating, sleeping, recreation, and work. By embracing such regulations, we free ourselves from the discomfort and challenges that arise from irregular routines and unbalanced lifestyles. Practising self-control encourages positive changes and helps us avoid harmful patterns. With mindful choices and disciplined actions, we create a foundation for a healthier, happier, and more fulfilling life.

Reflect to Realize

Think of a bowman getting ready to shoot an arrow. Before letting the arrow fly, he pulls the bowstring back, which might seem strange at first—why pull back when you want to move forward? But this action is key for the arrow's speed and accuracy. Just like the bowman needs both the tension of pulling back and the release to hit the target, we need a balance between work and play to achieve our goals. It's this balance, like the bowman's, that helps us navigate life's challenges and succeed.

2

The Role Models

A leader's influence extends far beyond the present moment.
It shapes the attitudes, behaviours, and dreams of future generations.

Leadership comes with responsibility. Leadership isn't only about steering the ship but also about setting a course that others can follow with confidence. Elders or leaders are inherently influential, whether they realize it or not. Their actions, decisions, and behaviour ripple through the lives of those around them, especially the younger generations or followers who look up to them for guidance and inspiration.

Lord Krishna highlights this same message in the following verse,

yad yad ācarati śreṣthas
tat tad evetaro janaḥ
sa yat pramāṇaṁ kurute
lokas tad anuvartate

"Whatever actions great persons perform, common people follow. Whatever standards they set, the whole world pursues." (3.21)

Leaders need to serve as role models not just through their words but through their deeds. In doing so, they inspire others to follow their dedication and strive for excellence. A leader has to exhibit resilience in the face of challenges, humility in times of success, and a commitment to continuous improvement. Leaders embody virtues that inspire and guide, and thus ensure the welfare of their followers.

Setting a good example involves embodying the values we talk about, embracing accountability for our actions and demonstrating inspiring behaviour. By consistently adhering to principles of honesty, fairness, and compassion, leaders cultivate a culture of trust and respect within their communities.

Here are a couple of stories for your inspiration—one a good example and another a bad one—to know what a leader must adopt and avoid.

Narada Muni Visits Krishna's Palaces

In the magnificent city of Dwarka, Lord Krishna dwelled amidst opulent grandeur alongside his 16,108 queens, each adorned with her regal palace. These palaces witness the extraordinary loving relationships between Krishna and his wives.

Once the great sage Narada Muni was eager to find out how Lord Krishna was able to please thousands of his wives and spend time with each of them. Thus, Narada Muni embarked on a curious journey to witness first-hand the divine interactions of Lord Krishna with his queens.

As Narada Muni gracefully stepped into the first queen's palace, he found himself witnessing a beautiful scene. Rukmini Devi, the first queen, stood fervently fanning Lord Krishna with a golden-handled yak-tail fan. Despite the presence of numerous maidservants, Rukmini chose personal service as an expression of her profound love for the Lord. The air in the palace seemed to shimmer with devotion as Narada Muni beheld this extraordinary sight.

Despite being the Almighty Lord, Krishna bowed with humility upon the sage's arrival and extended to him a royal seat. He personally washed Narada Muni's feet and sprinkled the purifying water on his own head. This act served as a profound example for all, underscoring the importance of humbly honoring brahmanas and teachers. With Narada Muni's arrival, Krishna's compassionate nature shone brightly as he eagerly inquired about the sage's well-being and sought ways to serve him. This divine exchange exemplified Krishna's benevolence and willingness to reciprocate with love and respect with His devotees.

Continuing his enchanting exploration, Narada Muni traversed through various palaces of Krishna's queens, each revealing a unique facet of Krishna's divine persona. In one palace, the playful side of the Lord unfolded as he engaged in a game of dice with his queen Satyabhama and cousin Uddhava.

In another palace, the paternal love of Krishna was on full display as he affectionately patted his children. In this way, each palace echoed with the diverse activities of Krishna—from performing fire sacrifices and feeding brahmanas to participating in evening worship and honing martial skills.

As Narada Muni observed Krishna's different roles, he marveled at the Lord's ability to seamlessly balance divine duties with the responsibilities of a noble King and a family man. In every palace, Krishna exemplified the righteous conduct expected of a householder (*grihastha*). Narada Muni, with a heart full of reverence, acknowledged Krishna's supreme greatness, recognizing the Lord's unparalleled capacity to set an example for humanity.

Although not obliged, the Lord performs duties to set a good example.

Brahmanas Kill King Vena

Anga was a righteous and virtuous king, deeply loved by his people. However, his son, Vena, grew into a cruel and tyrannical ruler, instilling fear among the citizens. Despite King Anga's tireless efforts to guide and reform his son, Vena's wickedness remained unchanged. Heartbroken and disillusioned, Anga made the painful decision to relinquish his throne. Embracing a life of meditation and devotion to Lord Vishnu, he renounced all worldly attachments. In time, through his unwavering spiritual practice, King Anga attained the eternal bliss of Vaikuntha, the divine abode of Lord Vishnu.

In Anga's absence, the kingdom was plunged into anxiety. Citizens, priests, and ministers searched fruitlessly for their king. Fearing a political crisis, Bhrigu Muni and other concerned sages reluctantly decided to enthrone Vena. Despite knowing Vena's cruelty, they felt they had no other choice.

Once in power, Vena ruled ruthlessly, disrespecting the sages and brahmanas. He prohibited sacred rituals, obstructing the citizens' spiritual lives. Witnessing the kingdom's perilous state, the sages decided to counsel Vena on his wicked activities. They resolved that if their advice was ignored, they would use their powers to eliminate the wicked king. They believed supporting him was like nurturing a poisonous snake with milk.

Approaching Vena with concealed anger, the sages emphasized the importance of facilitating the worship of Lord Vishnu and the devatas for the kingdom's prosperity. Blinded by arrogance, Vena proclaimed himself as God and dismissed the sages' wisdom. In a fit of anger, he insulted the sages. Enraged by Vena's behaviour, the sages killed him merely by chanting *mantras*. Thus, in a swift turn of events, Vena met his end due to the sages' angry words, leaving the kingdom free from the tyranny of an impudent ruler.

When a leader doesn't set the right example for others, he is unfit to be a leader.

Leadership is not just about authority; it's about setting an exemplary standard of behaviour. Lord Krishna, as a householder king, showcased humility, compassion, and devotion, earning the admiration of sage Narada Muni. On the contrary, Vena's cruel and arrogant conduct led to his downfall.

Reflect to Realize

Does the leadership Krishna talks of in this verse apply to us, because we don't hold formal leadership positions? Upon closer examination of our lives, we can realize that we do influence others through our actions, whether it's our friends, dependents, subordinates, or anyone else. Moreover, we are leaders of our own lives, through our choices and behaviours. Our actions serve as a beacon, guiding us either towards fulfilment or despair. Sensible actions pave the path to joy and contentment, while heedless actions lead to disillusionment and sorrow. Let us, therefore, strive to be good examples.

3

Detachment in Duty

Responsibility shouldn't lead to attachment, and detachment doesn't mean irresponsibility.

You can prepare for an exam diligently, but can you determine the exact questions that will appear on the paper? You can write the exam to the best of your ability, but can you predict your precise score? Similarly, a sportsman may exhibit incredible skill and prowess, but the outcome of the game is ultimately beyond his control, isn't it? This illustrates a fundamental truth about life: while we have the responsibility to fulfil our duties, the results are not entirely within our grasp.

This is precisely what Lord Krishna emphasizes in the Bhagavad Gita when he says:

karmaṇy evādhikāras te
mā phaleṣu kadācana
mā karma-phala-hetur bhūr
mā te saṅgo 'stv akarmaṇi

"You have the right to perform your duty, but the outcomes are not in your control. Do not consider yourself the sole cause of the results of your actions, and never be attached to inaction." (2.47)

Understanding this profound teaching, we should conscientiously carry out our responsibilities yet remain detached from the outcomes. This detachment doesn't imply a lack of effort or responsibility; rather, it means performing our duties with full dedication and leaving the results to the divine will. By doing so, we cultivate inner peace and satisfaction, knowing we have done our part to the best of our abilities. This balanced approach allows us to navigate life's challenges with grace and equanimity, fulfilling our roles without the burden of undue stress about the outcomes. Did this concept seem challenging to grasp? Not to worry, we'll understand it with a couple of exciting stories!

A Frightful Feast

King Janaka, the esteemed ruler of Mithila and father of Sita Devi, exemplified both worldly responsibility and spiritual detachment. Despite his authority and opulence, he remained devoted to Lord Hari, dedicating all his actions to the divine.

Once, some brahmanas asked him how he could balance his rulership with spiritual consciousness and detachment. King Janaka smiled and invited the brahmanas for a feast the next day, promising them to reveal his answer after the feast. The next day, Janaka presented the brahmanas with a lavish spread of delicacies in his royal palace. The brahmanas were wonderstruck with the elaborate arrangements for their meal. However, they were astonished to notice sharp swords hanging above their heads, suspended by weak strands of horsehair. They were anxious thinking that the swords could fall on their heads at any moment. Despite the sumptuous food items before them, the brahmanas couldn't fully enjoy the feast as they were preoccupied with fear of the swords falling upon them. After the meal, King Janaka approached the brahmanas and inquired, "Dear Brahmanas, I trust you found the feast to your liking? Were the dishes to your satisfaction?"

One of the brahmanas nervously replied, "Your Majesty, the food may be delicious, but our minds were focused on the swords hanging above us. We were not even aware of what was going into our mouths."

With a gentle smile, King Janaka responded, "Ah, I see. Although you were eating, you couldn't relish the feast due to fear. Similarly, although I am surrounded by many luxuries, I remain detached from them due to my devotion to Lord Vishnu. Despite life's comforts, the inevitability of death reminds us to prioritize spiritual pursuits over worldly pleasures."

Through this powerful analogy, King Janaka illustrated the importance of performing duties with detachment from both results and worldly pleasures. The brahmanas comprehended the profound lesson, recognizing the necessity of remaining focused on spiritual pursuits amidst worldly responsibilities.

We can be in the world but not of the world. We should fulfil our responsibilities, but our focus should be on the Lord, our ultimate goal.

Vritrasura's Dutiful Fight

Once, a great war erupted between the devatas and the asuras. The devatas, led by Indra, faced off against the formidable Vritrasura, leader of the asuras. Vritrasura, in his past life, was a king named Chitraketu. He was a great devotee of Lord Vishnu. But unfortunately, he once passed a remark on Lord Shiva that angered Mother Parvati, who then cursed Chitraketu to become an asura. Thus, Chitraketu was reborn as Vritrasura.

Despite his demonic form, Vritrasura never forgot his devotion to Lord Vishnu. He reflected, "The Lord has kindly punished me for my mistake. I must fulfil my duty as a warrior without attachment to the results and maintain my devotion to the Lord to ultimately attain Him."

In the battlefield, Vritrasura stood with a massive army of demons, while Indra led the devatas. The demons launched their attack with mountain peaks, tridents, axes, swords, and other deadly weapons. However, the devatas swiftly destroyed these weapons before they could cause harm. Frightened, the demons fled, leaving Vritrasura alone.

Vritrasura then spoke to his retreating army, "O powerful asuras, listen to me. Dying on the battlefield while fighting bravely ensures promotion to higher realms. Do not run away. Fight!"

Despite his encouragement, the demons continued to flee. Seizing this opportunity, the devatas pursued and attacked them from behind. Vritrasura scolded the devatas, "How shameful to attack fleeing enemies! Face me if you have the courage."

Roaring like a lion, Vritrasura terrified the devatas, who nearly fainted. He trampled them like a mad elephant crushing hollow bamboos. Indra, unable to tolerate Vritrasura's rampage, hurled a great club at him. Vritrasura caught it with ease and struck Indra's carrier elephant, Airavata, on the head, causing it to bleed and retreat.

Seeing Airavata's condition, Vritrasura refrained from further attack. Indra used his mystic touch to heal Airavata and regain composure. Vritrasura then rebuked Indra, "You are shameless and heartless. I will pierce your stone-like heart with my trident, and vultures will feast on your body. But if you kill me, I will go to Vaikuntha."

Indra had a powerful Vajra (thunderbolt) weapon that was capable of killing Vritrasura, but he hesitated to release it, thinking Vritrasura might nullify the Vajra's power as he had with the club. Vritrasura reassured him, "Your victory is assured. The Vajra has been blessed by Lord Vishnu. Use it to kill me."

Indra still did not release the Vajra. Vritrasura felt that he was wasting time motivating Indra, and started praying to Lord Vishnu, "O Lord, may my mind always think of You, may my words praise Your qualities. I seek neither heavenly pleasures nor mystic powers, only Your service." Indra was astonished to witness the devotion of a demon, that too on the battlefield.

To provoke Indra, Vritrasura threw his trident, declaring, "I shall finish you off!" Indra cut the trident to pieces and severed Vritrasura's right arm with the Vajra. Despite his injury, Vritrasura struck Indra with an iron mace, causing Indra to drop the Vajra.

Ashamed, Indra hesitated to pick it up, but Vritrasura encouraged him, "Take your Vajra and kill your enemy. Only Lord Vishnu is always victorious, and all others are sometimes victorious and sometimes defeated. Focus on your duty, without concern for victory or defeat. Look at me, even with a severed arm, I am fighting without discouragement."

Moved by Vritrasura's words, Indra resumed the battle, cutting off Vritrasura's left arm as well. Though bleeding profusely, Vritrasura's gigantic form still intimidated the devatas. In a final act of defiance, he swallowed Indra and Airavata whole, like a python swallowing an elephant.

Inside Vritrasura's belly, Indra remained unharmed due to his protective armour called Narayana-kavacha. As Vritrasura entered a trance and his soul joyfully ascended to Vaikuntha,

Indra pierced his way out with the Vajra. Vritrasura, having completed his destined role, attained liberation through his unwavering devotion to Lord Vishnu.

We can responsibly perform our duties, but the results are not in our hands.

Both King Janaka and Vritrasura epitomize the essence of performing duties with detachment from results, teaching us to offer our actions to the divine. King Janaka ruled Mithila with integrity, yet remained detached, dedicating all to Lord Hari. Vritrasura, once Chitraketu, fought as a warrior, unwavering in his devotion to Lord Vishnu. Their lives exemplify the path of detachment and devotion, reminding us that true fulfilment lies in dedicating our actions to the divine and relinquishing attachment to outcomes.

Reflect to Realize

Why shouldn't I expect results from my hard work, and what's wrong with becoming attached to those results? Lord Krishna's counsel to avoid attachment to the fruits of our labour holds a profound logic. When we achieve something, are we solely responsible for the outcome? Not quite. Numerous individuals support, guide, and facilitate our endeavours. Moreover, nature provides essential resources for our work. Thus, credit for success extends beyond ourselves; we are but one contributor among many. Therefore, it's essential to share the credit. Ultimately, the fruits of our labour are a collective effort, attributable to God, nature, and the contributions of many.

4

From Detachment to Devotion

When "working with detachment" matures into "working with devotion", it brings satisfaction to the heart.

Imagine a tree—when you nourish its roots, every part of the tree thrives. Similarly, when we dedicate our efforts to God, the root of all existence, every aspect of our life flourishes.

The Gita highlights the incredible power of dedicating our actions to God. By acting selflessly and focusing on the divine, we naturally find personal joy and fulfilment. Everything is connected to the Lord. God is like the root from which everything grows. Just as branches and leaves become strong and healthy when the root is watered, serving God brings prosperity and happiness to the world.

When we work for God, we move beyond our ego's limits and find true spiritual fulfilment. By embracing this teaching from the Gita, spiritual growth becomes attainable and real.

In this verse, Lord Krishna counsels Arjuna directly, saying,

mayi sarvāṇi karmāṇi
sannyasyādhyātma-cetasā
nirāśīr nirmamo bhūtvā
yudhyasva vigata-jvaraḥ

"Perform all your tasks as an offering to Me. In spiritual consciousness, without desiring selfish gains, without claiming yourself to be the doer, without any laziness, perform your duty of fighting." (3.30)

This advice of the Lord doesn't talk about mere detached action. Rather, it delves into the essence of spiritual consciousness (*ādhyātma-cetasā*). By surrendering selfish desires, by abandoning complacency, and giving up the notion of being the sole doer, one enters a state of profound alignment with the Lord's will.

To illustrate the practical application of this principle, let's explore the stories of individuals who wholeheartedly worked for God. These narratives provide tangible examples of the profound connection between selfless service to God and the ensuing joy it brings.

The Mysterious Young Man

Jayadev Goswami was a great poet and a true devotee of Lord Krishna. He wrote the famous book of epic poem *Gita Govinda* praising Lord Krishna.

Once, Jayadev wished to weave his poem *Gita Govinda* on a nice cloth and offer it to the deity of Lord Jagannath at Jagannath Puri, a holy place in the Indian state of Odisha. Jayadev approached a group of weavers and requested them to weave the verses on a cloth. The weavers agreed and said, "We will do it, but on one condition. You must sing the *Gita Govinda* while we work."

Jayadev Goswami agreed and started singing. The weavers happily started stitching the song onto the cloth. As Jayadev continued singing the song, he suddenly entered deep meditation on the Lord, and was replete with spiritual joy. He suddenly stopped singing and became unconscious of the external world. The weavers also stopped stitching. They wondered what had happened to Jayadev.

Suddenly, one young man appeared there and said, "I am Jayadev's brother. I will continue singing the song while you work." Saying this, he started singing and the weavers resumed working. After a while, Jayadev Goswami came out of his trance, reviving his external consciousness. And just as this happened, the young man immediately disappeared.

Jayadev looked at the weavers and asked them, "What just happened?"

One of the weavers answered, "Well you went into a trance, but we continued working, because your brother came here and sang the song. Oh! He has such a divine voice!"

Surprised, Jayadev Goswami said, "I don't have a brother. And only my wife and I know the verses of *Gita Govinda*. Then who is this young man who came and sang the song?"

Suddenly, it dawned on Jayadev that the young man was actually Lord Jagannath, Lord Krishna Himself. He personally sang those songs because He loved them, and He was happy to accept this service. Thus, as a result of Jayadev Goswami's constant devotion to the Lord, the Lord Himself revealed His identity to His dear devotee.

The Lord reciprocates His devotees' love.

Hanuman's 'Long' Jump

Mighty Hanuman's adventurous journey to find Mother Sita reveals his deep devotion. Yet, driven by his love for Lord Rama and the sacred mission, Hanuman, the mighty monkey-hero, prepared to jump across the 800-mile-wide ocean.

Encouraged by the monkey-chiefs, Hanuman expanded into a gigantic form, radiating divine power. His fellow monkeys were enthralled by the spectacle, witnessing the embodiment of strength and determination. In a gesture of humility and reverence, Hanuman bowed to the devas and his beloved Lord Rama, seeking blessings for the success of his crucial mission: to locate Sita.

As Hanuman soared through the sky, Mount Mainaka rose from the water's depths, offering Hanuman a brief resting place. Despite the generous offer of hospitality, Hanuman, single-minded in his mission, politely declined Mainaka's proposal, explaining the urgency that propelled him forward.

Continuing his journey, Hanuman encountered Surasa, a formidable demoness and mother of snakes, whose ominous presence threatened to obstruct him. She had a divine boon from Lord Brahma that granted her the ability to consume anything before her. She demanded Hanuman to enter her mouth, but Hanuman requested her to allow him to accomplish his mission first. He promised her that he would enter her mouth after completing his service. But she expanded her mouth to block his movement. Hanuman, maintaining focus on his mission, outwitted Surasa by swiftly adapting to her expanding size.

When Surasa's mouth expanded to an insurmountable 100 yojanas, Hanuman, in a masterstroke of intellect, shrank to the size of a thumb and quickly entered and exited her mouth.

Surasa, impressed by his intelligence, shed her antagonistic demeanour and blessed him for success in Lord Rama's service. This encounter shows Hanuman's ability to navigate challenges with intelligence, avoiding unnecessary conflict.

However, the journey was far from over. Soon, Simhika, a menacing rakshasi, emerged to thwart Hanuman's progress. She grabbed his shadow and pulled him back. In a swift and strategic move, Hanuman, tactically entered Simhika's mouth, and dismantled her heart. This victory over Simhika marked another triumph in Hanuman's quest, celebrated by celestial beings for his unwavering resolve.

With each obstacle surmounted, Hanuman's heart, fuelled by love for Lord Rama, remained undeterred. His eventful leap of 100 yojanas only strengthened his determination. As he reached the city of Lanka, Hanuman stood resolute, ready to fulfil his sacred mission—to bring tidings of Mother Sita to Lord Rama. This timeless tale of devotion, courage, and triumphant love continues to inspire generations, reminding us of the boundless power of dedication and the spirit of selfless service.

One who is determined to achieve one's goal can overcome all obstacles by God's grace.

Hanuman's heart overflowed with boundless love for Lord Rama, propelling him to overcome every obstacle in his path. While singing the *Gita Govinda*, Jayadev Goswami entered a meditative trance, immersed in profound thoughts of Lord Krishna. In the same vein, when we selflessly serve the Lord with unwavering love, He becomes our guiding force, empowering us to confront and conquer every difficulty that crosses our spiritual journey.

Reflect to Realize

While advising Arjuna, Krishna prescribes a mindset of detachment rather than a literal renunciation of duties. True renunciation lies not in forsaking external possessions but in relinquishing attachment to outcomes. But mere renunciation of results of work doesn't bring as much satisfaction to the heart as offering those results to the Lord with devotion. By working in a spirit of devotion and detachment, one can be a monk without adopting traditional ascetic practices.

5

Meditation in Action

Meditation is not just an act of the mind, but an absorbed action for the Lord's pleasure.

Irrespective of the nature of one's work—whether it be teaching, studying, cooking, trading, or any other pursuit—one can infuse spirituality into it by making it as an offering to the Lord. This mindset transforms trivial tasks into acts of devotion, elevating the mundane to the sacred.

In the Gita, Lord Krishna instructs Arjuna that his duty of fighting is also a sacred activity when he works in a spirit of dedication. In the verse, Lord Krishna instructs,

tasmāt sarveṣu kāleṣu
mām anusmara yudhya ca
mayy arpita-mano-buddhir
mām evaiṣyasy asaṁśayaḥ

"Always think of Me and at the same time carry out your prescribed duty of fighting. Dedicate your mind and intelligence to Me, and thus you will attain Me without doubt." (8.7)

How can someone "always" think of Krishna, and yet attend to one's responsibilities on a practical plane? Why is the Lord instructing us to do so in the above verse? Actually, thinking of Krishna or being conscious of Krishna doesn't just mean ignoring all other duties. One can perform one's duties with the thought of satisfying the Lord with those very duties. That is Krishna consciousness—dedicating not only one's mind, but also one's intelligence and body in the Lord's service.

Arjuna's role in the Kurukshetra war stands as a beautiful example of responsible action done with a devoted mind and dedicated intelligence. Thus, every aspect of life can be filled with a spiritual purpose when approached with the right mindset. By aligning our actions with the Lord's instructions, we naturally transcend the ego and find inner fulfilment.

Two exemplary devotees stand out as illustrations of this teaching, showcasing how we can dedicate their minds and intelligence to thc Lord while diligently fulfilling their duties.

Mighty Hanuman's Fight

Hanuman's heroic venture into the golden city of Lanka is an adventure of valour and devotion. Each movement was etched with daring feats and a spirit of dedication. Having met Mother Sita in the groves of Ashoka, Hanuman became the beacon of hope in the gloom of her arrest. Sita devi, once despondent, found hope and reassurance in Hanuman's presence, her eyes gleaming with tears of joy.

Before embarking on his return journey to Lord Rama, Hanuman had a burning desire to confront Ravana himself. So, he started creating great disturbance in the Ashoka grove. It was nothing short of spectacular. The air resonated with the crash of uprooted trees, the ripple of disturbed lakes, and the thunderous echoes of crushed hilltops. The once serene grove was transformed into a chaotic battleground of monumental proportions. The rakshasas, trembled at the colossal might of Hanuman, hurrying to Ravana with reports.

Ravana, his pride wounded, unleashed a formidable army of 80,000 fierce rakshasas to capture the audacious monkey. Hanuman roared defiantly remembering Lord Rama. With each battle cry, he invoked the name of his beloved Lord Rama, a mantra that echoed through the garden which was now a battlefield. Hanuman, cutting through the rakshasa army like a storm, left only dead bodies.

Undeterred by the annihilation of his forces, Ravana, a shrewd strategist, sent Jambumali, a formidable rakshasa warrior, to engage the relentless Hanuman. As Hanuman clashed with Jambumali, the ancient structures of the Ashoka grove further crumbled. Their battle shook the very foundation of Earth. Yet, Hanuman swiftly defeated Jambumali, adding to the growing tally of the fallen adversaries.

Refusing to yield, Ravana recognized the need for a more formidable warrior. He summoned his eldest son, Indrajit. The stage was set for a fierce duel, as Indrajit, wielding mystic weaponry, attacked Hanuman. Yet, the mighty devotee of the Lord stood undeterred. In a desperate move, Indrajit deployed the Brahmastra, the ultimate weapon, binding Hanuman and rendering him momentarily unconscious.

Actually, Hanuman voluntarily decided to get caught by Indrajit, firstly to honour lord Brahma's weapon, and secondly to see Ravana face-to-face. Soon Hanuman was presented before Ravana. The enraged king, blinded by fury, ordered his ministers to interrogate the audacious monkey. Hanuman, undaunted, declared his mission as Rama's messenger, urging Ravana to return Sita and avoid impending doom.

In response to this counsel, Ravana, his ego unyielding, opted to humiliate the messenger with a punishment. He ordered his soldiers to set fire to Hanuman's tail. Then the rakshasas bound Hanuman's tail with cotton rags, soaked in oil, setting it ablaze. The spectacle unfolded through the city streets, a long procession announcing the capture of a defiant spy.

Yet, in a moment, Hanuman, the servant of Lord Rama, slipped from his bonds. He leaped from rooftop to rooftop, setting fire to the towering structures of Lanka, the flames licking the heavens. As Hanuman's triumphant flames consumed Lanka, his unwavering chant of Lord Rama's names reverberated through the city.

After thus creating a fiery spectacle in the enemy's kingdom, Hanuman reached Lord Rama and delivered the good news of Sita's safety. The stage was set for the grand finale, the impending clash between the forces of Rama and the tyrannical reign of Ravana.

A devotee who works in God consciousness is always blessed with success.

Mother Yashoda's Churning

On the auspicious day of Diwali in the enchanting land of Vrindavan, Mother Yashoda woke up early. She decided to start churning butter before her darling child Krishna awoke, anticipating that His playful presence would make the task more challenging.

Little Krishna was famous for stealing butter from the houses of the gopis. The gopis often came to Mother Yashoda to complain about Krishna's antics. She was puzzled by Krishna's excitement for butter theft and thought deeply about it. Feeling that her maidservants were not preparing butter to

Krishna's satisfaction, she decided to personally churn butter for him. She thought that only her hands could make the perfect butter to please her naughty boy.

In her vast Goshala, which housed around nine lakh cows, Mother Yashoda had a special affection for eight cows known as the Padma-gandha cows. These cows were given exceptional care, fed the best grass, and their milk was reserved for making butter for Krishna.

Clad in a saffron-yellow sari with a waist belt, Mother Yashoda positioned herself before a large earthen pot filled with curd made from the milk of the Padmagandha cows, ready to begin churning. The churning rod, tied securely with a soft rope, moved rhythmically in the pot as she pulled the rope with vigour. Engrossed in this simple yet divine household activity, her thoughts, words, and actions were entirely dedicated to Lord Krishna. She sang melodious songs about Krishna's exploits, from vanquishing demons like Putana and Trinavarta to His playful butter thefts. The rhythm of her churning created a melody, complemented by the harmonious jingle of her bangles, earrings, ankle bells, and golden waist-belt.

As Mother Yashoda lost herself in the ecstasy of her devotion, little Krishna, stirred by His mother's intense love, awoke from His sleep. Seeking her presence, He cried out and rubbed His lotus-like eyes. His search led Him to His mother who was churning butter, the rhythmic sound resembling a divine mridanga drum. Eager for her attention, Krishna, with His tiny hands, tried to stop the churning. Delighted by this endearing interruption, Mother Yashoda welcomed Him into her lap, offering Him her milk—the culmination of her meditation on Krishna.

Thus, Mother Yashoda seamlessly blended her simple household duties with her unwavering remembrance of

Krishna. In turn, Krishna reciprocated her boundless motherly love, by identifying Himself as her darling son, rather than the Almighty God.

The Lord always loves to be bound by the love of His devotees.

Devotees, whether engaged in simple household chores or undertaking extraordinary feats, epitomize dedication to the divine. Mother Yashoda, while churning butter, turned this simple task into a sacred meditation and love for her beloved Krishna. Similarly, Hanuman, in his fearless pursuit of service to Lord Rama, showcased unwavering focus amidst challenges, inspiring us to transform our daily activities as a meditation on the Lord.

Reflect to Realize

Lord Krishna promises our entry into His eternal abode after death, if we work in this world while absorbed in His love. Even if, due to intense pain, we forget to remember Krishna at that crucial moment of death, the Lord will recall us and ensure we reach the supreme destination. That is His boundless mercy. Recognizing His immense compassion, let us dedicate our lives to Him with sincere and humble devotion. Let us wholeheartedly commit to serving the Lord, trusting that His grace will lead us to our ultimate spiritual home.

6

Work as Worship

Find the higher purpose of your work rather than viewing it as an obligatory chore.

There is a way of integrating our daily pursuits and spiritual journey. Lord Krishna reveals it in the following verse,

yat karoṣi yad aśnāsi
yaj juhoṣi dadāsi yat
yat tapasyasi kaunteya
tat kuruṣva mad-arpaṇam

"Whatever you do, whatever you eat, whatever you offer, whatever you give, and whatever penance you undertake, oh Kaunteya, dedicate it all to Me." (9.27)

Devoting our work to God can turn even the most mundane tasks into meaningful acts of profound significance. When we need to approach our jobs with dedication and integrity, seeing them as opportunities to serve a higher purpose, rather than chores for personal survival or enjoyment. This perspective transforms our daily tasks into acts of worship, where each action becomes an offering to the Lord.

Pleasing God through our work goes beyond specific professions or roles. Whether we are teachers, doctors, engineers, artists, or homemakers, our activities can be made spiritual through devotion to God. It's not about changing what we do but changing our consciousness in which we do it—working with a spirit of dedication, detachment, and devotion.

By integrating spiritual principles into our work ethics, we build a deeper connection with the Lord. This approach fills our hearts with fulfilment and purpose, as we realize our efforts are part of a larger divine plan. Ultimately, when we offer the fruits of our labour to God with sincerity and humility, we invite His blessings into every part of our lives, enriching our hearts.

To illustrate this verse, consider two inspiring stories of individuals who offered the fruits of their labour to Lord Krishna and, in turn, were showered with His generous blessings.

Sudama–The Garland Maker

Sudama was a humble florist in the bustling city of Mathura. He often travelled to Vrindavan to gather rare, fragrant flowers. Vrindavan was the divine village where Lord Krishna spent His childhood. During Sudama's visits to Vrindavan, he not only gathered special flowers but also caught a glimpse of the joyful, rustically dressed blue boy, Krishna, playing with His friends.

Years later, Krishna came to Mathura with His elder brother Balarama and some cowherd friends. The city, with its towering structures and busy marketplaces, was a stark contrast to their quaint village. Krishna's tour equally excited His friends and the city dwellers who had eagerly awaited

His visit. As Krishna walked by, even those engrossed in their daily chores rushed out, hoping for a glimpse. Yet, amidst this excitement, Sudama, the florist, remained in his home, making a garland for his beloved Lord Krishna.

Drawn by the devotion of the florist, Krishna soon found His way to Sudama's house. Unaware of his visitor, Sudama was deeply engrossed in crafting a garland. It wasn't until he sensed a divine presence and saw a pair of beautiful blue lotus-like feet that he realized Krishna had entered his modest dwelling. Sudama's joy was uncontainable as he looked up to meet Krishna's gaze.

"O Lord," Sudama exclaimed, his voice trembling with emotion, "today, my family, my home, and I are truly blessed. All my ancestors are fortunate. How may I serve You? Nothing would honour me more."

Krishna, embodying pure love and joy, just asked for garlands. Understanding Krishna's heart, Sudama offered Him and His friends fresh garlands. A splendid, half-completed garland caught Krishna's eye. Sudama swiftly finished it and presented it to Krishna. Decorating Krishna with the garland, Sudama's happiness knew no bounds, especially as he bathed Krishna's feet with lotus-petal-infused water.

Krishna, with a grace that filled the room, blessed Sudama, saying, "My dear florist, your life will be marked by strength, longevity, fame, beauty, and prosperity. And at the end of this journey, you will join Me in the eternal world, enjoying an everlasting life together."

Sudama's encounter with Krishna transformed not only his material circumstances but his spiritual destiny, illustrating the profound impact of devotion and the humble offering of one's gifts to the Divine.

When we are eager to serve God, God becomes eager to receive our service and blesses us in return.

Kubja–The Sandalwood Pulp Maker

As Lord Krishna continued his journey through the picturesque streets of Mathura, his attention was captured by a young hunchback woman. She was delicately holding a plate of fragrant ointments and cosmetics. The aroma was so compelling that Krishna couldn't resist asking, "Who are you, and what are those fragrances you carry?"

Upon seeing Krishna, the woman was instantly mesmerized by His divine presence, and His charming beauty. She responded, "My name is Kubja, a servant of King Kamsa. He likes the sandalwood pulp and cosmetics that I prepare."

Intrigued, Krishna expressed his desire, "Could you share some of your cosmetics with Me? We've come all the way from Vrindavan, and it's our first visit to the grand city of Mathura."

Without a moment's hesitation, Kubja offered Krishna generous amounts of the ointment. She selected shades that complemented His divine complexion. Despite being in close proximity to the fearsome King Kamsa's palace (Kamsa being an enemy of Krishna), Kubja showed no fear. Her admiration for Krishna eclipsed her dread of Kamsa. Disregarding her role as the king's servant, she openly applied the sandalwood pulp on Krishna. She adorned His plump cheeks, broad chest, and slender arms with beautiful patterns.

Moved by Kubja's act of devotion, Krishna resolved to transform her bent body. He gently placed His foot upon her toes and with His right hand, tenderly grasped her chin. Supporting her back with His left hand, He slowly straightened her bent figure.

The moment Lord Krishna's divine touch graced her, Kubja was transformed into a beautiful woman. No longer hunched, she stood straight and radiant. Her beauty was unmatched, and her limbs perfectly aligned. This miraculous healing, a testament to Krishna's divine power, left all who witnessed it in awe.

Having blessed Kubja with a new lease of life, Krishna resumed his exploration of the city, leaving behind a trail of wonder and divine love.

Any work, if done with devotion, attracts the Lord's boundless love and blessings.

The stories of Sudama and Kubja show us that true devotion and selfless service are keys to connecting with the Lord, no matter our social status or physical condition. It's not about how grand our offerings are, but about the sincerity of our devotion. Let's make every action an act of devotion, enriching our spiritual journey.

Reflect to Realize

Pilgrims often flock to the sacred Ganga, where they immerse themselves and collect holy water in their hands, reverently offering it back to the river. Intriguing, isn't it? In the same way, let's recognize that all our abilities, talents, and resources are gifts from the Lord, and channel them back into His service. By doing so, we derive deep satisfaction and honour the source of our blessings.

7

The Art of Eating

Recognizing God as our ultimate provider,
let's express our gratitude to Him.

The journey of food, from its humble beginnings in the fields to its final destination on our dining tables, is indeed an interesting one. As it travels through various stages, passing through markets, kitchens, and restaurants, each step plays a vital role in bringing nourishment to our lives. Yet, behind these visible sources lies a deeper, and a more profound cause and source of nourishment—the grace of God.

Knowing well that God is the ultimate supplier of all our necessities, wise people express their gratitude to Him by offering all that they eat before partaking of it. This act of offering is more than a physical ritual; it is an acknowledgement for the divine Lord's mercy that looks after us. In a revealing verse, Lord Krishna says,

iṣṭān bhogān hi vo devā
dāsyante yajña-bhāvitāḥ

tair dattān apradāyaibhyo
yo bhuṅkte stena eva saḥ

"One who enjoys the gifts or eats the food provided by the gods without first offering it to them is a thief." (3.12)

Here, the emphasis is not on the external act of offering, but on the sentiment behind it—the love, devotion, and gratitude with which it is offered. By offering our food to the divine, we fill our meals with sacredness. Every bite is infused with a sense of reverence and appreciation. This practice serves as a constant reminder of the interconnectedness of all life and our dependence on the grace of the divine. Through this simple yet profound gesture, we cultivate a deeper spiritual connection, enriching not only our body but also our souls.

But the question arises, "Does the Lord actually consume the offerings we make?" This question invites us to explore the relationship between the material and the spiritual, and the ways in which our acts of devotion are received and blessed by the divine.

Does God Eat the Food We Offer?

In a school, a dedicated teacher took on the task of imparting spiritual wisdom to his students. One day, he explained the significance of a Gita verse, emphasizing that if you offer simple things like a flower, fruit, leaf, or water to Lord Krishna, He would graciously accept it.

However, doubts lingered in the mind of one pupil who questioned, "Does Krishna really consume our offerings? Despite daily presentations of various items, they seem untouched."

In response, the guru patiently explained, "The Lord doesn't have to physically consume your offerings. He eats in a spiritual way just by merely glancing your food, when you offer it with sincerity and devotion."

Yet, the pupil, harboring doubts, persisted, "How can he have consumed the offerings when the food remains visibly intact?" The teacher wisely decided to continue the discourse the following day and instructed the students to memorize the verse before the next class.

That night, the intelligent student diligently memorized the verse seeing the book, as instructed by his teacher. In the next day's class, he confidently recited it, impressing his teacher.

The teacher asked him, "How did you learn this verse?" The boy candidly responded, "I learned it from the book, reciting it repeatedly until it became ingrained in my memory."

Seizing this opportunity to deepen the lesson, the teacher drew a parallel between the verse and the act of offering. With a smile, the guru remarked, "The verse entered your memory, right?" The boy said yes. The teacher questioned back, "Does it mean that the verse has disappeared from the book?"

The boy, quick-witted, clarified, "No, the verse is still in the book, but it's also in my memory."

Capitalizing on this insight, the guru gently questioned, "Why then can't the food offered to God exist on the plate and simultaneously be in his belly?"

The boy, momentarily speechless, absorbed the analogy. Sensing the readiness for a deeper understanding, the teacher expounded, "The Lord partakes of the offerings in a spiritual dimension. What remains visible is the physical representation, but spiritually, the offering is consumed. The remnants are left for us as prasadam, a divine blessing."

Slowly, but surely, the student's doubts transformed into conviction as he embraced the profound wisdom of offering with faith and love.

God graciously accepts our offerings and bestows his blessings upon us.

When God Steals Our Offerings

In the sacred realm of devotion, the narrative of Madhavendra Puri, an ardent devotee of Lord Gopala, unfolds as a testament to the profound encounters one can have while on a spiritual journey. Once he travelled from Vrindavan to Jagannath Puri, fuelled by the desire to procure some cooling sandalwood paste for his beloved deity. He stopped at the enchanting village of Remuna, where there was a beautiful temple of Lord Gopinath. It was here that a beautiful incident occurred.

Overcome by the divine presence of the deity, Madhavendra Puri was swept into a wave of ecstatic devotion, singing and dancing in the temple. Drawn by his love for Lord Gopinath, he approached a brahmana priest to learn about the offerings made to the deity. The priest shared that Lord Gopinath is offered a delectable milk sweet known as *amrita-keli*, also celebrated as *Gopinatha-kshira*. Hearing of this heavenly delicacy, Madhavendra Puri felt an intense desire to taste it—not out of personal craving, but to prepare a similar offering for his beloved deity, Gopalji, in Vrindavan.

However, a profound realization struck Madhavendra Puri. He questioned himself the appropriateness of desiring to taste the food before the deity had partaken of it. Distressed by the perceived offense, humble Madhavendra Puri silently departed from the temple after the *aarati*. He sat in a marketplace and became immersed in chanting the holy names of Lord Krishna.

That night the priest of Lord Gopinath's temple had a divine dream, where Gopinath told the priest, "I have stolen a pot of *amrita-keli* sweet, for my sincere devotee Madhavendra Puri. Please take that pot and give it to him. He is chanting in the marketplace now."

The priest hastily got up from his sleep, took a bath, and entered the temple. He was astonished to find a pot of *amrita-keli* behind the deity of Gopinath. He took it and at once ventured into the village marketplace, proclaiming the Lord's benevolence and calling out to Madhavendra Puri.

Responding to the calls, Madhavendra Puri was led to the temple by the priest, who then handed him the pot of *amrita-keli*. Overwhelmed by the Lord's compassionate gesture, Madhavendra Puri partook of the sweet rice with a heart brimming with gratitude. He even cherished the earthen pot as a display of the Lord's extraordinary love. Each day, he savored a piece of the earthen pot, reflecting on the Lord's mercy.

This sweet episode not only revealed Madhavendra Puri's devotion, but also left a great mark on the sanctity of the temple. Lord Gopinath, having exhibited boundless grace, earned the endearing name 'Kshir-chor-Gopinath'—the sweet-thief Gopinath.

The Lord knows the innermost desires of His devotees and fulfils them.

These tales beautifully illustrate the reciprocal love between the devotees and the Lord, who graciously accepts their heartfelt offerings and bestows His *prasadam* (mercy). Let's embrace the joyous practice of cooking, serving, and partaking of the remnants of our offerings to the Lord. Let's embark on the uplifting journey of offering our meals to the Lord, transforming the act of eating into a sacred activity of spiritual bliss.

Reflect to Realize

It's a distressing reality that countless people worldwide go hungry each day, with some even succumbing to starvation. Amidst the escalating global crisis, the future remains uncertain, and many in impoverished regions resort to consuming inedible substances for survival. In light of these stark realities, it's truly remarkable that many of us enjoy full meals every day. How blessed we are! Let us deeply acknowledge and express our gratitude to Lord Krishna for providing us with everything we have. Let's first offer Him the food before we eat and partake of his prasadam and even share that sanctified food with the hungry and bring them closer to the Lord.

8

Fight for Him

Being instrumental for a noble cause brings profound inner fulfilment.

Take a soldier, for example. When they fight in battle, they're honoured for their service, even if they kill. But if that same soldier harms someone in anger outside of battle, he's punished. Therefore, Lord Krishna teaches us in the Gita on doing our duties on behalf of the divine not to satisfy our own whims. He says,

yajñārthāt karmaṇo 'nyatra
loko 'yaṁ karma-bandhanaḥ
tad-arthaṁ karma kaunteya
mukta-saṅgaḥ samācara

"Work as an offering to the Lord for His satisfaction, otherwise it causes bondage in this world." (3.9)

Just as a soldier fights for the country or an employee works for the company, we're encouraged to do our tasks as a service to the Lord. This approach frees us from the cycle of karma (the bondage of actions and reactions) and fills our hearts with satisfaction.

Initially, in the Bhagavad Gita Arjuna declined to fight. But Lord Krishna reminded Arjuna of his responsibility to act as his instrument in establishing virtue by subduing vice. So, Arjuna was expected to fight on behalf of the Lord, rather than being overwhelmed by his own emotional attachment to his relatives who committed innumerable offenses.

It is important to understand our roles and responsibilities in life. It's not just about what we do, but why and how we do it. When we perform our duties with detachment, seeing them as contributions to a noble purpose rather than mere personal gains, we naturally feel a sense of selflessness and spiritual joy. Thus, the focus shifts from external outcomes to internal intentions. By aligning our actions with the higher principle of service to the Supreme, we rise above ego. Moreover, by being detached from the results and focusing more on the process, we often achieve better outcomes.

The forthcoming episodes will shed more light on this profound teaching.

The Beginning of Govardhan Puja

In the serene landscapes of Vrindavan, excitement filled the air as the residents busily prepared for an elaborate ceremony. Seven-year-old Krishna, curious as ever, approached His father, King Nanda, seeking to understand the purpose behind the grand arrangements.

King Nanda explained that the ceremony, known as Indra-puja, was a time-honoured tradition performed to appease Indra, the celestial king responsible for bestowing the invaluable gift of rain upon the land—a lifeline for agriculture and sustenance.

However, Krishna, deeply connected to the essence of Vrindavan, proposed a paradigm shift. With a compelling argument, He redirected their focus from worshipping Indra to worshipping the Govardhan Hill, which sustains everyone. Krishna ardently suggested a departure from the traditional Indra-puja, advocating instead for the worship of the Govardhan Hill, the unsung hero providing all essential needs to the community—water, lush grazing grounds, natural shelter, fruits, and more.

Initially met with hesitation from Nanda Maharaj, Krishna, in His charming and persuasive manner, asserted that the preparations already made for Indra-puja could seamlessly be adapted for Govardhan-puja. The simple-hearted residents of Vrindavan, deeply enamored by Krishna's wisdom and love, joyfully embraced this alternative. Thus began the meticulous preparations for a unique celebration, marking the initiation of the enchanting tradition of Govardhan-puja.

As the day unfolded, Krishna assumed a divine four-handed form atop the Govardhan Hill, declaring Himself to be Govardhan, the mountain-god. The majestic spectacle unfolded as He gracefully accepted the food offerings extended by His devotees with outstretched arms. The atmosphere buzzed with awe and reverence as the divine communion between the residents of Vrindavan and the Govardhan Hill unfolded in a spectacle of love and devotion. This unprecedented celebration delighted the hearts of the Vrindavan residents. It became a symbol of their unwavering devotion and a testament to the unique connection they shared with the Govardhan Hill.

In a fascinating twist, Krishna's decision to divert from Indra-puja served a dual purpose—to humble the proud celestial king Indra, and to establish the cherished tradition of Govardhan-puja. When Indra learned that his worship had stopped, he unleashed huge torrential rains upon Vrindavan in a fit of rage, wanting to submerge the entire village. Unfazed, Krishna, the eternal protector, effortlessly lifted the Govardhan Hill with the touch of His little finger, shielding the residents from the relentless downpour. All the Vrindavan residents took shelter under the uplifted Govardhan Hill that rested on Krishna's little finger.

As the waters receded and the skies cleared, Indra, humbled by Krishna's acts, approached Krishna with regret. This enchanting episode not only showcased Krishna's supreme prowess but also served as a profound lesson in devotion, humility, and the boundless rewards of surrendering to the divine Lord.

Actions performed to please God provide us with happiness, while disobedience to Him causes distress.

The King Who Became a Lizard

In the enchanting surroundings of Dwarka, one day, Lord Krishna's young sons, while playing, stumbled upon a peculiar sight, an enormous lizard struggling in a dry well. Driven by their innocent curiosity, they sought the intervention of their benevolent father, Lord Krishna. Responding to their plea, Lord Krishna came to the well and gracefully extracted the creature from the well with His left hand.

The touch of Krishna's divine hand worked wonders. The lizard underwent a miraculous transformation. It transformed into a celestial human being, adorned with resplendent garments, dazzling ornaments, and fragrant garlands. Krishna's sons, witnessing this celestial miracle, stood in awe of the divine display before them.

Though omniscient, Lord Krishna, in His divine *lila* (pastime), chose to assume the role of one seeking knowledge. With curiosity, He inquired about the identity and story of the celestial being who had once taken the form of a lizard. The celestial revealed himself as King Nriga, a noble ruler from the illustrious lineage of King Ikshvaku. He then began recounting his story, a tapestry of acts marked by charity, virtue, and an unintended transgression that ultimately led to his cursed transformation.

King Nriga, renowned for his benevolence, had generously donated countless cows and valuable possessions to learned and sincere brahmanas. He desired to gain a lot of piety. However, a seemingly inconspicuous lapse occurred when a cow, previously donated, found its way back to King Nriga's cowshed. Unaware of this, he inadvertently donated the same cow to another brahmana, triggering a heated dispute between the two recipients.

The ensuing quarrel left King Nriga despondent, despite his earnest attempts to resolve the situation. Tragically, the consequences of this unintentional error manifested after his demise, as the soldiers of Yama escorted him to hell for the perceived sin of appropriating a brahmana's property unknowingly.

Facing Yama in hell, King Nriga chose to experience the consequences of his sinful actions before his past piety. Granting his request, Yama declared that King Nriga should fall and become a lizard. Consequently, King Nriga lived a life of repentance, devoted to brahmanas. However, he was bereft of true devotion to Lord Krishna. The essence of spiritual life that is devotion to God was missing.

It was only through the divine touch of Lord Krishna that King Nriga, the once lowly lizard, shed his reptilian form and assumed a heavenly body. Grateful for his release, King Nriga sought permission to depart, signifying the culmination of his karmic journey. This tale of King Nriga serves as a poignant reminder of the intricate interplay between piety, charity, and the subtle nuances of intention behind one's actions. While King Nriga's generosity was abundant, the absence of selfless devotion to the Supreme resulted in the unfolding of his destiny, teaching profound lessons about the essence of true spiritual service.

Howsoever great the work, if not performed as a service to God, and done with expectations in return, will not set us free.

The tales of Vrindavan and King Nriga convey the profound impact of intentions behind actions. In Vrindavan, the residents selflessly devoted every activity to please Lord Krishna, embodying unconditional love. Conversely, King Nriga's benevolence, though abundant, was tinged with a desire for personal gains. These stories inspire us to introspect on our purpose behind our activities.

Reflect to Realize

Just as a householder constantly strives for the family's welfare, constantly thinking of them even while working at the office, we should nurture our devotion to constantly contemplate on Lord Krishna even while doing our trivial duties. This devotion grows by immersing ourselves in His pastimes, chanting His names, serving His devotees, and maintaining integrity in all our endeavours. Through such practices, our mundane activities become offerings of love and service to the Supreme.

9

Five Great Actions

Selfless actions lead to satisfaction, while selfish actions destroy one's peace.

In the vast expanse of God's divine realm, there exists an eternal place, where spiritual bliss flows endlessly. That spiritual abode is far beyond the material world, and is unaffected by the temporary problems of the earthly realm. One can gain entry into that beautiful place by working in a spirit of devotion as encapsulated by Lord Krishna personally in the following verse.

mat-karma-kṛn mat-paramo
mad-bhaktaḥ saṅga-varjitaḥ
nirvairaḥ sarva-bhūteṣu
yaḥ sa mām eti pāṇḍava

"You can effortlessly attain My abode by following these five principles – (1) Dedicate your endeavours to Me, (2) Make Me the focal point of your life, (3) Embrace devotion to Me, (4) Let go of all worldly attachments, and (5) Refrain from harboring envy towards others." (11.55)

According to this beautiful verse, devotees are encouraged to engage in actions that are brimming with devotion. It is a journey guided by acts of kindness, compassion, and unwavering faith. However, amidst this journey, there lies a cautionary note: the peril of envy. For those who harbor envy towards the Lord, His devotees or any living entity, their spiritual journey becomes spoilt and tainted. Envy, with its corrosive nature, acts as a barrier to spiritual elevation, clouding our hearts with bitterness.

Thus, the verse not only offers a pathway to spiritual fulfilment but also serves as a beacon of wisdom, reminding us to cultivate virtues of humility, gratitude, contentment and non-envy. Through sincere devotion and a heart free from envy, we can aspire to live in the spiritual world, where bliss reigns supreme in the loving company of the Lord. Now let's read stories of a few devotees who lived up to these principles.

A Pearl for Gopal

King Purushottamdev ruled the state of Odisha in Eastern India and was a devout follower of Lord Krishna. After a victorious battle against the kingdom of Vidyanagar, he visited a temple dedicated to Lord Gopal (Krishna) in Vidyanagar. Filled with devotion, King Purushottamdev bowed before the deity and fervently prayed, "O Lord, please come to my kingdom." Moved by his devotion, Lord Gopal accepted his prayer.

The king then transported the deity of Lord Gopal from Vidyanagar to Cuttack in Odisha, where he constructed a magnificent temple and arranged for elaborate worship rituals. King Purushottamdev's wife, also a devoted follower of Lord Gopal, offered numerous jewels to the deity. Among her treasures was a beautiful nose ring adorned with a valuable pearl. She longed to offer this to Lord Gopal and thought, "Lord Gopal is the master of the universe. He deserves the finest offerings. This radiant pearl would look stunning on Him. If only there was a hole in His nose, I could present this pearl to Him."

That night, while she slept, Lord Gopal appeared to her in a dream and spoke in a gentle voice, "Dear queen, when I was a child, my mother Yashoda pierced my nose and set a pearl there. The hole is still there. I would be delighted to accept the pearl you wish to offer Me with so much love." Astonished, the queen awoke and the following morning, she went to the temple and offered the pearl to Lord Gopal. Her heart was filled with immense satisfaction from Gopal's loving reciprocation.

Thus, Lord Gopal fulfilled the desires of both the king and the queen, responding to their sincere devotion with divine grace.

The Lord always answers the heartfelt prayers of His devotees.

The Two Boatmen

Once, Lord Rama, along with His beloved wife Sita Devi and His loyal brother Lakshmana, came to the banks of the sacred Ganga. They needed to cross the river. A humble boatman was ready to take them to the other side. This simple-hearted boatman was a devotee of Lord Rama. His heart was filled with love and reverence for the divine trio, and he was thrilled to serve them. Bowing before Rama, the boatman expressed his devotion through heartfelt prayers and humble gestures.

In a remarkable display of humility and reverence, he offered his own hands for Rama to step on before boarding the boat. The boatman's love and dedication shone brightly, deeply touching Rama, Sita, and Lakshmana. Impressed by his devotion, Sita took a ring from her finger and handed it to Rama to give to the boatman. Rama took it and offered it to the boatman, saying, "My dear friend, please take this. It is a small token of our gratitude for your kind service."

The boatman replied, "No, my dear Lord! I cannot accept this."

Surprised, Rama asked, "Why can't you accept it?"

The boatman explained, "I am a boatman, and you are also a boatman. People of the same profession shouldn't charge each other for their services."

Puzzled, Rama inquired, "How can I be of the same profession as you?"

The boatman explained, "O Lord, I take people across the Ganga to the other shore. You take people across the ocean of material existence (*samsaara*) to Vaikuntha. Just as I am taking you in my boat today, when my time comes, You will take me across the ocean of life."

Deeply moved by the boatman's wisdom and devotion, Rama hugged him. Because of his loving service, the boatman was later liberated from the cycle of birth and death, finding eternal peace and joy.

By doing even the smallest task for the Lord, one can benefit eternally.

The tales of Purushottamdev's queen and the humble boatman remind us that the Lord responds to genuine love and selfless service with boundless grace. In every sincere act of devotion, we can find divine reciprocation, guiding us towards the ultimate spiritual bliss.

Reflect to Realize

There are many negative qualities in this world: lust, anger, greed, pride, envy, etc. Interestingly, with little effort, we can transform all these bad qualities into positive attributes. For instance, instead of desiring things for ourselves out of lust, we can redirect that desire to serve the Lord. Similarly, anger can be justified when it arises in defense of the Lord's devotees or against unjust acts. Likewise, we can be eager or "greedy" for opportunities to serve the Lord and humanity. We can be happy to be able to follow a spiritual path rather than being proud in our material accomplishments. And we can convert envy into genuine appreciation. Thus, when Lord Krishna refers to *mat karma* we can transform all our ordinary material actions into spiritual acts.

10

Spirituality in Occupation

It's not the nature of our work but the intention and dedication behind it that determine our spiritual progress.

Anyone, regardless of their occupation, can connect with God. Unless one's occupation is inherently sinful or forbidden, there is no need to change it. Remaining faithful to one's occupation while nurturing a connection with the divine is entirely possible. Thus, work performed in devotion can bring anyone to spiritual fulfilment and unity with the divine. By integrating devotion into everyday tasks, we maintain a constant connection with God, regardless of our profession.

Lord Krishna, in this verse says,

yataḥ pravṛttir bhūtānāṁ
yena sarvam idaṁ tatam
sva-karmaṇā tam abhyarcya
siddhiṁ vindati mānavaḥ

"By worship of the Lord, who is the source of all beings and is all-pervading, a man can attain perfection through performing one's work." (18.46)

Through this practice of dedicating the fruits of one's labour to God, work becomes a form of worship, and we can achieve spiritual growth while fulfilling our worldly responsibilities. It transforms mundane activities into sacred acts. By offering our work to God, even routine tasks gain higher purpose, and facilitate our spiritual growth. This holistic integration of spirituality into daily life balances material responsibilities and spiritual aspirations, allowing us to experience spiritual satisfaction at every moment. Now, let's read a few stories of people who achieved life's perfection by integrating the spiritual with the material.

The Cobbler's Faith

Once, Narada Muni wandered through a tranquil village, his heart attuned to the melodies of devotion. During his contemplative stroll, he chanced upon a learned brahmana, who eagerly asked him, "O great sage, when you go to Vaikuntha, can you please ask Lord Vishnu if I can get liberation from the cycle of birth and death?" Ever compassionate, Narada Muni promised to carry the brahmana's plea to the Lord.

Continuing his journey, Narada Muni's path intersected with that of a simple cobbler. He toiled tirelessly beneath the expansive canopy of a banyan tree. Like the brahmana before him, the cobbler's gaze, though fixated on earthly tasks, harbored a profound longing for liberation. In a humble yet hopeful voice, the cobbler entreated Narada Muni to inquire Lord Vishnu about his liberation. Moved by the sincerity of the cobbler's plea, Narada Muni pledged to convey his supplication to the Lord.

Arriving in the abode of Lord Vishnu at Vaikuntha, Narada Muni stood in the resplendent presence of the Lord and asked, "O Lord, on my way here, a brahmana and a cobbler asked me about their liberation. Can you please tell me when they will be liberated?"

Lord Vishnu replied, "The cobbler will come to Me right after his current life."

Narada Muni then questioned, "O Lord, what about the brahmana?"

Lord Vishnu said, "He will have to remain there for several more lifetimes."

Narada Muni was surprised and asked, "Why so? The brahmana is very learned, engaged in conducting sacrifices, teaching scriptures, worship and so on. And the cobbler's occupation is just to stitch damaged shoes. He doesn't even know the scriptures. How can he reach You before the brahmana?"

Lord Vishnu replied, "You will understand soon. When they ask you about Me, just tell them that I am threading the eye of a needle with an elephant."

Narada Muni returned to earth and met the brahmana. The brahmana eagerly asked, "O sage, have you seen the Lord? What was He doing?"

Narada Muni answered, "He was threading an elephant through the eye of a needle."

The brahmana replied, "I don't believe it. How can an elephant enter the eye of a needle?" Narada Muni understood that although the brahmana was performing his occupational duties, he had no faith in the Lord's potency.

Narada Muni then went to the cobbler. The cobbler eagerly asked, "Pranam, O great sage. Have you seen Lord Vishnu? What was He doing?"

Narada Muni replied, "He was threading an elephant through the eye of a needle."

The cobbler had tears in his eyes. He said, "My Lord is so powerful, nothing is impossible for Him."

Narada Muni asked, "Do you really believe that the Lord can push an elephant through the hole of a needle?"

The cobbler replied, "Of course. Why not? As I sit under this banyan tree, I see so many fruits falling daily. In each fruit, there are many seeds, and in each seed, there is a huge banyan tree like this one. If my Lord can put a huge tree inside a small seed, why can't He push an elephant into a needle's eye?"

Narada Muni was impressed with his devotion and faith in the Lord. He then understood why Lord Vishnu told him that the cobbler would reach Vaikuntha after that very lifetime.

Unflinching faith in the Lord is more important than one's occupation.

The Banana Leaf Seller's Fortune

Sridhar Kolevacha was a humble and poor brahmana residing in Bengal. His modest livelihood depended on selling bananas and banana leaves, yielding a meagre profit. Half of his earnings were devoted to worshiping the sacred Ganga, while the other half sustained his basic needs. Sridhar lived in a dilapidated hut with a leaky roof and relied on a cracked iron pot for his drinking water. Despite his hardships, he spent his nights chanting the names of Lord Krishna, his devotion unwavering. Neighbours misconstrued his sleepless nights as the result of poverty and hunger.

Every day, Nimai Pandit, who was none other than Lord Krishna incarnated as a brahmana, visited Sridhar's shop to purchase bananas and leaves. Although Sridhar always quoted fair prices, Nimai would playfully argue, "Sridhar, you are selling these bananas at unreasonable rates. I will pay only half of what you're asking." This playful banter would escalate into a tug-of-war over the bananas, with Sridhar trying to reclaim them, sometimes even pushing Nimai. Nonetheless, Nimai would pay only half and take the goods.

This routine continued daily, with the two engaging in spirited debates over the prices for more than an hour. On occasion, Nimai would even request the items for free, and eventually, Sridhar would concede, offering some bananas at no cost. Nimai delighted in eating from the small bowls made of banana bark that Sridhar provided. Despite Nimai taking away all his goods, Sridhar never grew angry, captivated by Nimai's beauty, unaware that he was, in fact, Lord Krishna in a fair complexion.

One day, Nimai Pandit visited Sridhar's humble hut and inquired, "O Sridhar, why do you remain so poor? You worship Lord Vishnu, the consort of Goddess Lakshmi, yet you lack sufficient resources for food and clothing, and your house is in ruins."

Sridhar responded, "A bird builds its nest in trees and roams in search of food, while a king enjoys the luxuries of a palace. Yet, there is no difference in their pleasure, as everyone's capacity to enjoy is limited, regardless of the abundance of facilities."

Nimai replied, "Dear Sridhar, though you appear to be poor, you are truly wealthy. One day, I will reveal your riches to the world."

On a momentous day, Nimai Pandit disclosed His divine identity to Sridhar, who fainted upon the revelation. Regaining consciousness, Sridhar praised the Lord with heartfelt hymns. Pleased with his devotion, the Lord offered him eight mystic powers as a boon. However, Sridhar declined any material boon. Despite the Lord's repeated insistence, Sridhar finally requested, "O Lord, I ask for just one thing. May you, in the form of this brahmana, continue to come and take my banana leaves and bark, life after life. May you argue with me over the price of my wares, allowing me the privilege to serve you."

The Lord smiled and granted his simple-hearted wish, revealing to all the depth of Sridhar's selfless devotion and his true wealth. Sridhar's occupation of selling bananas and leaves, combined with his simplicity and devotion, won the Lord's heart, and their sweet, loving interactions continued eternally.

One can win the Lord's heart even by simple occupational activities.

The stories of the cobbler and Shridhar Kolavecha remind us that the Lord treasures faithful devotion, regardless of our worldly status. Despite their humble occupations, both deeply touched the heart of the Lord. The Lord values the sincerity of our hearts above all else, reminding us that His grace is accessible to all.

Reflect to Realize

Everyone aspires to be perfect in life, whether in relationships, work, or academics. Yet, even when they achieve this worldly perfection, they often find themselves dissatisfied and unhappy. This obsession with perfection leads to perpetual dissatisfaction. Therefore, the greatest perfection in life is to develop and nurture a spiritual connection with God. By sincerely striving to serve God, being humble, and serving His devotees, we naturally attain true perfection. This spiritual pursuit brings the real happiness and satisfaction that has always eluded us.

SECTION II: JNANA–KNOWLEDGE

Who are we—bodies or souls? How can we know God? What is the role of a guru or teacher? When and why does God appear on earth? Is He partial? If so, how? If not, why does He support His devotees and kill the demons?

Knowledge about this world, our own selves, the Lord and the interconnection between all these, helps us live a more meaningful and purposeful life. Thus, pursuing pure, authentic and enlivening knowledge is a vital aspect of spiritual life. This section presents simple yet authentic answers to such questions based on the shlokas of the Bhagavad Gita, intertwined with inspiring stories.

11

Trust in a Teacher

Knowledge cannot be truly absorbed without faith in the one who imparts it.

Who among the following is indeed more knowledgeable?

a. A school topper who gets excellent grades but is very proud, arrogant and disrespectful towards teachers; or

b. A humble student who studies sincerely, who may not score top grades in class, but is respectful and grateful towards the teachers.

The second one, isn't it? Acquiring knowledge is not just about gathering information and becoming a scholar. Knowledge, when devoid of humility, can lead to pride and arrogance. Real knowledge requires humility, good conduct, and respect for teachers.

In the Bhagavad Gita, Lord Krishna describes the characteristics of a person who is qualified to receive knowledge:

śraddhāvān labhate jñānaṁ
tat-paraḥ saṁyatendriyaḥ

jñānaṁ labdhvā parāṁ śāntim
acireṇādhigacchati

"One who has faith (shraddha), devotion, and self-control can easily gain knowledge, and thus attain peace." (4.39)

This verse emphasizes that true knowledge is accessible to those who possess faith, devotion, and self-discipline. These qualities are essential for a deeper understanding and internalization of knowledge.

Although teachers may impart great wisdom, if we lack faith in their teachings, we wouldn't truly absorb the knowledge. Identifying a wise and realized teacher, and keeping faith in the teacher's teachings is crucial for effective learning. It is this faith, coupled with humility and self-control, that allows a student to not only acquire knowledge, but also apply it in a way that brings peace and inner fulfilment.

Therefore, when comparing two students, the humble student who studies sincerely and helps others is more aligned with the path of true knowledge as described by Lord Krishna. This student embodies the qualities of faith, devotion, and humility, which are essential for genuine learning and personal growth. The school topper, despite excellent grades, lacks these crucial qualities, which limits the depth and value of their knowledge.

True knowledge transforms the individual, fostering a sense of inner peace and fulfilment. It is not measured by external accolades but by the quality of one's character and the positive impact one has on others. In this light, the humble student is indeed more knowledgeable, as they embody the spirit of learning and growth that Krishna extols.

Here are some stories of great people who had deep faith in their gurus and thus easily attained knowledge about God.

The Uneducated Scholar

In the sacred region of Srirangam in South India resided a simple brahmana. His daily ritual included a visit to the temple where he enthusiastically attempted to recite the Bhagavad Gita. Because he lacked formal education, his pronunciation was not perfect, inviting mockery, criticism, and laughter from onlookers. Undeterred and unperturbed, he neither took offense nor wavered in his devotion. With each recitation, he experienced goosebumps, and tears of joy welled up in his eyes.

During this time, Lord Chaitanya Mahaprabhu, an incarnation of Lord Krishna touring South India, arrived at the same temple. Observing the emotional state of the brahmana, He inquired, "My dear friend, why are you crying? Surely, your tears aren't a result of pain or distress. Please tell me which part of the Bhagavad Gita brings you such profound joy?"

The brahmana, with innocence in his voice, replied, "I am an uneducated man. I don't know the meaning of the words I read. Sometimes I pronounce them correctly, and sometimes not, but still, I read the Bhagavad Gita only to honour my guru's instructions. Whenever I open the Gita, I see Lord Krishna driving Arjuna's chariot, taking the reins in his hands. I feel so delighted seeing how affectionate the Lord is towards His devotees."

Appreciating the brahmana's humility towards his guru and his sincere love for Krishna, Lord Chaitanya continued, "You are the best reader of the Bhagavad Gita. Whatever you know constitutes the real essence of the Gita." Speaking thus, Lord Chaitanya embraced him. Lord Chaitanya, actually an incarnation of Lord Krishna in the form of a sanyasi, revealed this understanding to the brahmana through His mercy.

Scholarship isn't essential for understanding scriptures, but faith in the guru along with devotion to God is.

The Kitchen of Humility

In ancient India, there once lived a great scholar named Dasarathi. He was a disciple of the great saint Ramanuja Acharya. Once, Dasarathi asked Ramanuja to explain the meaning of the topmost verse of the Bhagavad Gita. At the same moment, Ramanuja's sister, Atulai, arrived distressed at the scene. Witnessing his sister in a state of anxiety, Ramanuja inquired, "What happened? Why are you so sad?"

In response, Atulai explained, "Dear brother, my father has sent me here. At my father-in-law's house, I had to fetch water daily from a lake that was over two miles away, making the journey twice a day. The road to the lake was rough and deserted, causing fear and exhaustion."

Ramanuja attentively listened as Atulai continued, "I shared these difficulties with my mother-in-law, but instead of offering sympathy, she became enraged and insisted that I should procure a servant from my father's house for the task. Faced with such harsh treatment, I returned to my father's house, and he suggested that I seek your assistance."

Ramanuja Acharya promptly replied, "Dear sister, please don't worry. I will send a brahmana along with you, who will fetch water and also assist with cooking." With this assurance, he directed a meaningful glance at scholarly Dasarathi, indicating that he was to accompany Atulai as a servant during her trips to the lake. Understanding the desire of his guru, Dasarathi gladly accompanied Atulai to her father-in-law's house and diligently began working in the kitchen. Six months passed in this manner.

One day, a gathering of villagers assembled to attend a lecture by a learned speaker, and Dasarathi was among the audience. During the discourse, the speaker provided inaccurate explanations of a Sanskrit verse, prompting Dasarathi to speak up against these errors. The speaker, irate at being corrected by a servant, rebuked Dasarathi, saying, "Stop, you fool! How can a servant like you explain the scriptures? Go back to the kitchen and display your talents there."

Undeterred and composed, Dasarathi continued to elucidate the correct meaning of the verse. His flawless presentation, grounded in various scriptures, left everyone in the assembly, including the angered speaker, in awe. Recognizing his mistake, the speaker humbly begged Dasarathi's pardon and fell at his feet.

Curious, the speaker inquired, "How is it that such a learned scholar and devotee as yourself is engaged in such menial work in the kitchen?"

Dasarathi calmly replied, "I am simply following the orders of my guru."

Upon learning that Dasarathi was the renowned devotee-scholar, the entire assembly collectively went to Srirangam to meet Ramanuja Acharya. In unison, they addressed the great saint, "O revered sage, it is inappropriate for your esteemed disciple to serve in the kitchen any longer. He possesses great knowledge, yet his heart remains devoid of pride. Please permit us to bring him back to you."

Pleased with the praises showered upon his disciple, Ramanuja Acharya responded, "I shall come with you to bring back Dasarathi!" Personally undertaking the journey, Ramanuja Acharya went to fetch Dasarathi. Upon reaching him, Dasarathi bowed down, and Ramanuja embraced and blessed him. Together, they returned to Srirangam.

During their return journey, Ramanuja Acharya expounded on Lord Krishna's final instruction to Arjuna in the Bhagavad Gita. This teaching revealed how a devotee completely takes shelter of the Lord. Through his selfless and humble service, Dasarathi imbibed the profound teachings of the Bhagavad Gita from his guru.

A true disciple doesn't doubt his guru's instructions but accepts them with faith.

The uneducated brahmana steadfastly followed his guru's instructions despite facing mockery from others. Similarly, Dasarathi, a learned scholar, willingly undertook the menial services assigned by Ramanuja Acharya. This exemplifies how obedience and unwavering faith in the guidance of teachers pave the way for receiving divine knowledge.

Reflect to Realize

Throughout countless ages, we've placed our trust in the transient pleasures of this material realm. Journeying through 8.4 million species, our souls have encountered nothing but disappointment. It's indeed repugnant for a pure, eternal soul to be ensnared in such a state within the material world. After enduring the trials and tribulations of this material existence, why not bestow a fraction of our faith in Krishna and His teachings? Even little devotion towards Him renders the Lord indebted to us. Having served the illusions of maya for aeons and reaped only unspeakable consequences, why not invest our faith in the Lord and experience His boundless love in the spiritual domain?

12

Devotion Gives Knowledge

True knowledge isn't about gathering information; it's about undergoing transformation.

The qualification to truly know God transcends worldly attributes such as wealth, beauty, scholarship, or strength, as emphasized by Lord Krishna in this profound verse:

bhaktyā mām abhijānāti
yāvān yaś cāsmi tattvataḥ
tato māṁ tattvato jñātvā
viśate tad-anantaram

"One can understand Me as I am only by devotion. And when one is in full consciousness of Me by such devotion, one can enter into My eternal spiritual kingdom after death." (18.55)

Lord Krishna imparts the wisdom that it is through loving devotion to Him alone that one can attain true knowledge of His essence. When we approach God with a pure heart, developing a more personal connection with Him, we are blessed with His divine grace, which illuminates our understanding and brings us closer to Him. This loving devotion is what allows one to truly understand and experience God's infinite nature, leading to inner peace and ultimate happiness. This relationship is not merely intellectual but is deeply experiential, allowing the devotee to live in constant awareness of God's presence and to act as a vessel of His divine love and wisdom.

Thus, the path to true knowledge of God is marked by humility, faith, and unwavering devotion. These qualities open the heart and mind to receive divine knowledge and experience the profound joy and peace that come from a close relationship with God. This is the essence of the teaching in the Bhagavad Gita and a guiding principle for anyone seeking to understand and connect with the divine.

To further elucidate the profound significance of this verse, let us delve into a series of illuminating stories that exemplify this point.

Little Mouth, Mighty Insight

About nine centuries ago, in Srirangam, a holy place in Southern India, a five-year-old child named Parashara lived. One day, a renowned scholar named Digvijay Pandit, known for his expertise in logic, grammar, and philosophy, arrived at Srirangam. Traveling across India, he challenged scholars in debates, gaining wealth and fame by defeating many. Accompanied by four strong men carrying him in a decorated palanquin and brahmanas chanting mantras, he instilled fear wherever he went. Upon his arrival at Srirangam, little Parashara approached him, expressing, "Sir, I have a question for you." The Pandit, looking down from his palanquin, dismissed the child, claiming to be too young for serious debates. Unyielding, Parashara argued, "If you're enlightened, why emphasize the size of my body? I am not just my body; please answer my question." Exasperated, the Pandit asked, "What is your question?" The child then picked up a handful of sand, held it before the Pandit's face, and asked, "Tell me, sir, how many grains of sand are there in my hand?" The scholar, speechless and perplexed, had never encountered such a question.

Parashara continued, "A person with real knowledge sees the presence of God in everyone's heart, like a tree with delicious fruits. If you lack respect for others, if you are not humble before God and His devotees, I consider all your knowledge as worthless as this handful of sand." Saying this, the boy let go of the sand.

These profound words from a five-year-old pierced the scholar's heart. Humbly, he descended from his palanquin, bowing at the child's feet. With tears of humility, he pleaded, "I want to be your disciple." Thus, he became the young boy's disciple.

One who is humble learns even from younger people.

The Mystical Manuscript

Once, the King of Jaipur faced a challenge from scholars who questioned the authenticity of the Gaudiya Vaishnavism school. Despite having commentaries on scriptures like the Bhagavad Gita, *Srimad Bhagavatam*, and the Upanishads, the absence of a commentary on the *Vedanta Sutras* by sage Vyasa was pointed out. Desiring to respond to the challenge, the king sought help from his guru, Srila Vishvanath Chakravarti Thakur, a devoted follower of Lord Krishna.

Due to his old age, Srila Vishvanath Chakravarti could not personally travel to Jaipur. Instead, he sent his scholarly disciple Baladev Vidyabhushan to represent and address the situation. Initially hesitant, Baladev pondered how he could write a commentary when Vyasa himself had already provided one through the *Srimad Bhagavatam*. However, feeling the urgency to establish the authenticity of the Gaudiya Vaishnava school, he decided to give it a try.

Baladev Vidyabhushan prayed at the temple of Lord Govindaji, seeking direction and guidance. In response, Lord Govindaji's garland fell on him, a divine sanction and blessing. Filled with gratitude, Baladev Vidyabhushan completed the commentary in a much shorter time than the given month.

In declaring his work, Baladev Vidyabhushan humbly stated, "What I have written as the commentary to the *Vedanta-Sūtra* are not my words; I have written whatever Lord Govindaji made me write. Therefore, this commentary will be known as the *Govinda-bhashya*." The *Govinda-bhashya*, inspired and blessed by Lord Govinda in reciprocation to Baladev Vidyabhushan's devotion, became a renowned and profound explanation of the *Vedanta Sutra*.

The Lord is very eager to reveal rare knowledge to His sincere devotees.

The contrast between proud Digvijay Pandit's defeat in a debate by a devoted child and Baladev Vidyabhushan's empowered writing of a scholarly commentary highlights the significance of devotion in acquiring knowledge. Devotion, at times, proves to be more crucial than knowledge itself in spiritual understanding and growth.

Reflect to Realize

In some sections of the Gita, Lord Krishna explains that no one can understand Him. However, at some places, He says that He can be completely understood. Why this seeming contradiction? Because Krishna reserves a special seat for His devotees. He cannot be known by others. Only devotees can know Him through the path of devotion. Therefore, for His devoted followers, the Lord reveals about Himself without any reservations. Undoubtedly, the Lord reserves a special affection for His sincere devotees!

13

Nature of Soul

Celebrate your real existence beyond birth and death.

Celebrating birthdays and mourning deaths are common human experiences, deeply ingrained in emotional and cultural expressions. However, these events often prompt us to deeply reflect on the true essence of "birth" and "death". In a philosophical and spiritual context, birth signifies the soul's entrance into a new physical body, while death marks the soul's departure from the body, transitioning into another body. These events are merely transitions for the soul, which is eternal and transcendental to the cycle of birth and death.

This profound concept forms one of the foremost teachings of Lord Krishna in the Bhagavad Gita. The Gita eloquently illustrates the soul's immortality through a simple, yet powerful analogy presented by Krishna.

vāsāṁsi jīrṇāni yathā vihāya
navāni gṛhṇāti naro 'parāṇi
tathā śarīrāṇi vihāya jīrṇāny
anyāni saṁyāti navāni dehī

"As a person puts on new clothes, giving up old ones, the soul similarly accepts new bodies, giving up the old and useless ones." (2.22)

This verse describes the transient nature of the material body and the enduring nature of the spirit soul. The body is like clothing—temporary and replaceable—while the soul is eternal, moving from one physical body to another upon death and rebirth. Birth and death are mere phases in the soul's eternal journey.

How long does the soul transmigrate from one body to another? As long as one has selfish material desires to be fulfilled, and as long as one doesn't take to spiritual life. While responsibly maintaining the body, we need to simultaneously cultivate detachment from the body and its belongings and give up a sense of possessiveness and selfishness. Rather, one must prioritize engaging oneself in spiritual activities, such as worshiping God, chanting His names, and hearing about Him, and by His mercy put an end to the cycle of birth and death. Thus, one can enter the eternal spiritual world and attain the loving association of the Lord in spiritual body that's never subject to birth and death.

This deep philosophical idea, while complex, can be made accessible through the following stories. So, why wait? Dive into these narratives to grasp the enduring nature of the soul as taught in the Gita.

Chitraketu's Bitter-sweet Journey of Parenting

Once, in the prosperous Surasena province, there lived a king named Chitraketu. Despite his wealth, education, fame, and the affection of ten million wives, his heart was heavy with sorrow—because he didn't have a child.

Once, a revered sage named Angiras visited his palace. King Chitraketu welcomed him with great respect and warmth. Sage Angiras was pleased with the loving reception, and inquired about the king's well-being, noticing the visible sorrow on his pale face. The king confided, "O Holy Sage, though you possess knowledge beyond mortals, let me share my situation. My vast wealth and kingdom bring me no joy, for I lack a heir. I request you to help me beget a son who can look after my kingdom."

Responding to the king's plea, Angiras conducted a sacred ritual. From the sacrificial fire, a celestial being emerged, bearing a pot of mystical sweet. Chitraketu gratefully accepted it and presented it to his first wife, Kritadyuti. Angiras assured her that the consumption of the sweet would bestow her with the power to beget a child.

Before departing, Angiras warned Chitraketu, "Your son shall bring both joy and sorrow." The king, interpreted these to mean that the only child would bring him great happiness but he might be naughty or disobedient thus bringing him some sorrow as well. Still Chitraketu felt that having a disobedient child is better than having no child.

In due course of time, Kritadyuti gave birth to a beautiful son, bringing immense joy to the kingdom. Chitraketu, overjoyed, celebrated the long-awaited occasion by generously showering gifts—gold, silver, ornaments, garments, villages, horses, and more, similar to a bountiful rain from a benevolent cloud.

Chitraketu's affection for his son and Kritadyuti grew day by day. He slowly began neglecting his other wives. This made the remaining queens envious. They thought, "The new-born child is the cause of our condition." Their jealousy made them lose their minds and do the unthinkable. They poisoned the baby to death!

Unaware of the sinful act of her co-wives, Kritadyuti thought that her son had been sleeping for a long time. Later, she sent her maid to wake him up, only to realize that the child was dead. Shocked at seeing the lifeless boy, she cried profusely and fell to the ground unconscious. All the palace residents gathered there and began to cry. The queens who had poisoned him also cried pretentiously.

When Chitraketu heard of his son's death, he became almost blind with grief. Slipping and falling, he approached the dead child and fell unconscious. Kritadyuti loudly cried and blamed God for her son's death.

At that time, sage Angiras arrived there along with Narada Muni. The two sages spoke to Chitraketu. While Chitraketu lay like a dead body next to his son's dead body, Narada Muni and Angiras Muni spoke to him, "Dear Chitraketu, what relationship does this dead body have with you? Did this relationship exist before? Does it truly exist now? Will it continue in the future?"

Chitraketu was confused to hear such questions. Due to deep grief, he was unable to reply. Narada Muni continued, "As sand particles on a seashore come together and get separated by the force of waves, the living beings also sometimes come together and get separated by the force of time. We were not together before birth and will not be together after death. God brings people together and disperses them as they deserve."

Narada Muni then spoke to the soul of the dead boy, "Dear child, just look at your father and mother. Everyone is grief-stricken because of your passing away. Re-enter your body and enjoy life with your relatives. Accept your father's royal throne and be a good king to your people." So saying, he brought the son back to life with his mystic powers.

The boy spoke, "O great sage, in which birth were these persons my parents? I have been wandering in the bodies of devas, animals, and human beings. In many lifetimes, I had many parents from different species. In different births, different people become our friends, relatives, enemies, well-wishers and so on. All these relationships are valid only when one is within a body. But no one is permanently related." Saying this, the boy again left, and people saw only his dead body.

Chitraketu and all others were amazed on hearing the unpalatable facts of life taught by the child. Giving up their sadness, they dutifully arranged for the funeral ceremony of the dead boy, as a matter of custom. Kritadyuti's co-wives were ashamed of their sinful act. They atoned for the killing of the child on the banks of the Yamuna as directed by brahmanas.

Thereafter, Chitraketu chanted a mantra given by Narada Muni continuously for one week. His mind thus calmed down and he became increasingly attached to Lord Vishnu. Eventually, the Lord appeared before him and blessed him.

One shouldn't get too elated in happiness, or too depressed in distress. Both situations are temporary.

Transcending Tears

In the kingdom of Ushinara, there lived a powerful king named Suyajna. Once he valorously fought in a battle, and unfortunately died leaving his kingdom in mourning. As the sun dipped below the horizon, his queens rushed to the battlefield, their hearts breaking at the sight of their fallen husband. Their grief was palpable, their cries a testament to their profound loss. They lamented their fate, unable to envision a life without their beloved.

Their refusal to part with the king's body halted the funeral rites. Their sorrow echoed everywhere until it reached Yama, the lord of death, the deity who oversees the afterlife for the departed souls. Moved by their plight, Yama came to the earthly plane, assuming the guise of a young boy.

Addressing the queens, the boy said, "See the depth of their confusion over the nature of life and death. Although they had seen so many people die in front of them, they are still lamenting. The separation of the soul from the body is inevitable. The soul is eternal as distinct from the temporary vessel of the body. Dear queens, please try to overcome your grief, by recognizing the futility in mourning the loss of what was always meant to pass."

Yet, the queens remained enveloped in their sorrow. This prompted Yama to share a tale of a hunter and a pair of kulinga birds, illustrating the futility of lamentation and the harsh cycles of life and death. He said, "Once a male and female bird were enjoying each other's company when suddenly a hunter's arrow killed the female bird. The male bird then lamented for the death of his mate and failed to notice that the hunter's next aim was he. The hunter then shot an arrow and kill the male bird too."

Thus, Yamaraja tried to bring out the importance of focusing on spiritual devotion rather than being consumed by grief. He concluded, "Dear ladies, even if you lament for a hundred years, your departed husband will not come back. So, please allow the last rites to be performed at the prescribed time." Saying this he departed.

Yama's words, profound and enlightening, left everyone in awe. With Yama's departure, the air cleared, allowing Suyajna's family to proceed with his last rites. This tale serves as a poignant reminder of the transient nature of life, urging the living to seek solace in the eternal, rather than being stuck to the material world.

Emotions are common when we lose our dear ones. But that shouldn't make one dysfunctional.

Both King Chitraketu and the wives of King Suyajna experienced deep sorrow upon the departure of their loved ones. In these moments of despair, devotees of the Lord, such as Narada, Angiras, and Yama, stepped in to share insights about the realities of life. It's natural to feel a profound sense of loss when close friends or relatives pass away, enveloping one in grief. However, it's essential not to let this grief render us incapable of moving forward. Instead, embracing the truth of the situation and carrying on with our duties and responsibilities is a testament to our resilience and understanding of life's transient nature.

Reflect to Realize

Take pictures of yourself from when you were young to your current age. Arrange them in ascending order on a chart paper. Observe how your body undergoes constant change while the essence of who you are remains unchanged. Think about how fleeting our body is and why it's time that we put an end to our transmigration and serve Lord Krishna.

14

Who Controls Nature?

Spirituality doesn't just include worshiping God, but respecting nature as well.

Stones can't float on water, and a child can't lift a mountain. These actions go against the laws of nature we know. Nature, with all its different parts, follows fixed rules that seem unchangeable. Gravity pulls objects down, water flows downwards, and mountains are heavy and sturdy. These rules are strong and don't easily change.

But there's a higher power and authority, the Supreme Being, who created and controls everything in the universe, and is the cause of various natural functions of the universal elements. In this verse, Lord Krishna says,

mayādhyakṣeṇa prakṛtiḥ
sūyate sa-carācaram
hetunānena kaunteya
jagad viparivartate

"Dear Arjuna, this material nature works under My direction, producing all moving and non-moving beings. Every change and effect in nature comes from Me." (9.10)

This means that the Supreme Lord has the power to direct and change the natural world as He wants. Elements like earth, water, air, fire, and sky follow the Lord's commands. He gives them their unique properties: earth is solid, water flows, air moves, fire burns, and the sky is vast. He can change these properties whenever He wishes, showing His ultimate power.

So, while natural laws seem strict, they are actually under the control of the Supreme Being. The things that seem impossible to us, like stones floating or children lifting mountains, can happen if He wills it. This shows that the divine power is above all natural laws.

To delve deeper into this profound concept, here are two captivating tales illustrating the divine's influence on the natural order.

Floating Stones

Upon learning that Sita Devi was held captive in Lanka, Lord Rama, driven by the urgency to rescue her, gathered a vast army of monkeys. Standing on the shore that separated them from Lanka, the immense ocean posed a formidable obstacle. Lord Rama, contemplating the daunting task of crossing, turned to the ocean God, Samudra, for a solution.

After a prolonged wait, the ocean God emerged, radiating brilliance similar to the dawn sun. Adorned in a red dress, a garland of red flowers, and a flower crown, his eyes resembling lotuses, Samudra, accompanied by river goddesses, humbly addressed Lord Rama, "O Lord, my waters cause no impediment to You or your army. Yet, I request you to construct a bridge across the ocean, so that the future generations praise you for this inconceivable act." Lord Rama approved the plan. The monkeys, led by the skilled architect Nala, eagerly began their task. Huge rocks and tree trunks were thrown into the sea, and instead of sinking, the rocks miraculously floated on water by the power of Lord Rama. Binding trees and rocks with creepers, the monkeys constructed an expansive bridge towards Lanka.

Just within a few days, the monkeys crafted a huge bridge spanning several miles, connecting to the shores of Lanka. Riding on the backs of Hanuman and Angada, Lord Rama and Lakshmana crossed the bridge, reaching Lanka's shores. This remarkable feat, where even heavy stones defied their natural sinking tendency, became an enduring testament to the divine power of Lord Rama, earning eternal praise.

The Lord performs superhuman acts to please His devotees.

A Rainy Rebellion

Once, Indra, the king of heaven and the lord of rains, succumbed to ego due to his power and position. Observing this unwarranted pride, Lord Krishna decided to divert the traditional worship of Indra in Vrindavan and instead initiated the worship of the Govardhan Hill. The cowherd community in Vrindavan embraced this new Govardhan puja with immense joy.

Indra, angered by the shift in worship, unleashed a devastating downpour on Vrindavan, fuelled by his pride and forgetfulness of Krishna's mercy. He sent dense Samvartaka clouds accompanied by seven fierce winds capable of destroying the entire world. The sky was filled with colourful clouds, resembling huge elephants moving side by side. Lightning, thunder, and wild winds accompanied the continuous rain, similar to piercing arrows, along with large, heavy pieces of ice. The heavy downpour resembled long hanging branches of a banyan tree, submerging all the lands in water. The cows sought shelter for their calves, and the distressed cowherd community sought refuge at King Nanda's palace.

Seeing the distress of His beloved cowherds, Lord Krishna displayed His omnipotence. He temporarily halted the rain over the path from King Nanda's house to the Govardhan Hill. With divine speed, Krishna ran from His home to the Govardhan Hill without a single raindrop touching His divine body or clothes. Effortlessly, like a child picking a mushroom or an elephant lifting a clump of grass, Krishna lifted the Govardhan Hill, touching the clouds. He became Giridhari, the lifter of the hill, and laughed off the mighty power of the foolish Indra. All the devatas, except Indra, rejoiced and praised this act. The Govardhan seemed to celebrate the destruction of Indra's fame, with flowers falling from the trees as Krishna touched the hill.

A large stone separated from the hill, and Krishna comfortably lifted the Govardhan with His left hand's little finger. Under the Govardhan, King Nanda, Mothers Yashoda and Rohini, gopas, gopis, thousands of cows, calves, bulls, buffalos, and the entire cowherd community gathered. Through Krishna's touch, the Govardhan expanded to thirty-two miles, providing comfortable shelter for all. As Krishna held the Govardhan, chunks of earth formed a natural boundary wall around it, preventing water from flowing underneath. Seshanag coiled around the Govardhan to stop the flow of water, and the Sudarshan Chakra hovered above, drinking up falling streams. Despite Indra's fierce rain, not a blade of grass moved in Vrindavan.

After seven days, Indra was humiliated and humbled, the sky cleared, and the sun shone. While these seven days were like seven yugas of pain for Indra, they were like seven joyous hours for Vrindavan's residents. Krishna placed the Govardhan back on the ground, restoring the divine harmony in Vrindavan.

Whether the Lord protects or punishes, all His activities are merciful and enchanting.

Given that the Lord governs nature, He possesses the ability to defy natural laws—making stones float and effortlessly lifting a massive hill with His little finger. Moreover, Krishna does not hesitate to admonish the devatas if they deviate due to pride or greed. Lord Krishna, the repository of all superpowers, utilizes His divine abilities to safeguard and bring joy to His devotees. Thus, it is essential for us to earnestly pray to Him, serve Him diligently, and, above all, cultivate a profound friendship with the Divine.

Reflect to Realize

Often, people may believe it's acceptable to worship God while disregarding the well-being of nature. However, in this Gita verse, it's revealed that all of nature is Lord Krishna's energy. Do you think Krishna would be pleased if we honour Him but disrespect His creation? No! Alongside directly pleasing God, let's also strive to conserve and protect the nature, His energy. Let's take a moment to express our apologies to Mother Earth for the injustices we've consciously or unconsciously inflicted upon her. Let's show gratitude for all that she provides us and commit to rectifying our past wrongdoings. By honoring and preserving nature, we honour and please the divine.

15

The String behind Pearls

Recognize how the divine thread unites and sustains the universe.

Have you ever taken a moment to admire a beautiful pearl necklace? Each pearl has its own unique shine and shape, forming an intricate design that catches your eye. But there's something vital in it that often goes unnoticed—the invisible thread that holds all the pearls together. This delicate string weaves through each pearl, turning them into a harmonious piece of art. Each pearl, with its individual charm, adds to the necklace's overall beauty, but it's the unseen thread that brings it all together, giving it structure and unity.

In the same way, the universe, in all its splendour, is intricately threaded by the divine string of Lord Krishna, the Supreme Being. His energy permeates every atom, sustaining and governing the vast expanse of creation. His declaration resounds in the Bhagavad Gita,

mattaḥ parataraṁ nānyat
kiñcid asti dhanañ-jaya

mayi sarvam idaṁ protaṁ
sūtre maṇi-gaṇā iva

"O Arjuna, there is no one superior to Me. Everything rests upon Me, as pearls are strung on a thread." (7.7)

While the individual components of the universe, much like the pearls, may seem autonomous and distinct, they are in reality interconnected and supported by the omnipresent and omnipotent Lord Krishna. He is the taste of water that quenches our thirst, the brilliance of the sun and the moon, the natural fragrance of the earth from which all sweet-smelling flowers emanate. Thus, He is present inside and outside of everything, and is the source and sustenance of all that exists, as He Himself had mentioned in the Gita.

Now, let's dive into two enchanting stories that explore the mysteries of Krishna's all-pervading nature.

The Gateway to Infinity

One day in the beautiful surroundings of Vrindavan, little Krishna, adorned with innocence, played with His companions and elder brother Balarama. Mother Yashoda, engrossed in her daily chores, witnessed the joyous acts of her divine son's play.

Suddenly, Balarama and Krishna's playmates rushed to Mother Yashoda, their faces etched with concern. "O Mother," they exclaimed, "Krishna has consumed mud!" Worry creased Mother Yashoda's brow as she apprehensively approached her mischievous yet beloved child Krishna.

Inquisitively, she asked Krishna, "Why have you eaten mud, my dear? Am I not feeding You delicious milk products at home? Your friends, even Balarama, are distressed. What is the truth?"

Krishna, innocence resonating in His voice, replied, "Mother, I never ate mud. Their accusations are false. Balarama, in a fit of playfulness, joined the others against Me. If you doubt, look into My mouth and decide the truth."

Amidst a mix of concern and determination, Mother Yashoda agreed, "Well, open your mouth wide for me to see." Krishna, like any ordinary child, obliged. However, within His mouth was something astonishing. The Lord unveiled a cosmic spectacle within His tiny mouth. Mother Yashoda, peering into His tiny mouth, witnessed the entire cosmos—outer space, celestial bodies, mountains, rivers, the village of Vrindavan, and even herself and her son—all encapsulated within Krishna's divine oral cavity.

Bewildered and scared, Mother Yashoda questioned her senses. "Is this reality or a dream? Have I lost my sanity, or is my child endowed with unimaginable power?" Yet, by the divine will of Krishna, a transformation swiftly swept over her mind. The cosmic vision faded from her memory and she quickly cradled Krishna, in her affectionate arms.

In the land of Vrindavan, Krishna, as a cherished child, relished the warmth of maternal scolding, feeding, and affection. The cosmic revelation, a fleeting glimpse into the majesty of the Supreme, dissolved, leaving behind the simplicity of motherly love.

Krishna enchants us with His delicate interplay of being the infinite and the intimate.

A Jaw-dropping Gaze

While imparting the teachings of the Bhagavad Gita to Arjuna, Lord Krishna proclaimed, "I am the origin of the entire universe; everything emanates from Me and is dependent upon Me. Recognizing this truth, My devoted followers serve Me with unwavering dedication and speak of Me with love. Then I gift them with the intelligence to seek Me."

In response, Arjuna inquired, "My dear Krishna, I know that You are the Supreme God—pure, transcendent, and the source of all. Not only do I recognize this, but sages like Narada and Vyasa have also confirmed Your divinity. Now, You Yourself have also said it. Could you please explain to me the glories of Your divine power?"

Lord Krishna replied, "O Arjuna, I am the Supersoul (Paramatma) residing in the heart of all living beings. I am the start, end, and everything in between. I am the sun among luminaries, the moon among stars, Indra among devas, and the mind among the senses. I am Meru among mountains, the ocean among water bodies, and the banyan tree among trees. I am Ananta among many-hooded serpents and Ganga among rivers. My grandeur knows no bounds. What I've shared with you is but a glimpse of My infinite power. Anything beautiful, potent, or majestic in this world is but a small fraction of My omnipotence. I pervade every corner of the universe, sustaining it with My divine energy."

Arjuna, overwhelmed by the cosmic revelation of Lord Krishna's vishva-rupa, spoke with awe and reverence, "O Lord, I feel truly blessed and privileged to understand Your inconceivable spiritual powers. After learning about Your omnipresence and support for the entire universe, my sole desire is to behold Your universal form, in which You pervade and sustain everything."

Responding to Arjuna's earnest request, Krishna granted him divine vision, allowing him to witness the vishva-rupa. As Arjuna beheld this extraordinary form, he saw unlimited faces, eyes, hands, legs, arms, and bellies extending in all directions. The effulgence emanating from this form surpassed the brilliance of thousands of suns simultaneously rising in the sky. The entire universe, comprising sages, deities, humans, animals, birds, and all forms of life, manifested within the various parts of the vishva-rupa.

Mesmerized and deeply moved, Arjuna bowed down to the Lord, his heart filled with reverence. With folded hands, he exclaimed, "O Lord, within Your divine body, I perceive the presence of Brahma, Shiva, the sages, and divine serpents, along with all living beings. This form is the origin of the entire universe. I see countless arms, bellies, mouths, and eyes extending endlessly. There is no discernible end, middle, or beginning to this awe-inspiring form. The radiant glow, adorned with numerous clubs, discs, and blazing weapons, is challenging for me to behold. Witnessing the devas and sages offering prayers, I am simultaneously filled with fear and awe. Your colossal form, touching the sky with vibrant colors, numerous mouths, and radiant eyes, leaves me awestruck."

Arjuna continued, expressing his distress, "I observe the sons of Dhritarashtra, Bhishma, Drona, Karna, and other prominent warriors rushing into Your fearsome, blazing mouths, similar to rivers merging into the ocean or moths meeting their demise in the fire. Some are trapped with their heads crushed between Your teeth, a sight that evokes both terror and sorrow within me."

Arjuna, recognizing the magnitude of his friend Krishna's divine manifestation, humbly sought forgiveness, saying, "My dear Krishna, I repeatedly bow down in front of You. Please forgive my offenses. I treated You like my friend without fully understanding Your divine glory. There were times when I joked with You and made light of You as one does with a friend. Yet, in Your infinite kindness, You have consistently tolerated and forgiven my ignorance and playful jokes. The sight of Your formidable vishva-rupa both delights and terrifies me. This is indeed an awe-inspiring manifestation unseen by anyone before. I earnestly request You to withdraw this overwhelming form and reveal Your pleasant four-armed form as Vishnu."

In response, Lord Krishna, with a reassuring smile, replied, "You were able to witness this vishva-rupa because of My pleasure with you. Such a divine vision has never been seen before. Now, let this extraordinary sight conclude. May you see the form that brings you comfort." Krishna then gracefully unveiled His four-armed form as Vishnu, radiating tranquility, and subsequently revealed His sweet two-handed form as Lord Krishna. Arjuna, regaining his composure, prepared himself for the impending battle with new-found strength and determination.

Krishna is omnipresent, and everything in the universe stems from Him.

Lord Krishna embodies a harmonious fusion of supreme greatness and supreme sweetness. Indeed, He stands as the ultimate source of everything in the universe, as revealed in His interactions with both Mother Yashoda and Arjuna. Despite His cosmic significance, Krishna delights in friendly exchanges and loving bond with His devotees, who hold Him above even their own lives. His divine nature transcends mere cosmic magnitude, as He intimately connects with His devotees on a personal and affectionate level.

Reflect to Realize

Krishna, the supreme and all-great, encompasses infinite universes, while we, as living beings, are but specks within this vast cosmos. Our insignificance in comparison is undeniable. Yet, despite our finite nature, Krishna's boundless love for us shines through. In this verse, Krishna refers to us as pearls, signifying the preciousness He sees in each of us. Despite our imperfections and countless misdeeds against Him, His love for us remains unwavering. It beckons us to ponder: "If the Lord can love us so deeply, despite our flaws, why can't we dedicate our lives to Him wholeheartedly?"

16

Is God Partial?

When God treats different people in different ways, there is a reason behind it!

Consider a loving mother with two children. In her eyes, both children are equal, and her love for them is unwavering. However, her actions might differ based on their behaviour. If one child is well-behaved while the other is mischievous, she may express her affection differently. This isn't partiality; it's a tailored response to their moods and deeds. Similarly, Krishna's special favour towards devoted worshippers is a reflection of their sincere connection with Him, akin to a mother's response to her children's behaviour. In either case, the underlying sentiment is one of unconditional love.

This verse from Lord Krishna provides profound insight into the apparent disparities in people's lives. Krishna asserts,

samo 'ham sarva-bhuteshu
na me dveshyo 'sti na priyah
ye bhajanti tu mam bhaktya
mayi te teshu capy aham

"I am equal to everyone. I envy no one, nor am I ever partial to anyone. However, I show special favour to those who worship and serve Me with devotion. I consider such selfless and dedicated devotees as my dear friends." (9.29)

Lord Krishna is also the creator of the principle of karma, where everyone reaps the consequences of their own actions. His special favour towards devoted worshippers stems from their selfless dedication and alignment with dharma. These devotees, through their sincere worship and service, create a profound connection with Krishna, which naturally invites His loving response.

This dynamic interaction between Krishna and His devotees highlights the reciprocity inherent in spiritual practice. Devotion and righteousness invite divine grace, while actions contrary to dharma necessitate corrective measures. Yet, underlying all these interactions is Krishna's boundless love for all beings.

In essence, Krishna's divine actions are an expression of His eternal and unconditional love, tempered with justice and wisdom. By understanding this, one can appreciate the profound balance Krishna maintains between justice and compassion. Now, let's read a few stories that throw more light on this verse.

Love vs Might

Before the Kurukshetra war, both Duryodhana and Arjuna sought Krishna's assistance. Upon reaching Krishna's palace, they found Him asleep, attended to by one of His wives. Duryodhana went to the head of the bed, while Arjuna, as a devoted friend and cousin, stood at Krishna's lotus feet with folded palms. Overwhelmed with love, tears rolled down Arjuna's cheeks as he looked at Krishna's face.

When Krishna woke up, His eyes fell on Arjuna first, who stood at His feet. Later, Krishna noticed Duryodhana, who had taken a seat behind Him. Krishna welcomed both princes and inquired about the purpose of their visit.

Duryodhana, seeking Krishna's assistance in the war, argued that as he arrived before Arjuna, it was only fair for Krishna to support him. Krishna, smiling, responded, "While you arrived first, I saw Arjuna first. Moreover, scriptures advise helping the youngest first, so I will offer My assistance to Arjuna, who is younger than you." Duryodhana, feeling a sense of partiality, became somewhat upset.

Krishna then presented a unique proposal, offering either His invincible army, Narayani-sena, or Himself to one of them. However, He declared that He would not personally take up arms during the battle. Duryodhana, anxious and afraid that Arjuna might choose the formidable army over an unarmed Krishna, faced a challenging decision.

To Duryodhana's surprise, Arjuna expressed, "Krishna, I choose you. Your presence is more precious to me than any army." Duryodhana, delighted, thought Arjuna's decision was sentimental and not intelligent, considering Krishna's commitment to not personally fight. Duryodhana gladly accepted the powerful army, and with a mild smile, said, "It seems then that I am left with the army. I shall accept it," and took Krishna's leave.

The contrast in their choices reflected Arjuna's profound love and faith in Krishna, while Duryodhana lacked both. Despite Krishna's apparent partiality towards Arjuna, in reality, He merely reciprocated the genuine love and devotion Arjuna had for Him.

God is not partial; He is reciprocal. He will respond based on how we approach Him.

Mohini's Divine Strategy

Once, the asuras (demons) defeated the devatas (gods) and seized control of heaven. Faced with this dire situation, the gods turned to Lord Vishnu for guidance and support. Lord Vishnu advised, "Go to the demons and make an agreement. Collaborate with them to churn the milk ocean, using Mandara Mountain as the rod and Vasuki, the serpent, as the rope. This will yield amrit (nectar), granting you longevity and strength. Exercise patience and agree to their terms, as they currently hold more power."

Following Lord Vishnu's counsel, the gods engaged in the churning of the milk ocean (Samudra-manthan) alongside the demons. Lord Vishnu actively supported them throughout this endeavour. Eventually, when the amrit was obtained, the evil demons seized the pot and fled. However, instead of peacefully sharing the nectar among themselves, they started quarrelling with each other for the first share of the nectar.

Disheartened by the loss of the amrit, the devatas received solace from Lord Vishnu, who then assumed the enchanting form of Mohini Murti, a beautiful woman. Mohini approached the perplexed demons, who, captivated by her charm, trusted her individually, thinking she favored each one. The demons requested Mohini to personally distribute the amrit.

Agreeing to their request, Mohini instructed both gods and demons to form queues. With sweet words and gestures, Mohini cleverly deceived the demons and began distributing the amrit exclusively to the gods, ensuring their strength and longevity. The demons, hesitant to confront the charming woman, remained silent, reluctant to spoil their chances of impressing her.

Amidst the distribution, an asura named Raahu disguised himself as a god and silently consumed some amrit. The Sun-God (Surya) and the Moon-God (Chandra) detected this deception and informed Mohini. Instantly revealing his divine identity, Mohini, who was Lord Vishnu himself, swiftly severed Raahu's head with the Sudarshan Chakra before the amrit could bestow immortality. However, Raahu's head, having touched the amrit, became immortal. In retaliation, Raahu is believed to attack Surya and Chandra, leading to solar and lunar eclipses, respectively.

Upon distributing all the amrit among the gods, Mohini vanished. The gods, now empowered, reclaimed their positions in heaven. Despite the demons' diligent efforts in churning the milk ocean, they did not receive even a single drop of amrit. This outcome wasn't a result of Lord Vishnu's partiality or injustice; rather, it was a natural response to the devas' devotion and justice against the deceitful asuras who had attempted to run with the nectar.

Moreover, entrusting amrit to the asuras, inherently driven by malice and envy, would have posed a severe threat. Their propensity for causing harm to the innocent, including children, women, devotees, and cows, could have led to chaos in the universe. Thus, Lord Vishnu's prevention of the asuras obtaining amrit was a safeguard against potential havoc and a demonstration of divine wisdom.

The Lord ensures that people get what they deserve.

The narratives of Arjuna and the devatas exemplify the profound dynamics of divine reciprocation based on love and respect. Arjuna's sincere devotion and unwavering commitment on the battlefield led Lord Krishna to reveal the Bhagavad Gita. Similarly, the devatas, facing adversity, received divine assistance due to their humility and devotion. Conversely, Duryodhana and the demons, driven by ego and deceit, faced a different response from the divine, highlighting the consequences of malicious actions. For those seeking a deeper understanding, exploring the scriptures provides timeless lessons on the reciprocity between the lord and His devotees.

Reflect to Realize

Consider a Test match on its third day: two teams have been engaged in intense play. One team was bowled out for 200 runs in the preceding days, and on the third day, the second team is batting at 100 runs with the loss of 5 wickets. If someone were to glance at the scorecard at that moment, they might question why the team has already lost 5 wickets on the third day, unaware of the preceding events. Similarly, people's current situations are influenced by their past actions or karma. Judging divine impartiality solely based on present conditions overlooks the influence of past actions on the present. By acknowledging the ripple effects of past actions, we gain insight into the broader context of divine impartiality, where fairness is measured not only by current conditions, but by the echoes of yesterday's choices.

17

Time of God's Descent

The journey from vice to virtue becomes easy and quick with the Lord's support.

Dharma stands firm on four essential pillars: truthfulness (*satyam*), cleanliness (*saucham*), kindness (*daya*), and austerity (*tapa*). These virtues form the bedrock of a harmonious society and a balanced existence. However, when the scales tip towards adharma, negativity festers—envy, pride, anger, and greed corrode the fabric of righteousness. It is then, in the face of such imbalance and neglect of dharma, that the Lord incarnates, assuming a suitable form to impart teachings and realign humanity with righteousness.

The Lord's descent into this world stems from an infinite well of kindness and compassion, stirred by the plight of suffering humanity. It's a divine intervention, timed perfectly. Lord Krishna says in the Gita,

yadā yadā hi dharmasya
glānir bhavati bhārata

abhyutthānam adharmasya
tadātmānaṁ sṛjāmy aham

"Whenever there is a decline in righteousness (dharma) and an increase in unrighteousness (adharma), Myself." (4.7)

Thus, whenever the balance tips towards adharma and people neglect dharma, the Lord incarnates in a suitable form to impart teachings and reestablish righteousness on Earth. In each of His incarnations, Lord Krishna's divine presence serves as a beacon, illuminating the path towards righteousness and guiding souls back to the virtuous way of life. Whether as a fish (Matsya), tortoise (Kurma), boar (Varaha), half-man half-lion (Narasimha), a brahmana (Vamana), an ideal human being (Rama), the Supreme Lord's incarnations and His teachings resonate through the ages. Each incarnation serves as a testament to the Lord's boundless love and compassion for all of us, His children.

Now, let's read a few stories of the Lord's incarnations in this world.

Bhumi Devi's Ordeal

Once, the goddess of Earth, Bhumi Devi, was in profound distress. The rulers of Earth during that era were demoniac, cruel, and malevolent, with their massive armies tormenting innocent people. The pervasive adharma or vice weighed heavily on Mother Earth.

Unable to endure this plight, Bhumi Devi, assuming the form of a cow, approached Lord Brahma with tears in her eyes. She shared her anguish caused by the demoniac kings, prompting Brahma's compassion. Taking Bhumi Devi and several other deities, including Shiva and Indra, Brahma swiftly transported them to the ocean of milk, where Lord Vishnu resides.

Upon reaching the shores of the milk ocean on the planet called Sveta-dvipa, the assembled deities fervently offered prayers to appease Lord Vishnu, reciting the Purusha Sukta. Despite their earnest efforts, there was no immediate response from Lord Vishnu. In response, Brahma initiated meditation on the Lord, who transmitted a message to Brahma from within his heart.

Having received the divine message, Brahma proclaimed to all the devas, "The Supreme Lord, Krishna, will soon manifest on Earth within the Yadu dynasty. He will finish adharma by punishing the demons and safeguard dharma by protecting the virtuous. I urge all of you, devas and your consorts, to incarnate on Earth in different dynasties to assist Lord Krishna in His sacred mission. Lord Krishna Himself will incarnate as the son of Vasudeva, while Lord Ananta (Balarama), an expansion of Krishna, will precede His arrival."

After conveying this significant information and comforting Bhumi Devi with reassuring words, Lord Brahma returned to his celestial abode, Brahmaloka. Shortly thereafter, Lord Krishna manifested on Earth in human form. He dismantled adharma by vanquishing many formidable demons like Putana, Vatsasur, Aghasur, Vyomasur, Arishtasur, Narakasur, and Kamsa. Simultaneously, he established dharma on the planet and imparted profound teachings through the Bhagavad Gita.

The Lord descends to relieve His devotees from distress.

Lord Varaha's Call of War

Hiranyaksha and Hiranyakashipu, the offspring of the sage Kashyapa, were notorious demons known for their cruelty. Due to rigorous penance, Hiranyaksha earned boons from Lord Brahma and became immensely strong. Fuelled by a relentless desire to fight with others, he searched the entire universe in search of a worthy opponent. His fiery temperament and formidable power left even the heavenly deities trembling in fear, prompting them to flee.

After instilling terror among the celestial beings, Hiranyaksha dived into the depths of an ocean. With his mighty mace, he struck the ocean waves, sending all aquatic life into disarray. Upon encountering Varuna, the lord of the waters, Hiranyaksha, in a mocking tone, requested, "Great warrior, engage in a battle with me."

Perceiving the insincerity in his plea, Varuna responded, "Mighty warrior, I have aged, and my strength cannot match yours. Only Lord Vishnu possesses the power to fulfil your desire for a formidable opponent. He alone can humble your pride, laying you low on the battlefield to be consumed by dogs. Mercifully, in various incarnations, He manifests to punish the wicked, like yourself, and to establish righteousness."

Hiranyaksha set out in search of Lord Vishnu, and on his journey, he encountered Narada Muni. Inquiring about Vishnu's whereabouts, he received directions from Narada, who said, "Proceed to the Garbhodaka Ocean; there you will find Lord Vishnu, gracefully seated on His serpent couch."

Fuelled by anger, Hiranyaksha reached the Garbhodaka Ocean and was astonished to see a magnificent boar lifting the Earth on its tusks. Ridiculing the boar, he declared, "This Earth belongs to us, and as long as I am here, you cannot claim it.

Face me if you dare! Today, I will vanquish you. When you succumb to the blows of my mace, all the celestial deities and sages will wither away like trees without roots." With these words, Hiranyaksha began shouting at Lord Varaha.

Bhumi Devi, the Goddess of Earth, who was perched on Varaha's tusks, felt a sense of fear. Witnessing the impending conflict, Varaha gently placed Earth on the water's surface, granting her the ability to float. The anxious assembly of celestial beings observed, anticipating the unfolding events.

Lord Varaha sternly retorted, "O demon! I shall remain here as you wish, and I will not depart without displaying My power. Abandon your useless talk and now prepare for the battle."

Enraged by the challenge, Hiranyaksha, similar to a furious lion, swiftly attacked the Lord. He delivered a powerful blow with his mighty mace. Sensing the gravity of the situation, Lord Brahma intervened, addressing Lord Varaha, "O Varaha! This demon has transgressed against devotees, deities, and all innocent beings. Having obtained a boon from me, he now wanders the universe solely to torment the innocent. O Lord, please eliminate this demon without delay."

Responding to Brahma's plea, Lord Varaha leaped into the air, directing His mace towards Hiranyaksha's chin. The assembly of deities exclaimed, "May victory be Yours, O Lord!" In retaliation, Hiranyaksha hissed like a snake and clenched his lips, only to have the Lord effortlessly deflect and disarm his powerful mace.

The Lord challenged Hiranyaksha, saying, "Take up your weapon once again and try conquering Me." In response, Hiranyaksha invoked the deadly trident and hurled it at the Lord, only to have the Lord cut it to pieces with His Sudarshan Chakra.

Undeterred, Hiranyaksha resorted to creating several demonic illusions. He created fierce winds, clouds accompanied by lightning and thunder, and a mystic mountain that rained pus, blood, stool, urine, and bones. Various rakshasas emerged, voicing violent slogans. Yet, Lord Varaha effortlessly destroyed all the illusions with his Sudarshan Chakra.

Expressing his frustration, Hiranyaksha began striking the Lord's chest with powerful fists. Responding decisively, the Lord delivered a resounding slap at the root of Hiranyaksha's ear, causing his eyeballs to bulge out. With swift and overwhelming force, the Lord shattered Hiranyaksha's arms and legs. The final blow came as the Lord tore off the demon's head, and Hiranyaksha fell to the ground like an uprooted tree.

Observing the lifeless body of the defeated demon, Brahma, in awe, offered prayers to the Lord. Earth, carried on Lord Varaha's tusks, resembled a lotus flower held by an elephant with its trunk. In this powerful manner, the Lord safeguarded Mother Earth from the formidable demon Hiranyaksha.

The Lord punishes demoniac people who possess qualities like anger, pride and greed.

Bhumi Devi's story teaches us a powerful lesson. By following the path of righteousness (dharma), we connect with the Lord, much like Bhumi Devi did when facing adversity. The story of Lord Varaha vanquishing Hiranyaksha further emphasizes how the Lord can destroy vice (adharma) and support virtue. So, the key takeaway is to live by good values, be kind, and align ourselves with dharma, trusting that it invokes the divine protection of Krishna in our lives.

Reflect to Realize

Although the Lord resides blissfully in His eternal spiritual abode and is not obliged to come to the material world, He descends out of His boundless mercy solely to deliver and enchant us with His divine pastimes. Like a loving father, He endeavours to draw us away from the entanglements of material existence. Acknowledging His causeless mercy, let us dedicate ourselves to the path of *bhakti* and bring a smile to Krishna's face. Let's perform all our acts of devotion with a desire to please Krishna!

18

Purposes of God's Descent

God operates with the framework of divine justice and compassion.

The primary purpose of Lord Krishna's incarnations on Earth is to protect and nurture the righteous. However, in doing so, he also addresses the forces of evil that threatens the harmony of the universe. This involves chastising those who act against the principles of dharma (righteousness) and disrupt the cosmic order. Thus Lord Krishna elucidates on the purposes of His incarnations in the Bhagavad Gita, stating,

paritrāṇāya sādhūnāṁ
vināśāya ca duṣkṛtām
dharma-saṁsthāpanārthāya
sambhavāmi yuge yuge

"I manifest in different ages for three reasons – (i) to protect the virtuous, (ii) to punish the vicious, and (iii) to establish righteousness." (4.8)

The Lord not only performs these three activities when He descends but also empowers His devotees like Arjuna to perform these three activities. Thus, although Arjuna initially declined to fight in the battle of Kurukshetra, Lord Krishna encouraged him to fight, ultimately to accomplish the above three purposes. Krishna also informed Arjuna (in the Chapter 11 of the Gita) that He had already killed all the miscreants like Duryodhana, and that Arjuna was just meant to act as an instrument to manifest their death.

Lord Krishna, as the universal father, loves all His children equally. Yet, just as the government protects law-abiding citizens and penalizes criminals, Lord Krishna's actions are driven by the principles of justice, and vary based on individuals' behaviour and choices. He protects and blesses those who lead righteous lives, while corrective measures are taken against those who engage in immoral actions.

Of these three, protecting the virtuous people is the primary reason for the Lord's descent. Although the Lord doesn't rejoice punishing the sinful people, He does so, out of His compassion, only to rectify their degraded mentality, just as a loving father sometimes chastises his mischievous children. Through His divine interventions, Lord Krishna ensures that righteousness prevails and that the forces of darkness are subdued, thereby upholding the balance and harmony in the world. Let's explore instances of how the Lord safeguarded some of His greatest devotees from formidable demons.

Krishna Knocks Out Kamsa

Once in Mathura, King Kamsa organized a lavish wrestling festival with a sinister motive to kill Krishna. He extended an invitation to Krishna under the guise of the festival. As the city residents and nearby visitors filled the galleries, Kamsa occupied the royal dais in anticipation. Krishna, accompanied by His brother Balarama, arrived just before the festival began.

At the entrance of the wrestling arena, Kamsa stationed a formidable elephant named Kuvalayapida to kill Krishna. The massive elephant struck Krishna forcefully, but Krishna retaliated, cleverly hiding among its legs. Although Kuvalayapida caught Krishna using its sense of smell, Krishna playfully teased and provoked the elephant until it became irritated with rage. In a remarkable turn, Krishna extracted one of the elephant's tusks and, using it as a weapon, defeated Kuvalayapida, putting an end to the menacing threat.

Bedecked with the blood of Kuvalayapida and carrying the conquered tusk on His shoulder, the invincible Krishna made a grand entrance into Kamsa's wrestling arena. The residents of Mathura were captivated by Krishna's beauty, and their admiration turned into joyful praises.

Upon Kamsa's command, the formidable wrestlers Chanura and Mushtika were unleashed to confront Krishna and Balarama. The audience, particularly the women, felt compassion for the charming boys, perceiving the match as unfair. Vasudeva and Devaki anxiously watched as their children faced the powerful wrestlers.

To reassure the concerned onlookers, Krishna and Balarama demonstrated their extraordinary strength and wrestling skills. One by one, Chanura and the other wrestlers were defeated by the boys' might, none able to withstand their power. The entire assembly, except for Kamsa, erupted in joyous celebration.

In a fit of rage, Kamsa ordered the arrest and execution of Vasudeva, Nanda, Ugrasena, and all the cowherds. Krishna, incensed, leaped onto the elevated royal dais. Swift as a hawk, Kamsa armed himself with a sword and shield. But Krishna seized him by the hair and flung him into the wrestling ring. Overpowering Kamsa, Krishna stood on his chest and delivered the fatal blows with his bare fists. He brought an end to the reign of terror. Subsequently, Krishna freed his parents, Devaki and Vasudeva, and reinstated his grandfather, Ugrasena, as the King of the Yadus. Thus, the tyrannical chapter closed, marking the triumph of righteousness and justice.

The Lord destroys the wicked and protects the righteous.

Lord Parashurama's Conquest

In the kingdom of the Haihayas, resided a formidable and handsome king named Kartaviryarjuna, with his capital in Mahishmati. Bestowed with a thousand arms through his devotion to Lord Dattatreya, he took great pride in his immense power. During a hunting expedition, Kartaviryarjuna ventured into a forest and stumbled upon the hermitage of Sage Jamadagni. The sage graciously welcomed the king, his soldiers, and ministers, providing them with exceptional hospitality and ensuring their comfort.

Amazed by the sage's ability to offer such elaborate facilities in the forest, Kartaviryarjuna discovered the secret. There was a mystic cow named Kamadhenu, owned by Jamadagni, which fulfilled all his needs. Envy overpowered Kartaviryarjuna, leading him to forcibly seize Kamadhenu and its calf. Unfortunately, being a brahmana sage, Jamadagni found himself powerless in the face of this injustice.

Jamadagni had a formidable son named Parashurama, an incarnation of Lord Vishnu. Upon learning of Kartaviryarjuna's sinful act of stealing a cow from a brahmana, Parashurama, furious like an injured tiger, armed himself with a fierce axe, shield, bow, and arrows.

He pursued Kartaviryarjuna with relentless determination, resembling a tiger chasing its prey.

Clad in black deerskin with matted locks shining like the sun, Parashurama proved a terrifying sight. Despite Kartaviryarjuna sending thousands of soldiers equipped with various weapons, elephants, chariots, and horses, Lord Parashurama, with incredible speed, single-handedly annihilated the entire army.

Undeterred, Kartaviryarjuna himself entered the battlefield, utilizing his thousand arms to fix arrows on five hundred bows. However, Parashurama, with astonishing skill, released enough arrows with just one bow, dismantling Kartaviryarjuna's weaponry. Resorting to uprooting trees and hurling rocks, Kartaviryarjuna's efforts were in vain as Parashurama deftly dodged and eventually severed all his thousand arms with his axe. In the culmination of the battle, Parashurama beheaded Kartaviryarjuna, putting an end to the conflict.

Kartaviryarjuna had 10,000 sons who, witnessing their father's demise, fled in fear. Parashurama, in an act of justice, reclaimed Kamadhenu and its calf, restoring them to Jamadagni. Upon this, Jamadagni, though deeply aggrieved, emphasized the principle of forgiveness inherent in their brahmana lineage and urged Parashurama to undertake a year-long pilgrimage to purify himself from the act of killing.

During Parashurama's absence, seeking revenge for their father's death, Kartaviryarjuna's sons attacked Jamadagni's hermitage. Finding the sage in meditation on Lord Vishnu, they shamelessly severed his head. Renuka, Jamadagni's wife, in her pain, cried out to Parashurama.

Though far away, Parashurama swiftly responded to his mother's cry. Discovering his father's lifeless body, he took up his axe with a determination to end the pride of the warrior class. Journeying to Mahishmati, Parashurama executed justice by slaying the 10,000 sons of Kartaviryarjuna. He created a chilling monument of their severed heads in the heart of the city.

In Mahishmati, where justice was served, a river of blood flowed as a stern reminder to those who disrespected brahmanas. Parashurama, driven by the pursuit of righteousness, continued his mission. He vanquished numerous sinful Kshatriyas, repeating this act twenty-one times. The bloodshed led to the creation of nine lakes at Samanta-Panchaka, instilling fear in those who dared to harm the brahmanas.

In a profound display of power and devotion, Parashurama then reunited his father's severed head with his lifeless body, miraculously reviving him. This extraordinary act affirmed Parashurama's divine nature and unwavering commitment to upholding dharma, leaving an indelible mark in the history of the world.

The Lord doesn't tolerate any offence against devotees.

Vasudeva, Devaki, and Sage Jamadagni exemplified virtue, and the Lord, being the protector of the righteous, could not tolerate the transgressions of Kamsa and the arrogant Kshatriyas against them. Consequently, He did the needful to eliminate the threats in His incarnations of Krishna and Parashurama. The next chapter presents another profound Gita verse on similar lines.

Reflect to Realize

All living beings are indeed God's children, yet why does He sometimes appear to punish them? Consider a teacher with two students: one obedient and the other mischievous. If the teacher disciplines the wayward student, is he right or wrong? He's right, for his actions stem from a desire for the student's well-being. Similarly, when God chastises someone, it's an act of His boundless mercy and compassion. He doesn't punish out of anger or hatred, but out of profound concern for His children's ultimate welfare. It's an expression of His deep love, guiding us away from harm and towards our highest potential.

19

God's Reciprocation

Our approach to the divine shapes His response: kindness begets grace, while indifference invites distance.

Isn't it natural to befriend someone who treats us kindly? Similarly, we tend to react differently to someone who behaves rudely. This instinctive human behaviour is also reflected in the way the Lord interacts with us. When we approach Him with love and respect, He responds with boundless compassion and grace. Conversely, if we act with indifference or disrespect, we distance ourselves from His divine presence.

In the Bhagavad Gita, Lord Krishna elucidates this concept in the following verse:

ye yathā māṁ prapadyante
tāṁs tathaiva bhajāmy aham
mama vartmānuvartante
manuṣyāḥ pārtha sarvaśaḥ

"I respond to individuals based on their approach, rewarding them in accordance with their actions. Everyone unknowingly or consciously follows My path." (4.11)

Lord Krishna's responses are inherently aligned with the nature and behaviour of individuals. Just as we naturally gravitate towards those who show us kindness and may react defensively towards those who treat us poorly, the Lord's treatment towards us reflects our own attitudes and actions. Those who seek Him with sincere devotion and righteousness are met with His grace and protection. Conversely, those who engage in negative or unrighteous actions encounter corrective measures, not out of favouritism or vengeance, but as a reflection of their own deeds.

In summary, Krishna's interactions with us are a direct reflection of our own behaviour and attitudes. This understanding encourages us to align our actions with dharma, knowing that our sincere efforts in devotion and righteousness will always be met with divine grace and favour.

Now, let's delve into the narratives of two individuals—one who interacted with Krishna rudely and another who approached Him with love. Let's explore the ensuing outcomes.

Clothed in Mercy

Lord Krishna took birth in Mathura, but he spent His childhood in the enchanting village of Vrindavan. After spending a decade with the gopas, gopis, and cows in Vrindavan, Krishna eventually returned to His birthplace, Mathura.

Upon entering the magnificent city, Lord Krishna and His elder brother Balarama encountered a washerman carrying a vibrant array of clothes intended for Kamsa, the ruthless king of

Mathura. With politeness, Krishna addressed the washerman, saying, "Dear friend, we are cowherds from Vrindavan. Could you please give us some clothes? We have a longing to adorn ourselves with the exquisite garments you carry. I assure you that offering us suitable attire will bring you abundant blessings and auspiciousness."

What a remarkable twist of fate! At a time when millions of devoted individuals yearn for the chance to present offerings to the Lord, here was Krishna Himself, humbly requesting clothes from a washerman.

Instead of acknowledging his incredible fortune, the haughty washerman responded with arrogance. "How dare you seek the king's attire? You, an uncivilized cowherd and villager, do you think you deserve such luxurious garments? If you dare make such a request again, the king's soldiers will not hesitate to beat, arrest, and even kill you. Leave this place immediately!"

While Krishna's request had been characterized by politeness and gentleness, the washerman's retort was harsh, rude, and filled with public ridicule. Despite the multitude of washermen in Mathura, this particular individual happened to be in the service of the king, contributing to his arrogant behaviour.

Upon hearing the malicious words from the washerman, Krishna responded effortlessly by beheading him with just His fingertips. The Lord, in His infinite power, need not exert Himself to address the arrogance of the disrespectful. Witnessing their master's abrupt demise, the washerman's assistants hastily dropped their bundles of clothes and scattered in different directions. Then the soul emerged from the washerman's body and merged with Lord Krishna, signifying the washerman's deliverance.

In His boundless mercy, Krishna, along with Balarama and the other cowherds, continued their journey after adorning themselves with the elegant garments. Despite the washerman's rude insults, Krishna exhibited mercy by liberating him from the cycle of life and death. Such is the compassion of Lord Krishna.

The Lord is kind enough to give us opportunities to serve Him, we need to be eager enough to grab them.

The Weaver's Delight

After liberating the washerman, Lord Krishna continued His tour of Mathura. His journey led Him to a weaver who, due to fear of Kamsa, had never ventured to Vrindavan. Despite not visiting the village himself, he had heard tales of its magnificent atmosphere and the miraculous deeds of the Lord from companions who had experienced Vrindavan first-hand. Eager to encounter Krishna and Balarama, the weaver finally had the opportunity.

Filled with profound affection for the divine young brothers, the weaver adorned them in soft silk garments adorned with jewels. He presented exquisite armlets, bracelets, and earrings that complemented their complexions. These ornaments were not only aesthetically fitting but also practical, considering that Krishna and Balarama were soon engaged in a confrontation with Kamsa's wrestlers. The soft ornaments ensured they would not cause harm to the brothers' bodies during the impending battle.

The brothers appeared truly amazing in their newly adorned attire. Pleased with the weaver's selfless service, Krishna bestowed upon him a blessing to attain a cowherd's form in the spiritual world. There he would get a chance to be a part of the Lord's divine pastimes.

In his previous life, the weaver had resided in Mithila, where he served as a devoted soul and an adept weaver. He had crafted exceptionally fine garments for Rama and Lakshmana to wear at their wedding. Witnessing the incomparable beauty of Rama and Lakshmana, the kind-hearted weaver harbored a deep desire to personally attire the two Lords with his own hands. Recognizing the sincere wish of His devotee, Lord Rama chose to fulfil it. Consequently, Rama and Lakshmana once again manifested in Mathura, this time as Krishna and Balarama, providing their ardent devotee with the opportunity to personally dress them.

The Lord remembers the heartfelt desires of His devotees and fulfils them.

The contrast between the washerman arrogantly rejecting the chance to serve Lord Krishna, and the weaver joyfully adorning Him is evident. Krishna reciprocates uniquely in each interaction. However, when Krishna administers punishment, it does not stem from hatred; rather, His discipline serves as a form of protection.

Reflect to Realize

Often, in our devotional practice, we may find ourselves questioning why we aren't experiencing reciprocation from Krishna, despite our dedicated efforts. Here, Krishna reveals that His response corresponds directly to the depth of our emotions towards Him. Is our devotion genuine, or are we merely going through the ritualistic motions without emotions? Indeed, when we practise with sincere and heartfelt devotion, we often find ourselves immersed in profound satisfaction and reciprocation from Krishna. However, many people perform rituals without the spirit behind it. The reason one may not experience Krishna daily is that the devotion isn't genuine enough. Therefore, to truly experience Krishna, we must sincerely practise this process, infusing our actions with genuine devotional emotion.

20

Your Dearest Friend

An ideal friend is someone who stands as our well-wisher in every circumstance.

Now, envision having the most powerful and affluent person as your closest friend—wondering who is that? It is none other than Lord Sri Krishna.

Who can be closer to you than someone who stays right inside your heart? Lord Krishna said more than once in the Gita that He stays within the hearts of all living beings as Paramatma or the Supersoul, giving them the guidance and inspiration they need, like a dear friend. Further, in the Gita, Krishna makes a profound declaration:

bhoktāraṁ yajña-tapasāṁ
sarva-loka-maheśvaram
suhṛdaṁ sarva-bhūtānāṁ
jñātvā māṁ śāntim ṛcchati

"I am the supreme enjoyer of all endeavours, the ultimate proprietor of all planets, and the dearest friend and

well-wisher of all beings. One who recognizes this about Me attains supreme happiness and peace." (5.29)

Lord Krishna's compassion is all-encompassing, extending not only to His devotees but also to those who oppose him, such as demons. His divine love and care are not limited by the actions or attitudes of individuals. Even those who act against Him are recipients of his divine mercy in different ways. This universal compassion highlights Krishna's role as the ultimate well-wisher and friend of all beings. His actions are always aimed at the greater good, whether through direct protection and blessings for His devotees or through corrective measures for those who act against dharma. In every circumstance, Krishna's underlying motive is the welfare and spiritual upliftment of all souls.

Recognizing Krishna as the supreme benefactor and well-wisher transforms one's outlook on life. It brings about a profound sense of security and peace, knowing that the most powerful and compassionate being is always there to support and guide us. This realization encourages us to cultivate devotion, and trust in Krishna's divine teachings, leading to a life of ultimate happiness and inner peace.

Thus, Krishna's role as the supreme friend and benefactor is central to the spiritual journey. This fosters a sense of fulfilment and serenity that transcends all worldly challenges and tribulations. Let's explore the tales of two demons who, despite attempting to harm Krishna, attained liberation through the Lord's unexpected kindness.

Monstrous Mother

In a notable incident, a rakshasi named Putana was sent by Kamsa to eliminate baby Krishna in Gokula. Upon entering the serene village, Putana skillfully transformed her appearance into that of a beautiful, motherly woman.

Observing her, the unsuspecting residents perceived her as none other than Goddess Lakshmi, believing she had arrived to visit her husband Narayana, who was adored in the household of King Nanda. Putana, despite harboring a heart filled with ferocity and cruelty, adeptly presented herself as a loving and caring mother, similar to a sharp sword concealed within a soft sheath.

She slyly entered King Nanda's house without seeking permission. Her beauty and apparent motherly love rendered even mother Yashoda hesitant to intervene. Proceeding to the inner chambers, Putana discovered baby Krishna peacefully asleep in His cot, His boundless power covered like fire beneath ashes.

Despite recognizing that this was no ordinary child, Putana, determined to fulfil her sinister purpose. She cradled Krishna on her lap, similar to a fool who mistakes a sleeping snake for a harmless rope.

The ruthless demoness then began feeding her own milk to baby Krishna. However, with malicious intent, Putana had coated her chest with a lethal poison of such potency that mere contact could lead to death. As Krishna took hold of her chest, He, with His tender hands, vigorously squeezed both the poison and life from her, extracting the harmful elements while simultaneously draining her life force.

Putana screamed in intense agony, pleading, "Release me! Stay away!" Drenched in sweat, her eyes wide open, and her limbs falling in all directions, she cried out loudly. The commotion she caused was so intense that people, fearing thunderstorms and thunderbolts, began to collapse to the ground. Putana could no longer sustain her deceptive form and reverted to her original, fearsome rakshasi state. Witnessing this transformation, everyone realized her true identity.

In this manner, Putana met her demise, collapsing onto the pasture ground and causing destruction to all the trees within a twelve-mile radius. Fearlessly, Krishna continued to play on Putana's huge body. The simple-hearted gopis promptly picked Him up and performed protective rituals for Krishna's well-being. Mother Yashoda, after offering her milk to Krishna, tenderly laid Him to rest in bed.

Through the touch of Krishna, Putana's body underwent purification, absolving her of all sins. As the people of Vrindavan cremated her lifeless form, the ensuing smoke carried a remarkably sweet fragrance, detectable by those miles away.

Initially angered by Putana due to her sinister intentions of harming infants, Krishna thought about her pretence of motherly sentiments. Acknowledging this, Krishna elevated Putana to the status of a nurturing mother in Goloka Vrindavan to assist Mother Yashoda. Such an act underscores Krishna's boundless mercy. As the supreme well-wisher of all, His fundamental disposition towards everyone is one of ultimate compassion.

Krishna tries to find some reason to shower His mercy even on demons.

Cart Carnage: Krishna's Divine Kick

Long ago, there lived a formidable demon named Utkacha, the son of the powerful demon Hiranyaksha. His immense strength fuelled his arrogance. One day, Utkacha entered the hermitage of the sage Lomasa. In an attempt to showcase his might, he recklessly began breaking trees.

Observing this unwarranted disruption, the sage, disturbed by Utkacha's actions, pronounced a curse upon him, stating, "O foolish one! Your pride in physical strength has led to your downfall. I curse you to become bodiless!"

In an instant, Utkacha's body shed away like an old snake's skin, leaving him in a ghostly, formless state. Realizing his error, Utkacha humbly prostrated himself at Lomasa's feet, pleading, "O great sage, I was unaware of your might. Please forgive me and restore my body." Lomasa responded, "Only the dust from the lotus feet of Lord Krishna can liberate you from this spectral existence."

Following this transformation, Utkacha, now wandering as a ghost, formed an alliance with another bad figure named Kamsa, the cruel maternal uncle of Lord Krishna. Kamsa, driven by his envy, dispatched numerous demonic associates in a bid to locate and eliminate Krishna. Then on Kamsa's order, Utkacha also arrived in Gokula with the intent of ending Krishna's life.

Within the confines of King Nanda's courtyard, the demon sought refuge in a household cart laden with various vessels crafted from gold, silver, and brass. In Sanskrit, a cart is termed *shakata*, and a demon is referred to as asura. Hence, Utkacha became known as Shakatasura, denoting the cart demon. Remaining invisible, Shakatasura patiently awaited the right time to carry out his sinister plan.

At that time, Krishna was merely three months old. Mother Yashoda gently laid Him beneath the household cart that the ghostly Utkacha had entered, and she reclined beside Him until He fell asleep. Once satisfied that Krishna was in a peaceful slumber, she rose with care and returned to her household responsibilities. Nearby, some playful children observed Krishna as He rested.

Due to the presence of Shakatasura, the wheels of the cart started sinking into the ground. Intent on falling upon Krishna to carry out his malevolent plan, Shakatasura triggered this disturbance. However, baby Krishna, waking up and craving His mother's milk, began to cry as typical for an infant. Engaged in her activities, Mother Yashoda remained unaware of the child's cries. In a moment of infantile anger, Krishna energetically kicked His little legs upward, and the red sole of His lotus-like foot coincidentally touched the cart, foiling Shakatasura's malicious intent.

Despite Krishna's foot being as tender as a newly grown leaf, His kick miraculously turned the cart upside down, completely dismantling it. The wheels and axle were dislocated, the handle was broken, and all the utensils scattered in disarray, resulting in the demise of the demon within.

Shakatasura, having entered the cart invisibly, met his end mystically. Unnoticed by all, when the cart shattered, Shakatasura departed from his subtle, ghostly form and transcended to a pure spiritual body. In a display of reverence, he bowed before Lord Krishna. Transported in a chariot drawn by a hundred horses, he journeyed to Krishna's divine abode, Goloka Vrindavan, in the spiritual world. Such is the boundless mercy of the Supreme Lord Krishna, who punishes demons for their liberation.

If Krishna is so merciful to demons, just imagine how merciful He would be towards His devotees.

Lord Krishna's boundless kindness is evident in His act of liberating demons like Putana and Shakatasura, who tried to vanquish Him. If this is the treatment accorded to demons, one can only imagine the unparalleled special love He bestows upon His devotees. Therefore, offering heartfelt prayers to

Krishna becomes a profound way to experience His sweet and divine friendship.

Reflect to Realize

If God is considered everyone's dear friend, why then does suffering exist in this world? To address this question, let's envision a country where the government imprisons murderers. Is it the fault of the government or the prisoners? Clearly, the fault lies with the prisoners. Despite the government's benevolence in providing education, subsidies, and healthcare to all the citizens, it withholds these privileges from those who engage in wrongful behaviour. Similarly, God is perceived as everyone's friend, yet for those who choose to inflict unnecessary suffering, God must intervene to help them recognize their errors. God's punishment in the form of suffering is only meant for people to realize their mistakes, and He is readily appeased by their genuine repentance.

SECTION III: DHYANA–MEDITATION

Meditation involves a profound and sustained focus on a particular object or thought. But what is the best object of meditation? What nurtures and deepens our meditation practice? Conversely, what distracts us from true meditation? And what are the transformative results of a dedicated meditative practice? In the Bhagavad Gita, Lord Krishna offers timeless wisdom on the art of meditation. This section provides simplified yet authentic answers to these profound questions through beautiful slokas intertwined with captivating tales.

21

Hearing Leads to Love

Our fascination with anyone or anything often begins by hearing about them.

Think back to the first time you heard about an exciting place and then decided to visit it. The stories and descriptions from others sparked your curiosity and made you want to experience it for yourself. Similarly, when we hear positive things about someone, they start to occupy our thoughts, and we develop affection and admiration for them. The same principle applies to our relationship with the Lord. Hearing about the Lord's qualities, activities, and teachings deepens our meditation on Him and devotion for Him.

Lord Krishna describes this principle in this verse,

mayy āsakta-manāḥ pārtha
yogaṁ yuñjan mad-āśrayaḥ
asaṁśayaṁ samagraṁ māṁ
yathā jñāsyasi tac chṛṇu

"Now hear, O Arjuna, how by practising yoga in full consciousness of Me, with mind attached to Me, you can know Me in full, free from doubt." (7.1)

Regular hearing about God (*sravana*) leads us to think about Him repeatedly, and thus get absorbed in meditation (*dhyana*) on His qualities, activities, and names. That deep meditation transforms into love (*bhakti*) for God, which is the culmination of all spiritual paths. This is the transformative power of hearing, which is the beginning of spiritual life.

But are there tangible instances of devotees who cultivated devotion to Lord Krishna solely through hearing about Him? Let's explore!

Simple Ladies with Sublime Devotion

Once in Vrindavan, young Krishna went out with His *gopa* friends to tend to His beloved cows. As they journeyed, the boys became very hungry and looked around for food.

Lord Krishna suggested, "Nearby, some brahmanas are performing a sacrifice. Go and ask them for some food." The boys hurried to the brahmanas and made their request, but the brahmanas ignored them completely. Disheartened, they returned to Krishna empty-handed.

With a gentle smile, Krishna told them to approach the wives of the brahmanas instead. These simple ladies have heard a lot about Lord Krishna's beauty and His activities from vegetable sellers and visitors. Thus they became captivated by His character and fell in love with the Lord.

When Krishna's friends approached these ladies and asked them for food, they became spontaneously blissful. Eager to see Krishna, they quickly gathered plenty of food items and sweets from their homes and rushed to the forest. They even ignored their families' protests.

When they finally saw Krishna, His divine presence captivated their hearts. Krishna welcomed them warmly, praised their selfless service, and accepted their offerings graciously. However, when He urged them to return home, the women pleaded to stay, declaring their devotion to Him alone.

Krishna reassured them, saying, "You can worship Me perfectly by always remembering Me, serving My deity, hearing about Me, and discussing My stories. Through such devotion, you will soon attain Me." Accepting Krishna's words, the women returned home, their hearts filled with devotion.

Meanwhile, by Krishna's grace, the husbands of the ladies found no fault with their wives when they returned. Reflecting on their own mistake, the brahmanas lamented their failure to recognize Krishna's divinity. Despite their scholarly knowledge, they acknowledged that their wives' devotion surpassed their own.

In Vrindavan, amidst the tranquil beauty of the forest, Krishna's divine pastimes continued, strengthening the bond between the Lord and His devotees and illuminating the path of devotion for all beings.

Love for Krishna blossoms through hearing, chanting His name, and worshiping Him.

The Original Love Letter

Princess Rukmini was the beautiful and wise daughter of King Bhishmaka, ruler of Vidarbha city. Her palace was often visited by many learned brahmanas and sages, including the regular visitor, Narada Muni. Even at a young age, Rukmini respectfully listened about Lord Krishna's captivating beauty and divine qualities from sages like Narada Muni. Thus, her heart was set on Krishna as her ideal life partner.

However, Rukmini's brother, Rukmi, envied Krishna. Influenced by his wicked friends like Sishupal, Jarasandha, and Dantavakra, Rukmi decided to marry Rukmini to the malicious Sishupal, against her will.

Feeling utterly helpless, Rukmini composed a heartfelt letter expressing her love for Krishna. She entrusted this message to a trustworthy brahmana, pleading with him to deliver it to Krishna. The brahmana journeyed to Dwarka, where he was warmly welcomed by Krishna. Upon reading Rukmini's plea, Krishna immediately set out for Vidarbha to honour her love.

With the brahmana by His side, Krishna swiftly travelled to Kundinapur, the capital of Vidarbha. The sight of Krishna brought immense joy to the citizens of Vidarbha, and they fervently prayed for Rukmini to become His consort.

Meanwhile, Rukmini, consumed by anxiety, lamented her misfortune as the hours passed without any sign of the brahmana or Krishna. Just as despair began to overwhelm her, a twitch on her left side—a favorable omen—indicated Krishna's imminent arrival. Overwhelmed with joy, Rukmini eagerly awaited His arrival.

Seeking divine blessings, Rukmini went to the temple of Goddess Ambika, a customary prelude to marriage. There, she prayed fervently for Lord Krishna to become her husband. As she emerged from the temple, her heart leaped with joy upon seeing Krishna approaching on His resplendent chariot. Without hesitation, Krishna took Rukmini away on His chariot, to the amazement of numerous onlookers.

However, the envious kings, including Jarasandha, Sishupal, and Rukmi, gathered their forces to challenge

Krishna. With unwavering determination, Krishna defeated their armies, forcing them to retreat. Rukmi, however, persisted in his pursuit. Krishna disarmed him but spared his life at Rukmini's plea. With Rukmini by His side, Krishna returned to Dwarka, where they were joyously united in marriage, marking the beginning of a happy life together.

Rukmini's love for Krishna, kindled solely through hearing about Him, blossomed into an enduring bond, making her His esteemed queen.

Contemplation on the Lord's attributes sprouts love for Him within the heart.

Princess Rukmini and the brahmana ladies cultivated their love for Krishna purely through hearing about Him. Thus, by absorbing their minds in the enchanting stories of the Lord from devoted individuals and scriptures, we naturally contemplate His divine qualities, fostering a longing to behold Him, converse with Him, and establish a profound relationship with Him.

Reflect to Realize

To the degree we are hungry, we digest the food we eat. Similarly, to the degree we are eager to hear from authentic sources, to that degree we acquire spiritual knowledge. We may sometimes mechanically listen to spiritual teachings without allowing them to deeply resonate within us. But to truly benefit from spiritual wisdom and cultivate love for Krishna, like Rukmini or the brahmana ladies, we must be enthusiastic and eager to hear. Consider that after countless lifetimes, we have attained this precious human life, along with the intelligence and blessings to absorb and apply spiritual wisdom. Should we disregard this opportunity when it stands at our doorstep?

22

Joyful Discussions

Enthusiastic discussions about God lead to a deep meditation on Him

When you love someone, it's only natural that they frequently occupy your thoughts and conversations. This same principle holds true for the devotees of Lord Krishna.

Devotees experience immense joy and satisfaction in discussing the Lord with other like-minded devotees. These discussions are not mere casual talks but are profound exchanges filled with love, reverence, and excitement. Sharing one's understanding about the Lord strengthens their own faith and deepens their spiritual understanding. It creates a supportive and nurturing community where everyone is uplifted and inspired by the shared devotion.

In the following verse from the Gita, Lord Krishna Himself describes this phenomenon, explaining what His true devotees do.

mac-cittā mad-gata-prāṇā
bodhayantaḥ parasparam

kathayantaś ca māṁ nityaṁ
tuṣyanti ca ramanti ca

"My devotees constantly immerse their minds in Me and dedicate their lives to Me. They find immense joy and satisfaction in discussing about Me with fellow devotees." (10.9)

This verse reveals the deep connection and unwavering devotion that Krishna's followers have towards him. Their minds are constantly focused on Krishna, meditating on His divine qualities, pastimes, and teachings. This deep, continuous contemplation naturally overflows into their daily lives. They find their ultimate purpose and fulfilment in serving Krishna, making their lives a testament to their devotion.

For Krishna's devotees, their thoughts, words, and actions become an unbroken chain of devotion. This divine connection brings them unparalleled joy, and a sense of spiritual fulfilment that transcends ordinary worldly pleasures.

Here are two episodes that illustrate the potency of discussing Krishna's pastimes.

Loving Complaints

Child Krishna's mischievous pastimes in Vrindavan knew no bounds. The gopis found great joy in observing, discussing, and meditating on Krishna's sweet pastimes. Although they enjoyed these moments internally, they would scold Him outwardly. Once, they collectively approached Mother Yashoda to lodge complaints against Krishna.

The gopis began narrating, "Your darling son Krishna visits our homes and releases the calves. They then rush to their mother cows and drink milk."

Yashoda responded, "But Krishna is merely caring for the young calves."

The gopis protested, "He does it when it's not time to milk the cows. The calves consume all the milk, leaving none for us when we attempt to milk the cows!"

Yashoda empathized, "Krishna is just a child. He acts innocently. Why don't your household members prevent it?"

The gopis explained, "He often comes when we're occupied with various tasks and releases our calves."

Yashoda suggested, "Why not scare Him away?"

The gopis said, "Even when we become angry and shout, 'Beat Him, tie Him up,' He simply smiles. Enchanted by His smile, we can only helplessly watch Him."

Yashoda questioned, "But why does He release the calves?"

The gopis revealed, "By releasing the calves, He makes us run about. Then, He enters our homes, steals our delectable milk products, and consumes them before our eyes! He doesn't even attempt to flee. Yet, we're powerless to stop Him!"

Yashoda proposed, "Why not offer Him some milk before He takes it himself? He might be hungry."

The gopis clarified, "It's not hunger driving Him. His belly is always full, as He's constantly fed by you. He craves stolen milk only, rejecting what we offer. If we give Him milk, He refuses to drink it. He only wants to steal."

Yashoda relented, "Very well, let Him take some milk. What harm is there in Him having a little?"

The gopis confessed, "He chooses the finest milk we've reserved for our husbands."

Yashoda reasoned, "An innocent child couldn't possibly steal like this. You're all very clever."

The gopis countered, "Innocent? Your son is remarkably cunning. He invents unseen methods of theft. He's a skilled thief!"

Yashoda reflected, "Your ancestors' good deeds have enabled Krishna's enjoyment in your homes. Embrace this joyfully."

The gopis lamented, "We're content if He enjoys our butter, even with His friends. Yet, He feeds it to monkeys, who refuse to eat, leaving Him distressed. Then, He blames us, 'Your butter is so worthless that even monkeys won't eat it!'"

Yashoda inquired, "If you know all this, why not hide the pots?"

The gopis explained, "We've tried, but Krishna becomes angry. He threatens, 'Give me the pots or I'll return tomorrow with a flaming coal. If you don't give Me butter, I'll burn your homes!'"

The gopis' complaints seemed endless. Sometimes as they spoke, Krishna would be present with an innocent face. Occasionally, Mother Yashoda would defend Him, while other times, she'd chastise Him to instill discipline. Such was her absorption as Krishna's mother, dealing with the Supreme God acting as the Supreme Thief.

If Krishna is God, why does He steal? His playful antics as a child serve to captivate our hearts. By stealing butter, Krishna steals the pure hearts of the gopis. He isn't hungry for milk but for their motherly love. In reality, the gopis prepare milk products in hopes of Krishna's thievery.

These simple gopis greatly admire Mother Yashoda's fortune as Krishna's mother. Yet, they suspect she misses the joy of witnessing Krishna's thefts, as He refrains from such acts in her presence. Therefore, to share their joy with Yashoda, the gopis relay Krishna's mischievous tales to her in the form of complaints.

The gopis' sweet complaints are expressions of their love for Krishna, the Supreme butter thief (*maakhan-chor*), who steals the hearts of all.

Discussions about the Lord's activities and qualities bring the utmost delight.

When God Hears about Himself!

Lord Krishna spent His childhood in Vrindavan, engaging in sweet pastimes alongside His elder brother Balarama. These cherished moments were witnessed by their mothers Yashoda and Rohini. As Krishna grew older, He relocated to Mathura and later to Dwarka, where He married 16,108 queens. Despite His royal status in Dwarka, Krishna often reminisced about His beloved friends in Vrindavan, even in the presence of His queens.

One day, Krishna's queens requested Balarama's mother, Rohini, to share stories of Krishna's mischievous antics in Vrindavan. Rohini agreed, and they gathered in a room, sealing the windows shut. Rohini stationed Krishna's sister, Subhadra, to guard the door and prevent Krishna and Balarama from interrupting.

Recalling her dear friend Yashoda, Rohini recounted Krishna's enchanting pastimes in Vrindavan. She depicted how the residents of Vrindavan perceived Krishna not as a deity, but as an innocent and playful boy, son, friend, and lover. Krishna, adorned simply as a cowherd boy with peacock feathers and a flute, was adored by all the gopas and gopis.

Everyone was delighted by Rohini's narration. Even Subhadra was so captivated that she neglected her guard duty. Meanwhile, Krishna and Balarama stumbled upon Subhadra and became intrigued, joining her to overhear Rohini's enthralling tales.

As they immersed themselves in the activities of Krishna's childhood, both Krishna and Balarama were overcome with intense feelings of longing for Vrindavan. Their hearts melted with ecstasy, their external appearances mirroring their internal bliss. Their eyes widened in amazement, and their physical forms exhibited signs of transcendental ecstasy.

At that time, Narada Muni also happened to come by. Krishna was so blissful that He told Narada Muni to ask for any boon Narada wished. Narada then replied, "My Lord, may you three remain in those forms somewhere in this world and let the whole world see these blissful forms. That is what I want."

Krishna graciously granted Narada's wish, agreeing to manifest in those blissful forms in the city of Jagannath Puri, on the ocean's bank.

Thus, the enchanting forms of Jagannath, Balabhadra, and Subhadra manifested in Puri, a testament to the divine ecstasy experienced by the Lord while hearing His own pastimes.

Indeed, the sweetness of God's pastimes is so irresistible that even He is drawn to them.

By delving into Krishna's pastimes, the motherly gopis of Vrindavan and Mother Rohini filled the hearts of Mother Yashoda, Krishna, Balarama, and Subhadra with boundless joy. Likewise, when we share these enchanting narratives with our friends and family, we too can experience unbounded happiness and satisfaction.

Reflect to Realize

The satisfaction and bliss of spiritual discussions is profound. However, some may doubt its validity. The root of this discrepancy often lies in a hidden secret overlooked in our spiritual practices. Beyond mere physical acts of spirituality lies a deeper truth: the conscious connection of our consciousness (*citta*) with the Supreme Lord. Are our thoughts genuinely absorbed in the Lord during our spiritual endeavours? Do we confine our spirituality to specific times and places, neglecting to integrate it into our daily existence (*prana*)? It is only when we find absorption in our everyday practice and learn to embody spiritual wisdom in our lives that the long-awaited spiritual bliss will finally blossom within the core of our hearts.

23

The Provider and the Protector

The Lord not only acknowledges your meditation,
but also cherishes it.

Does a mother perceive her child in her lap as a burden? No! She finds immense joy in carrying and caring for the child. Similarly, the Lord tenderly cares for His devotees who cherish His service. In the Bhagavad Gita, Lord Krishna provides profound assurance to His devotees, expressing the depth of His commitment and love towards them.

In this verse, Lord Krishna states,

ananyāś cintayanto māṁ
ye janāḥ paryupāsate
teṣāṁ nityābhiyuktānāṁ
yoga-kṣemaṁ vahāmy aham

"Those who always worship Me with exclusive devotion,
meditating on Me—to them I supply what they lack,
and I preserve what they have." (9.22)

Here, Lord Krishna emphasizes that those who engage in unwavering worship and single-minded meditation on Him are exceptionally dear to Him. This unwavering devotion signifies a deep, personal connection where the devotee's mind is entirely absorbed in the thoughts of Krishna, reflecting a profound level of spiritual dedication.

Krishna promises to safeguard what His devotees possess, indicating that He will protect their spiritual gains and the progress they have made on their path of devotion. Furthermore, He assures them that He will fulfil what they require, providing for their needs and ensuring their well-being. This divine assurance reflects Krishna's role as a loving guardian who takes personal responsibility for the welfare of His devotees.

By stating *vahamyaham*, Krishna expresses that He will personally carry the burden of their well-being. Just as a mother derives immense happiness from caring for her child, Krishna finds joy in personally taking care of His devotees, ensuring their spiritual and material needs are met.

In essence, this verse reveals the compassionate and protective nature of the Lord towards His devotees. It reassures them that their unwavering devotion is not only acknowledged but cherished by Krishna, who in return, provides them with love, protection, and fulfilment. This divine relationship is built on mutual love and devotion, where the devotee offers sincere worship and Krishna responds with His boundless grace and care.

Once, a question arose in the mind of a devoted soul, "Why does Krishna Himself undertake the responsibility of providing for His devotees' needs?" How do you think Krishna addressed this doubt? Delving into these stories provides a wonderful insight.

The Divine "Delivery" Boys

Arjunacharya, a devout brahmana, resided in a modest hut with his wife, sustaining their livelihood through daily alms. Despite their poverty, Arjunacharya, a learned scholar, dedicatedly studied the Bhagavad Gita and explained its verses in his commentary.

One day, while contemplating the shloka starting with "*ananyas cintayanto mam*," which includes the phrase *vahamyaham* (I will personally carry), Arjunacharya had doubts. He thought, "How could the Lord say, *vahamyaham*—I will personally carry? It is a mistake to think that the Lord would personally carry to every devotee whatever is needed. Maybe, he will get it done through some assistant." Arjunacharya therefore scratched out the word *vahami* (I carry). Later, he went out to beg, as he did every day.

Meanwhile, two charming boys arrived at the door of Arjunacharya's house and began to knock. Arjunacharya's wife opened the door and saw two sweet boys, one dark and one fair in complexion. She saw them carrying on their shoulders huge quantity of food—rice, vegetables, fruits, butter and so on. They looked fearful. They insisted, "O mother, please accept this food." They were anxious to leave as early as possible. She asked them, "Who are you? Who had sent this?" They replied, "We are Arjunacharya's students. You husband has sent these items. Please take them quickly. Otherwise, your husband will beat us again."

Arjunacharya's wife was happy that she could cook some food for her hungry husband. But she couldn't believe that he would punish children who had such sweet faces. She told them, "My husband is not so cruel to beat little boys." Then the dark boy turned around and showed her the marks on his back where he had been struck. He said, "See? Your husband makes us do hard work and when he becomes angry, he punishes us in this way."

Arjunacharya's wife was shocked. She invited the boys into her hutment and lovingly applied some sandalwood paste on the boy's back to relieve him of the pain. Then, the two boys left. She then cooked a meal with the ingredients the boys brought and started eating.

Meanwhile Arjunacharya returned, empty-handed. Because he went out to beg late that day, he couldn't get anything. Seeing his wife eating, he was surprised. She never ate before him. She would lovingly feed him and then eat herself. But today was different. She also looked very upset and neglectful. She didn't want to speak to him.

Arjunacharya asked her, "What's the reason for your strange behaviour today? Have I hurt you in some way?" She replied, "Not me! You have hurt small children. You have become so cruel." Arjunacharya replied, "I have never done so. Why would I do such a thing?" She then narrated what had happened when Arjunacharya was away.

Arjunacharya thought for a few moments and asked her, "How did the boys look like?" She replied, "One was darkish, and the other was fair." He then understood, "It was Krishna and Balarama who came to my house. My wife was so fortunate and blessed to have their darshan. The marks on the dark boy's back were a result of my scratching out the word *vahami*. Krishna had come personally to prove His words true. I was foolish, I couldn't trust his words." Arjunacharya was now completely convinced, beyond any doubt, that Krishna is the Supreme Provider and Protector of His devotees.

Krishna's promises are unwavering and true. Let us place our trust in His words.

From Rags to Riches

Lord Krishna had a childhood friend named Sudama, with whom he shared the same gurukul under the tutelage of Guru Sandipani Muni. Sudama was a poor brahmana who maintained his family with whatever meagre means came his way.

One day, Sudama's wife urged him to visit his friend Krishna in Dwarka and seek some charity. Initially reluctant, Sudama eventually agreed to her persistent requests. Wishing to present a gift to Krishna after such a long time apart, Sudama's wife managed to beg for a few handfuls of flattened rice. She tied the rice in a torn cloth, and Sudama took it as a humble offering to Krishna.

Upon arriving in Dwarka, Sudama approached the palace of Rukmini, Krishna's queen. Krishna saw Sudama from afar, stood up from His throne, and joyfully welcomed him. Embracing his old friend, Krishna made Sudama sit on His own bed, washed Sudama's feet, and sprinkled the water on His head as a gesture of deep respect. Krishna worshiped Sudama with incense and lamps, showering him with many gifts, while Rukmini fanned him. The people in the palace were astonished at the extraordinary honour Krishna bestowed upon his poor friend.

Krishna then eagerly asked Sudama if he had brought any gift for Him. Ashamed of his humble offering, Sudama hesitated to present the flattened rice. However, Krishna seized the bundle Sudama was hiding and joyfully ate a handful. When Krishna was about to eat another morsel, Rukmini lovingly stopped Him, as she and the other queens also wanted a share.

Sudama spent that night comfortably in Krishna's palace and set off for home the next morning without asking Krishna for any favour. Krishna, being omniscient, knew the true reason behind Sudama's visit but did not speak of it.

On his way home, Sudama reflected on his immense good fortune of being honoured by Krishna and felt deep gratitude for Krishna's loving treatment. Upon arriving at his home, he was astonished to find a grand palace in place of his dilapidated hut. His wife, now adorned with expensive jewelry, warmly welcomed him. Sudama realized that this transformation was Krishna's mercy, and he entered his new, splendid home with a heart full of gratitude.

Krishna treasures even the smallest offering from a devotee when it is given with pure love and devotion.

Both Arjunacharya and Sudama harbored a deep and natural love for Krishna. Consequently, Krishna comprehended their needs even before they articulated them. Those who constantly dwell upon the Lord effortlessly draw His grace and support. His affectionate shelter is the solace and aspiration of all devoted souls.

Reflect to Realize

How can we maintain our focus on the Lord while engaged in our daily tasks? Consider a devoted householder who always thinks of his family's welfare while at work. Although he may not be actively dwelling on his family members in his thoughts at every moment, his ultimate purpose of working and earning livelihood is their well-being. He thus performs his duties meticulously while keeping them in his heart. In a similar way, although a devotee is engaged in many works, a devotee's ultimate goal is to please the Lord. But how can we cultivate such a mindset? By developing a regular habit of hearing about God. As we allow the sound vibrations of Krishna's glories to enter our ears, He personally cleanses our hearts, drawing us closer to Him.

24

Remembering God While Dying

God is ready to open the doors of his eternal spiritual kingdom for us.

Why should we take to spiritual practices? What is the benefit of worshiping and thinking of the Lord? What is the result of meditating on Him? One who had practiced spirituality whole life will be able to remember the Lord at the time of death. What if one remembers God during their final moments? Lord Krishna addresses this in the following verse. He assures,

anta-kāle ca mām eva
smaran muktvā kalevaram
yaḥ prayāti sa mad-bhāvaṁ
yāti nāsty atra saṁśayaḥ

"Whoever remembers Me at the time of death undoubtedly reaches Me." (8.5)

This promise opens the door to the kingdom of God, providing a clear and hopeful trajectory for devotees.

But how does one ensure they recall Krishna in their dying moments? The answer lies in the cultivation of a habit of constant remembrance of Krishna throughout life. Consistently meditating on Krishna, by hearing and discussing about His divine qualities, activities, and teachings, devotees train their minds to naturally turn to Him, even in the final moments. This practice is not just for the end of life but is meant to be a continuous, lifelong endeavour that shapes the devotee's consciousness.

This verse highlights the importance of a life dedicated to spiritual practice and devotion. By integrating thoughts of Krishna into daily life, a devotee creates a mental environment that is inclined towards the divine, ensuring that when the final moment arrives, their mind instinctively turns to the Lord.

Here are two captivating tales for you to savour this in a better way!

Dying on a Bed of Arrows

Bhishma, the venerable grandfather of the Kuru dynasty, was a great devotee of Lord Krishna. Blessed with the boon of "*iccha-mrityu*" by his father Shantanu, Bhishma could depart from this world at his own will. Despite his virtuous nature and vast knowledge, Bhishma found himself compelled to fight alongside evil Duryodhana against the virtuous Pandavas in the Kurukshetra war. All this was according to the plan of the Lord, who wanted to teach humanity that vice cannot win over virtue.

During the battle, Arjuna's arrows pierced Bhishma's body, causing him to collapse onto a bed of arrows. As the war concluded with the Pandavas emerging victorious, Krishna, ever mindful of Bhishma's devotion, arranged for the Pandavas to visit Bhishma. With tears in his eyes, Bhishma urged the Pandavas to rule the kingdom justly, following Krishna's wishes.

As the auspicious time of uttarayana approached, Bhishma resolved to depart from his mortal body. Focusing solely on Lord Krishna, who stood before him in his beloved four-handed form, Bhishma offered heartfelt prayers. Reflecting on Krishna's divine presence on the battlefield, Bhishma expressed his devotion through his chivalrous worship, offering his loving thoughts and emotions to the Lord.

In his final moments, Bhishma transcended to one of the Vaikuntha planets, where the Lord resides in His eternal form as Partha-sarathi, the charioteer of Arjuna. The celestial beings celebrated Bhishma's divine journey, showering flowers from the heavens. Yudhishthira, the eldest Pandava, performed the last rites for Bhishma, marking the culmination of Krishna's compassionate grace upon His devoted servant.

Thus, in Bhishma's departure, Krishna manifested His divine presence, bestowing His darshan upon His beloved devotee, affirming the eternal bond between the Lord and His faithful followers.

Thoughts about the Lord lead one towards the Lord.

Driving Away the Yamadutas

Ajamila was a learned brahmana from Kanyakubja, known for his good culture and refined etiquette. Initially, he had no vices, but his life took a drastic turn when he accidentally saw a prostitute and became distracted. He willfully associated with her and that led him away from his path of devotion. He abandoned his parents, his virtuous wife, and his good manners, succumbing to a life of sin characterized by drinking, stealing, and cheating. Thus, eighty-eight years of his life passed in moral degradation.

Ajamila had ten sons and, providentially, he named his youngest son Narayana. This child was particularly dear to Ajamila and his wife. Ajamila took immense pleasure in Narayana's childish prattle and antics. Out of deep affection, he would often call out, "Narayana, Narayana," repeatedly. Whether he was eating or drinking, he would call his son to join him, "Narayana, come and sit, eat this food," or "Narayana, come and drink this juice."

In time, Ajamila fell seriously ill, and his wife neglected him. As he lay on his deathbed, he witnessed three terrifying figures with twisted faces and erect hairs—these were the Yamadutas, the fearsome emissaries of Lord Yama, who administer suitable punishments to sinners in hell. Given the multitude of sins Ajamila had committed in thought, word, and deed, the Yamadutas had come to drag him to hell.

Terrified and tearful, Ajamila desperately called out to his son, "Narayana, Narayana," who was playing nearby. Although the child Narayana did not understand his father's plight, Lord Narayana did. Despite Ajamila's lifelong neglect of Him, the Lord's heart melted upon hearing His name uttered in such desperation. In His mercy, Lord Narayana dispatched His servants, the Vishnudutas, to save Ajamila.

As the Yamadutas attempted to extract Ajamila's soul, the Vishnudutas intervened. Radiant and beautiful in their yellow silk garments, with faces glowing like lotuses and crowns dazzling, they wielded maces, bows, quivers, swords, clubs, conches, chakras, and lotus flowers. Their effulgence dispelled all darkness, and their presence was powerful enough to challenge even Yama if needed.

The Vishnudutas addressed the Yamadutas, saying, "Ajamila, in his helpless state, chanted the name of Lord Narayana on his deathbed. Throughout his life, whenever he called his son, he affectionately uttered the holy name of Narayana. Even unintentional and unconscious chanting of the Lord's name eradicates all sins. Therefore, do not take Ajamila to hell. Just as fire burns dry grass to ashes, the Lord's holy name, whether chanted knowingly or unknowingly, obliterates all sinful actions. Powerful medicine works regardless of the patient's awareness of its properties; similarly, the Lord's holy name is effective even when uttered unknowingly."

The Vishnudutas severed the Yamadutas' ropes and sent them away. Ajamila prostrated himself at the feet of the Vishnudutas, but before he could speak, they vanished. Saved from death and hell, Ajamila deeply repented for his sinful life. "Alas, I have degraded my family's tradition. I deserve to be cast into hell for my sins, but those effulgent beings saved me from the terrifying men who came to arrest me. Given this second chance, I will renounce my sinful ways and devote myself to bhakti unto Lord Narayana, chanting His names with love and affection."

Ajamila then went to Haridwar, a sacred place, where he dedicated himself fully to bhakti. After living a purely spiritual life for twelve years, he passed away on the banks of the Ganga. At that moment, a golden airplane from Vaikuntha arrived to transport Ajamila gloriously back to Lord Vishnu, where he attained a spiritual body suitable for an associate of the Lord.

God is always merciful to His devotees, even if they sometimes commit mistakes.

In moments of need, whether intentional or not, the Lord's compassion shines through, as seen in Bhishma's and Ajamila's salvation, reminding us to meditate on Him with love to find our way to His eternal abode.

Reflect to Realize

Our entire spiritual practice will be tested at the moment of death, reflecting the depth of our lifelong practices. Hence, it's imperative to approach our spiritual journey with sincerity and unwavering commitment. Taking a moment to introspect, we should stand before the mirror and ask ourselves: How well am I preparing for the inevitable ultimate transition to *death*? In spite of our practice, spiritual perfection may elude us in our final moments, yet we won't hold the regrets for neglecting our spiritual pursuits. After all, the anguish of remorse outweighs the pain of discipline required for spiritual growth. Therefore, let us strive to cultivate a daily connection with Krishna, embracing each moment with fervor and inspiration.

25

Thoughts While Dying

What goes in comes out.

What if one remembers something else other than the Lord at the time of death?

Life is a journey of preparation where each moment is an opportunity to shape our inner world. Our thoughts, actions, and aspirations continuously mould our consciousness, which reflects our desires and beliefs. And these desires and value systems overwhelm our minds at the time of death. This perspective is beautifully encapsulated in the Bhagavad Gita, where Lord Krishna reveals a profound principle about the power of our thoughts and their ultimate impact on our destiny and future destinations.

Lord Krishna shares a beautiful insight:

yaṁ yaṁ vāpi smaran bhāvaṁ
tyajaty ante kalevaram
taṁ tam evaiti kaunteya
sadā tad-bhāva-bhāvitaḥ

"Whatever one remembers while giving up his body, one attains that state, for one is always absorbed in such thoughts." (8.6)

Here, Lord Krishna emphasizes the significance of our final thoughts, which are not mere fleeting moments but the culmination of a lifetime of contemplation and focus. Whatever dominates our mind at the time of death reflects what we have been constantly absorbed in during our life. This ultimate moment of truth reveals our true inclinations and the state of our soul, guiding us towards our next state of being.

The principle is both profound and practical. It reveals the importance of cultivating a life filled with positive, spiritual, and purposeful thoughts. By consistently meditating on noble and divine aspects, we prepare ourselves for a transition that aligns with those aspirations. Therefore, we need to live with mindfulness while upholding spiritual teachings, ensuring that our thoughts and actions are in harmony with our highest spiritual goal of attaining the kingdom of God.

Life is a continuous process of inner cultivation. By immersing ourselves in thoughts of love, compassion, and spirituality, we can shape our consciousness in a way that prepares us for a graceful and auspicious transition, ultimately determining our future state. Now, let's read a few stories to get a deeper understanding of this verse.

The King Who Became a Deer

King Bharat, a mighty emperor, expressed his devotion to Lord Vishnu through various grand sacrifices. After an illustrious reign of several centuries, he divided up his wealth among his five sons and went to a tranquil forest, nestled by the flowing waters of the Gandaki. Here, amidst nature's embrace, Bharat built a modest hermitage, where he immersed himself in solitary worship, offering the Lord fragrant flowers, sacred Tulasi leaves, and the pure water of the river. He found sublime contentment in his selfless devotion.

Once, while being seated on the bank of the Gandaki, Bharat began to chant some prayers. At that time, a thirsty pregnant doe happened to come by. As she started drinking water from the river peacefully, she suddenly heard the roar of a lion. As a result, she became very frightened and quickly leapt across the river although her thirst was still unquenched. When she thus jumped in fear, her baby fell from her womb into the flowing waters. Thus, being distressed and separated from its flock, the doe died on the spot.

Meanwhile, Bharat's heart swelled with compassion as he rescued the helpless infant from the rushing waters, cradling it in his arms like a newborn child. This was indeed a noble act of kindness, but surprisingly this compassion led to an undesirable distraction.

Enveloped by an overwhelming fondness for the orphaned deer, Bharat's devotion to Lord Vishnu reduced as he increased his care upon his deer. His days became consumed with the deer's welfare, his worship taking a backseat. Fearful for the fawn's safety, Bharat became its constant companion, carrying it on his shoulders through the forest, sharing his meals, and even sleeping with it nestled close to his heart. He completely forgot his spiritual practices, the very purpose of his retirement from an opulent kingdom.

However, one day the deer vanished into the forest. When King Bharat couldn't find the deer anywhere his heart crumbled. Gripped by anxiety, he searched frantically, his thoughts consumed by the situation of his lost child. Lost in this obsession, Bharat's spiritual practices faded, replaced by a singular focus on the lost deer.

As time passed, Bharat's mind was completely absorbed in the deer. And as he breathed his last, his mind, consumed by thoughts of the deer, sealed his fate. He was born as a deer in his next life, amid the rugged terrain of the Kalanjara Mountain.

Yet, even in his animal form, the grace of the Lord shone upon Bharat. Through divine providence, he retained the memory of his past life. Bharat regretted the past mistake he made of neglecting his spiritual practices. This mistake inspired determination within him. Then, in his next life he was born as a brahmana, and then his unwavering dedication took front seat. He achieved complete perfection and attained the Lord's spiritual abode. He could have attained liberation in one life, but due to his distraction, he had to take two extra lives before entering the spiritual kingdom.

Our emotions and attachments should not lead us astray from our goals.

Some More Time Please!

Once, there lived a man named Kailash. The great sage Narada Muni once urged him, "It's time to dedicate yourself to spiritual pursuits and worship the Lord." Kailash responded, "Indeed, Guruji, I understand, but my children are still young. Let them mature and complete their education before I commit fully to bhakti."

Years passed, and Narada Muni revisited Kailash, reminding him of his spiritual journey. Kailash deferred again, citing his children's unmarried status. "Once my children are wed," he insisted, "I will focus more on devotion."

As time elapsed and his children married, Narada Muni returned once more, emphasizing the need for Kailash's spiritual commitment. However, Kailash, now engrossed in securing his family's financial future, pleaded for further delay.

Repeatedly postponing his spiritual pursuits, Kailash remained absorbed in familial concerns. When Narada Muni eventually returned, Kailash had passed away. Learning of his demise, Narada Muni encountered a dog nearby, which revealed itself to be Kailash, reborn in the same house due to his attachment to home and family. Narada Muni saw him and mercifully replied, "Oh! You have become a dog! Still, it's not too late. Come with me now. Take shelter of the Lord." The dog replied, "I am sorry Narada Muni, I have acquired lot of wealth and built this house in my human life. But my sons are very careless. They are not taking due care of the property. I have to protect it from thieves. Please come back later." Feeling pity for Kailash who was so attached to his home and family of his past life, Narada went away.

Despite Narada Muni's counsel, Kailash, now a dog, was preoccupied with safeguarding the property of his previous life. When Narada returned in subsequent years, Kailash had transmigrated into a snake. Narada told him, "What are you doing here, Kailash? You can still come with me. Take shelter of the Lord." The snake replied, "Dear Narada, my children and grandchildren are not taking care of the fields. They are lazy and wake up late in the morning. By that time all the grains and vegetables in the field are stolen by the neighbours. Therefore, I have become a snake to go round and protect the field from thieves. I am very busy now. I am sorry. I cannot come with you." Ignoring Narada's guidance, Kailash, as a snake, remained bound by his earthly attachments.

This time, Narada Muni didn't go back. He went into the house and told the people, "A poisonous snake is near your house!" Then the sons and grandsons of Kailash came there with sticks. Narada showed them the large snake (Kailash), and they immediately started beating the snake.

Kailash in his snake body hissed and tried to explain to his sons, "I am your father, why are you hitting me?" But the more he hissed, the more his sons beat him. Then Kailash spoke to Narada Muni, "O Gurudev, It's time! Now is the time for me to take bhakti seriously. I shall come with you. I shall take shelter of Lord Krishna."

By continually prioritizing temporary attachments, we miss the chance for spiritual perfection.

Bharat's constant preoccupation with the deer led to his rebirth as a deer, while Kailash's persistent attachment to his home and family resulted in his repeated births near that very place. However, if one directs their thoughts towards the divine, they will attain the kingdom of God after death. Fascinating, isn't it? Let's delve into the next verse and the accompanying stories to unravel more mysteries.

Reflect to Realize

Are you familiar with the renowned Jagannath Puri Rath Yatra, the grandest festival where Lord Krishna and His siblings are ceremoniously drawn out on massive chariots amidst an endless sea of devotees? Legend has it that witnessing the Lord's divine presence and participating in pulling His chariot on this auspicious day leaves an indelible impression on one's consciousness, offering profound solace during one's final moments of life. As one navigates the numerous images flashing before the mind at the time of death, it is believed that the Lord mercifully halts the reel, allowing one to focus on the cherished memory of standing before the majestic chariot. Thus, one can invoke the Lord's grace and journey to the divine abode. Not only this, but even a slight moment of remembrance of the Lord fills our mind with immense satisfaction and provides protection at the time of death. Therefore, let us continue to remember the Lord throughout our lives.

26

Absorption in Service

Connecting with God is a deeply personal and enlivening journey. Lord Krishna outlines four straightforward and effective methods to achieve this in the Bhagavad Gita. These practices are designed to cultivate a profound and enduring relationship with the divine, ensuring that devotees can attain God's loving protection both in this world and the spiritual realm.

Lord Krishna states,

man-manā bhava mad-bhakto
mad-yājī māṁ namaskuru
māṁ evaiṣyasi satyaṁ te
pratijāne priyo 'si me

"Always think of Me, become My devotee, worship Me, and offer obeisances to Me. By doing so, you will surely come to Me. I promise you, for you are very dear to Me." (18.65)

Here are the four methods in detail:

1. **Always Think of Me:** This involves cultivating a habit of constant remembrance of Krishna. By regularly meditating on His divine name, qualities, pastimes, and teachings, devotees keep their minds focused on God. This practice can be integrated into daily life through activities like chanting, reading sacred texts, and contemplating the divine.
2. **Become My Devotee:** One can constantly think of the Lord even with a negative emotion—like evil Kamsa, Sishupal and others. However, we need to think of Krishna with a positive emotion of devotion. Devotion, or bhakti, is central to connecting with God. This involves developing a personal relationship with Him, expressing love, trust, and devotion through daily prayers, rituals, and acts of kindness and service.
3. **Worship Me:** Worshiping Krishna involves performing rituals and offering services that honour Him, especially in His deity form. This can include temple visits, participating in spiritual ceremonies, and performing puja at home. Worship also extends to living a life of integrity and righteousness, as these actions honour God through our conduct.
4. **Offer Obeisances to Me:** Showing reverence and respect through physical gestures such as bowing or prostrating before Krishna is an expression of humility and surrender. It acknowledges His supreme position and one's devotion and gratitude towards Him.

By engaging in these activities with sincerity and devotion, devotees can foster a deep connection with Krishna. He assures that those who follow these practices will surely come to Him, highlighting the importance of these methods in achieving spiritual fulfilment. This divine promise reflects Krishna's boundless love and commitment to His devotees, offering them protection and guidance in all aspects of their lives. Let's explore stories of devotees who immersed themselves in these four practices and ultimately reached Him.

The Cure for Snake Bite

In the holy place of Tirupati lived a devout servant of Lord Venkateshwara (Balaji) named Anantacharya. He was a disciple of the revered saint Sripad Ramanuja Acharya from South India and was renowned for his exceptional devotion, particularly his dedication to growing fragrant flowers for the Lord's worship.

One day, while Anantacharya was in the garden gathering Tulasi leaves to create a garland for Lord Venkateshwara, a venomous snake bit him. Despite the bite, Anantacharya remained fearless and continued his task, confident in the Lord's protection and seeing no reason to fear.

His disciples, noticing the bite, were horrified. They approached Anantacharya urgently, saying, "Guruji, you must seek medical help immediately. Allow us to fetch a doctor and get you some medicine. The poison is spreading rapidly through your body." But Anantacharya, dismissing their concerns, continued with his service.

Perplexed and anxious, the disciples turned to Lord Venkateshwara's deity in the temple. They prayed fervently, "O Lord, our Guru has been bitten by a cobra. Please urge him to seek medical treatment. We fear for his life."

Moved by their plea, the deity of Lord Balaji spoke directly to Anantacharya, "My dear Ananta, you have been bitten by a venomous snake, and the poison is spreading within you. Please take the antidote immediately."

Anantacharya, with folded hands, replied, "My dear Lord, I am content and gratified to have Your divine darshan. But which poison are You referring to? I carry within me two kinds of poison: one is the physical venom of the snake, and the other consists of my vices—ego, pride, greed, and anger. The snake's poison can harm only my body, not my soul. However, the poison of ego and greed can severely damage the soul. Which poison should I be more concerned about? The venom of ego and greed cannot be cured by any earthly doctor. It can only be healed by Your grace. Therefore, I seek refuge in Your service.

The Lord, deeply moved, replied, "My beloved Ananta, you are very dear to Me. Your loss would cause Me great sorrow, as I would miss the fragrant flowers you cultivate for Me. Please take the medicine without delay."

Anantacharya responded, "O Lord, I am like a venomous snake, filled with poison. If the snake's venom is stronger than mine, I will perish. Should I survive, I will bathe in Swami Pushkarini at the Tirumala Hill and continue to serve You as Lord Venkateshwara. If I die, I will bathe in the Viraja at the entrance to Vaikuntha and serve You there. Thus, whether I live or die, my devotion and service to You will remain unchanged, for I am eternally Your servant."

Lord Venkateshwara, deeply pleased and impressed by Anantacharya's unwavering and simple devotion, bestowed His grace upon him. Anantacharya survived the snake bite and continued his dedicated service to Lord Balaji.

Devotees, immersed in the service of the Lord, remain undisturbed by any danger that may arise.

A Spiritual Recipe

In the ancient city of Pratisthanapur in South India lived a humble brahmana, who attributed his poverty to the sins of his past lives. Though he lived a life of material scarcity, he remained content and peaceful, deeply interested in spiritual discourse and the glories of the Divine.

One day, while attending a spiritual discourse by a revered devotee, he heard, "Even if one cannot offer expensive clothes, ornaments, garlands, and food to the Lord directly, one can achieve the same results through sincere meditation." Inspired by this, the brahmana resolved to serve Lord Vishnu through the power of his mind.

He began his ritual by bathing in the holy river Godavari, after which he would sit in a clean, serene spot by the riverbank. Immersed in deep meditation, he envisioned the Lord's resplendent form. In his mind, he dressed the Lord in vibrant clothes, adorned Him with glittering ornaments and a dazzling crown, and humbly prostrated before Him. He imagined meticulously cleaning the Lord's temple with water fetched in golden and silver vessels, not only from the Godavari but also from other sacred rivers like the Ganga, Yamuna, Narmada, and Kaveri.

In his meditation, he gathered fragrant flowers, ripe fruits, sweet incense, and sandalwood paste, offering them all to Lord Vishnu with profound devotion. He performed the aarati and prepared an elaborate feast for the Lord, continuing this routine of mental worship for many years.

One day, while cooking sweet rice for the Lord in his meditation, he used the finest milk, sugar, and ghee. As the sweet rice finished cooking, he waited for it to cool, knowing that the cooler it was, the better it would taste. To test its temperature, he dipped his finger into the pot and immediately felt the sting of a burn, abruptly breaking his meditation.

To his astonishment, the brahmana found his finger actually burnt. He pondered, "All of this occurred only in my meditation—how then is my finger truly burnt?" Meanwhile, in Vaikuntha, Lord Vishnu laughed heartily at this event. Goddess Lakshmi, intrigued by His laughter, asked, "My Lord, what amuses you so?"

Instead of answering her directly, Lord Vishnu instructed His attendants, "Go to Pratisthanapur and bring the brahmana here." The Lord's servants promptly descended, inviting the bewildered brahmana to board the celestial airplane to Vaikuntha.

Upon arriving in Vaikuntha and standing before Lord Vishnu, the brahmana listened as the Lord narrated his tale to Goddess Lakshmi, commending the brahmana's unwavering devotion and meditative service. As a reward for his pure and heartfelt devotion, Lord Vishnu granted the brahmana eternal residence in Vaikuntha.

The brahmana's joy knew no bounds as he was blessed with an eternal place in Vaikuntha, in the divine company of Lord Vishnu and Goddess Lakshmi. This story illustrates that the Lord, though residing in the spiritual realm, is omnipresent and observes all our sincere efforts. The brahmana's profound absorption in serving the Lord through meditation pleased Lord Vishnu, who graciously rewarded him for his devotion.

The Lord graciously accepts anything offered to Him with love, whether physically or within the depths of meditation.

Both Anantacharya and the brahmana exemplified great devotion by constantly meditating on the Lord, worshipping Him, and offering obeisances. In return, the Lord reciprocated with them in remarkable ways. Let us also embrace the four simple activities recommended by Krishna in this verse and attain His grace effortlessly.

Reflect to Realize

Consider this scenario: you have disobeyed, felt envy, and lacked respect towards someone, yet despite all this, that individual tells you, "You are dear to Me." Wouldn't their extraordinary love for you ignite a longing within you? Undoubtedly, it would. This sentiment echoes in this verse of the Gita. Throughout time, we have purposefully turned away from the heartfelt invitation of the Divine. Even now, as the Gita concludes, the Lord, our dear friend, implores us to return to Him, to bask in His loving presence. With such a compassionate friend, parent, and companion, shouldn't we decide to journey back to Him in the spiritual realm, by engaging in ceaseless and unconditional devotional service?

27

Seeing God Everywhere

For those endowed with spiritual vision,
nothing is unrelated to the Lord.

If God is everywhere, why can't we see Him? This question has intrigued seekers and philosophers for centuries. The answer lies in the depth of our spiritual awareness and the purity of our devotion. Those with profound love and unwavering faith in God, who constantly meditate on Him, are the ones who perceive His presence everywhere.

In the Bhagavad Gita, Krishna addresses this profound truth and explains the unique relationship between God and His devotees. He affirms,

yo māṁ paśyati sarvatra
sarvaṁ ca mayi paśyati
tasyāhaṁ na praṇaśyāmi
sa ca me na praṇaśyati

"My devotees perceive Me in all things and see all things in Me. They are never separated from Me, nor am I ever separated from them." (6.30)

For those who have cultivated deep love and unwavering faith, Lord Krishna's presence becomes evident in all aspects of life. Their constant meditation and devotion allow them to see the divine in every being, object, and experience. This perception is not limited to physical sight but extends to a profound inner awareness that recognizes the Lord in all aspects of creation.

Devotees understand that everything exists within God. This realization comes from a deep spiritual insight that all of creation is a manifestation of the divine. Such understanding brings a sense of unity and interconnectedness, where every action and thought is seen as part of the divine play.

In this verse, Lord Krishna emphasizes that His devotees are never separated from Him, nor is He ever separated from them. For the devoted, God is always present everywhere, guiding and protecting them. It reflects a state of constant communion, where the devotee feels the divine presence in every moment of their life.

Thus, the ability to see God everywhere is not about physical vision but about the clarity of spiritual perception. It requires a heart purified by love, a mind steadied by faith, and a soul constantly engaged in remembrance of the divine. When these qualities are present, the veil of illusion is lifted, and God's omnipresence becomes a living reality.

Let us explore the stories of two young boys who witnessed the presence of the Lord everywhere.

The "Inedible" Mango

One day, in a gurukul, the guru summoned his disciples and presented them with fruits. "My dear children," he said, "eat these fruits in a place where no one can see you."

The disciples scattered to various secluded spots to consume their fruits. Upon their return, the guru inquired, "Where did each of you enjoy your fruit?"

One boy replied, "I ate mine behind the tree," while another said, "Below the cot," and yet another claimed, "In the field behind the gurukul."

Each had found a hidden spot, except for one disciple who still held his fruit in his hands.

The guru asked him why he didn't eat the fruit. He explained, "I could not find seclusion. Everywhere I turned, I felt someone's gaze upon me. He seemed omnipresent, in every direction, observing me wherever I went. Unable to fulfil the condition, I returned."

Curious, the guru asked, "Who was this observer?"

The boy responded, "It was Lord Krishna! You taught us from the Bhagavad Gita about Lord Krishna's presence in every corner of the universe. Wherever I attempted to eat the fruit, I remembered this teaching, and felt that Krishna was watching me."

Impressed by the disciple's insight and devotion, the guru commended him. As the boy matured, his devotion and meditation on the Lord flourished, leading him to become a revered devotee.

Although the Lord is omnipresent, His presence is perceptible only to those who harbor profound love for Him.

God in a Pillar

Hiranyakashipu, the king of the asuras, had become invincible through boons granted by Lord Brahma. With his new-found power, he terrorized the devas, sages, and innocent people alike. Despite his tyrannical nature, Hiranyakashipu had a five-year-old son named Prahlada, whom he sent to study politics and diplomacy under the materialistic teachers Shanda and Amarka.

One day, curious about his son's progress, Hiranyakashipu asked Prahlada, "My dear boy, please tell me what you have learned from your teachers." To his dismay, Prahlada fearlessly spoke about bhakti (devotion) to Lord Vishnu. Hiranyakashipu was furious. He rebuked the teachers and scolded Prahlada for his unwavering devotion to Vishnu.

Infuriated by his son's devotion to his sworn enemy, Hiranyakashipu sought to kill Prahlada. He subjected the boy to numerous tortures: tossing him under the feet of elephants, throwing him among poisonous snakes, employing destructive spells, hurling him from a cliff, imprisoning him, poisoning him, starving him, exposing him to severe cold, wind, fire, and water, and even attempting to crush him with heavy stones.

Despite these brutal attempts, Prahlada's faith in Lord Vishnu remained unshaken. Moreover, he bore no ill will towards his father. Baffled by his son's unyielding courage, Hiranyakashipu asked, "You wretched child, you know that when I am angry, the entire universe trembles along with its rulers. By whose power do you dare defy me?"

Prahlada calmly responded, "The source of my strength is the same as the source of yours. That source, Lord Vishnu, is the origin of all strength for every being."

Enraged, Hiranyakashipu threatened to kill Prahlada and demanded, "Is your God present in this pillar?"

Prahlada confidently answered, "Yes, my Lord is present everywhere."

In a fit of rage, Hiranyakashipu struck the pillar. To uphold Prahlada's declaration, Lord Vishnu emerged from the pillar in a magnificent and terrifying form as Nrisimhadeva—half man and half lion. In this formidable form, Nrisimhadeva killed Hiranyakashipu with His nails, thus protecting Prahlada.

Despite his father's cruelty, Prahlada's heart was full of forgiveness. He requested Lord Nrisimhadeva to pardon his father's transgressions. The Lord, pleased with His young devotee's compassion, granted his wish.

One who wholeheartedly trusts in God perceives His presence everywhere and is untroubled by fear.

Indeed, the Lord's omnipresence transcends our material perception, yet those with profound love for Him can sense His presence constantly, even to the extent of personally perceiving Him when their devotion matures.

Reflect to Realize

Consider the scenario of an unassuming, selfless employee within a multinational corporation. Let's imagine that this individual diligently works, aiming to please the firm's owner. However, is it feasible for the owner to take note of the employee's efforts? Given the owner's immense responsibilities and engagements, it seems impractical for him to recall or acknowledge every employee's contribution. But the Lord, the master of all the entire universe, assures and eagerly anticipates remembering and reciprocating with every person who wants to connect with Him. Despite our seeming insignificance, he is enthusiastic and prepared to recognize us continually, provided we remain steadfast in our devotion to Him. Such is the remarkable nature of our personal master. With the blessed fortune of such a Lord and the priceless gift of devotion bestowed upon us by our spiritual teachers, let us wholeheartedly commit ourselves to the path of devotion with unwavering enthusiasm and fervor!

28

Dedicated Mind and Intelligence

Body and senses render physical services, but mind and intelligence develop an inner bonding with the Lord.

Indeed, there are diverse avenues through which we can serve the Lord, utilizing our body, mind, and intelligence. Lord Krishna, in His teachings, provides clear guidance on how we can dedicate our entire being to divine service. He instructs us to focus our minds solely on Him and dedicate our intellect to His service, ensuring our perpetual residence in His divine presence. Lord Krishna emphasizes,

mayy eva mana ādhatsva
mayi buddhiṁ niveśaya
nivasiṣyasi mayy eva
ata ūrdhvaṁ na saṁśayaḥ

"Focus your mind on Me and dedicate your intellect to My service. By doing so, you will always live in Me." (12.8)

This verse highlights the comprehensive approach to serving the Lord:

1. **Focusing the Mind:** Concentrating the mind on Krishna involves constantly thinking about Him, His qualities, and His pastimes. This can be achieved through practices like meditation, chanting His holy names, and thinking of His divine qualities. A focused mind is one that remains steady in its devotion, undistracted by worldly concerns.
2. **Dedicating the Intellect:** Using our intelligence in the service of Krishna means applying our cognitive abilities to understand and spread His teachings. It involves studying sacred scriptures, engaging in discussions on divine knowledge, and using our talents and skills for planning spiritual services. This dedication ensures that our intellectual pursuits are aligned with our spiritual goals.

Throughout history, countless devotees have exemplified deep love for the Lord within their hearts and have served Him through their exceptional intelligence. Great devotees not only focused their minds on the divine but also used their intellect to deepen their understanding of spiritual truths and to inspire others. Their lives demonstrate that true devotion involves a harmonious blend of heart and mind, where emotional love for the Lord is complemented by intellectual engagement in His service.

By following Lord Krishna's instructions to focus our minds on Him and dedicate our intellect to His service, we ensure that every aspect of our being is connected to Him. This holistic approach guarantees that we remain in Krishna's divine presence, experiencing the spiritual joy and fulfilment. Here are some stories of such deep absorption in the Lord.

The Absorption of Sri Radha

Once, in the serene environs of Vrindavan, Lord Sri Krishna and Srimati Radharani were seated together, basking in each other's presence. Suddenly, a bumblebee began buzzing around Radha's face, mistaking her reddish feet for lotus flowers. The incessant humming and hovering of the bee frightened Radha.

Noticing her discomfort, Krishna called upon his friend Madhumangal and requested, "Madhu, please chase this bee away so that it never returns!"

Madhumangal, a jovial and loving companion of Krishna, immediately responded to the call. With playful and humorous gestures, he managed to drive the bee away to a distant place.

Returning triumphantly, Madhumangal announced, "Now Madhusudan is gone. He will never come back!" The word "Madhusudan" refers to both a bee and is also one of Krishna's names. Misinterpreting Madhumangal's words, Radharani thought Krishna had left. Overcome with sorrow, she began to cry, repeatedly calling out, "O Krishna, the Lord of my life, where have You gone?"

Despite Krishna's presence right beside her, Radharani's heart was overwhelmed by the mere thought of his absence. Her intense love for Krishna was so profound that it eclipsed the reality of his physical presence. Attempting to console her, Krishna softly said, "Radha, I am here, right next to you! Please do not cry."

However, Radharani's mind remained consumed by the anguish of imagined separation. Witnessing her deep love and sorrow, Krishna's eyes too welled up with tears. In an expression of their mutual love and devotion, Krishna joined Radharani in her weeping.

Their heartfelt tears of love mingled and formed a lake, which came to be known as "Prema Sarovar." This sacred lake, a testament to their divine love, can be found in Vrindavan to this day.

The loving emotions of devotees melt the Lord's heart.

Hanuman's Intelligence

During the epic war between Lord Rama and the demon king Ravana, Rama and his brother Lakshmana effortlessly vanquished many formidable demons. Rama even slew the mighty Kumbhakarna, Ravana's formidable brother. Ravana, who never expected a few humans accompanied by monkeys to wreak havoc on his vast rakshasa army, was deeply troubled.

As Ravana sat pensively on his golden throne, his son Indrajit approached him and said, "Dear father, why are you so sorrowful? These humans and monkeys will not survive my attacks. I shall tear them to pieces with my weapons today." Feeling a glimmer of hope, Ravana sent Indrajit to the battlefield with his formidable army.

Indrajit ordered his soldiers to attack the monkeys with sharp arrows and lances while he mystically remained invisible. Unseen by everyone, he decimated the monkey army with razor-headed arrows, lances, and maces. With a single arrow, he could pierce through five, seven, or even a dozen monkeys. Yet, the monkeys, dedicated to serving Lord Rama, continued to fight valiantly.

Indrajit even wounded the chief monkey warriors like Jambavan, Sugriva, and Angada with his arrows, and completely covered Rama and Lakshmana with his missile assault. Rama said to Lakshmana, "This demon has released the Brahmastra weapon and has overpowered our army. We too will be affected by this." Then, both brothers fell to the ground, dropping their bows.

Believing Rama and Lakshmana to be dead, Indrajit rejoiced and observed only a few thousand monkeys remaining on the battlefield. As the sun began to set, Indrajit returned to Lanka to deliver the seemingly triumphant news to his father, Ravana.

The mighty Hanuman and Vibhishan, however, survived Indrajit's attack. Hanuman surveyed the battlefield and saw the chief warriors, including Rama and Lakshmana, lying unconscious. He immediately ran to Rama and Lakshmana and sat near them, tears rolling down his cheeks. Vibhishan placed a comforting hand on Hanuman's shoulder and spoke gently, "My dear friend, do not be despondent. Rama and Lakshmana have voluntarily fallen unconscious to honour the Brahmastra. They are virtue personified and will surely rise to defeat Ravana's evil forces."

Hanuman then noticed Jambavan lying injured and approached him. Jambavan said softly, "O Hanuman, only you can save this army. You must go to the Himalayas and bring the four precious herbs: Sanjivakarani, which revives the dead; Vishalyakarani, which heals all wounds; Sandhani, which restores broken bodies; and Suvarnakarani, which rejuvenates. These herbs grow together atop the Himalayas. Please leave at once and bring them here."

Immediately, Hanuman stood up, expanded his body, and shouted, "Victory to Rama!" He soared through the sky and eventually reached the mountain where the celestial herbs grew. However, the divine herbs, sensing his presence, hid themselves, becoming invisible to all but the devatas.

Despite his exhaustive search, Hanuman couldn't find the herbs. Deeply concerned for Rama, Lakshmana, and the monkey army, he became furious and roared, "O mountain, you show no compassion even for Rama and Lakshmana! I will not return without the herbs. I shall now tear away your shining peak."

With his mighty hand, Hanuman broke off the entire section of the mountain containing the herbs. Lifting the massive peak, replete with tigers, elephants, deer, and the herbs, Hanuman sprang into the air and soared back towards Lanka. With the shining mountain peak in hand, he resembled the sun moving across the sky.

Upon arrival near Lanka, Hanuman knelt beside Rama and Lakshmana. Slowly, Rama breathed deeply, inhaling the celestial fragrance of the herbs. Gradually, he opened his lotus-like eyes, saw Hanuman, and smiled. Hanuman, deeply relieved, felt immense joy in his heart. Quickly, he administered the herbs to Lakshmana, who also regained consciousness.

With tears in his eyes, Rama embraced Hanuman, expressing heartfelt gratitude for his devoted service. Subsequently, Rama and Lakshmana courageously re-entered the battlefield and decisively defeated Ravana and his wicked army.

How much we love God is seen in how much we extend ourselves for His service.

Srimati Radharani's heart couldn't bear the mere thought of separation from Krishna, showcasing the depth of her love for Him. Similarly, Hanuman, utilizing his exceptional intelligence, uprooted the summit of the mountain, unable to endure the sight of Lord Rama lying unconscious on the battlefield. Through the absorption of our mind and intelligence in the service of Krishna, we can deepen and strengthen our relationship with Him.

Reflect to Realize

The mind has a tendency to get distracted and swayed by temptations. However, intelligence sharpened by wisdom texts like the Bhagavad Gita can control the mind from these distractions. Ultimately, the mind is meant to develop an emotional bond with the Lord, while intelligence is meant to understand the philosophy and the Lord's greatness. By combining our mental and intellectual functions, we can develop a deeper relationship with the Lord and perfect our lives.

29

Reaching God

It is not impossible to be in this world of dualities, yet remain devoted to God, and thus reach Him.

Transcending life's hurdles and attaining God is a profound spiritual goal that requires mastery over the mind and equanimity in the face of life's dualities. In the Bhagavad Gita, Lord Krishna provides clear guidance on how one can achieve this state of transcendence. He states,

jitātmanaḥ praśāntasya
paramātmā samāhitaḥ
śītoṣṇa-sukha-duḥkheṣu
tathā mānāpamānayoḥ

"One who masters the mind, remains serene, and unperturbed by joy and sorrow, heat and cold, honour and dishonour—effortlessly reaches the Lord." (6.7)

One of the vital aspects of spiritual life is to gain control over the ever-turbulent mind. Our thoughts and emotions can often lead us astray, causing turmoil and distraction. By mastering the mind through practices such as meditation on the Lord's names, contemplation on His qualities, and disciplined thinking, we can achieve a state of inner calm and focus. This requires dedication to spiritual practices, such as meditation, prayer, and ethical living, which strengthen our connection to the divine and enhance our inner stability. When these qualities are embodied, reaching the Lord becomes easy. A person free from the disturbances of the mind and the dualities of the material world, can effortlessly achieve spiritual perfection.

Throughout history, many saints and sages have exemplified these qualities. They have shown that it is possible to live in this world, facing its challenges and dualities, yet remain unshaken and devoted to God. Their lives serve as an inspiration and a practical guide for anyone seeking to transcend material obstacles and attain spiritual fulfilment. Below are the stories of two illustrious individuals who exemplified these qualities and ultimately attained the Lord, despite facing numerous challenges along the way.

Krishna in the Heart

Once, there lived a poor maidservant with her five-year-old son as her sole friend. She loved her only son, and he, in turn, relied completely on his mother's love and care. Their world revolved around each other, sheltered and content.

During the rainy season, a group of revered sages known as the bhakti-vedantas decided to stay in their humble abode. These sages, deeply versed in the Vedas and devoted to Lord Krishna, stayed with them, and both the maidservant and her son served them diligently.

As the sages talked about Lord Krishna's enchanting pastimes, the young boy listened intently, soaking in their wisdom and devotion. His behaviour of discipline, humility, and respect earned him the admiration and blessings of the sages.

Over the course of the monsoon and autumn, under the guidance of the bhakti-vedantas, the boy blossomed into a devout follower of Krishna. They imparted to him the teachings of Srimad Bhagavatam and initiated him into the path of bhakti, even though he hadn't requested for it.

One evening, tragedy struck unexpectedly, when the boy's mother, while tending to a cow, encountered a venomous snake. In a cruel twist of fate, she perished from the snake bite, leaving her son bereft and alone.

However, even in the face of such a loss, the boy remained steadfast in his faith. Recognizing the hand of the Divine in every circumstance, he embarked on a journey to the north. He relied solely on the grace of Lord Krishna.

Through cities and villages, forests and mountains, he travelled, undeterred by fear or fatigue. His unwavering devotion guided him at every step. Bathing in rivers, resting beneath trees, he found peace in meditation, his mind solely fixed on the Supreme Lord.

In moments of profound devotion, tears of love flowed freely from his eyes, and he completely felt the presence of Lord Krishna. These sacred visions fuelled his longing to reach the ultimate goal.

Encouraged by the Lord's assurance and inspired by an unshakeable resolve, the boy devoted himself wholeheartedly to the chanting of the Lord's holy name. In his next life, he would emerge as the venerable sage Narada, his heart forever intertwined with love for the Lord.

By sincere meditation, one can attain great blessings of the Lord.

Liberation of a Cow-killer

Once, there was a courageous prince named Prishadhra. His family priest was the great sage, Vasishtha. Despite being a qualified royal prince, Prishadhra took a solemn vow to protect cows, following the command of his guru. Every night, he would stand guard with a sword in hand, ensuring the safety of the cows from any lurking dangers.

One dark night, a ferocious tiger invaded the cowshed, causing panic among the cattle. Amidst the chaos, the tiger attacked one of the cows, which cried out in distress. Determined to rescue the cow, Prishadhra swiftly ran behind the tiger. However, in the darkness, he mistook the cow for the tiger and tragically beheaded it with his sword. In the chaos, the tiger's ear was also severed, causing it to flee in pain. However, Prishadhra remained unaware of his mistake.

In the morning, the horrifying reality of his actions dawned on Prishadhra as he discovered the lifeless body of the cow. Overwhelmed with guilt and remorse, he realized the gravity of his unintentional sin. Knowing that killing a cow was a grave offense, Prishadhra was consumed by sorrow despite his genuine intentions to protect the cows.

Word of the incident reached the sage Vasishtha, who, despite the unintentional nature of Prishadhra's mistake, cursed him to be reborn as a low-born man in his next life. Rather than challenging the sage's curse, Prishadhra humbly accepted the curse. He acknowledged it as a consequence of his own actions. Embracing the path of celibacy, he devoted himself entirely to the worship of Lord Vaasudeva.

With unwavering focus and devotion, Prishadhra immersed himself in meditation upon Lord Vaasudeva. He cultivated detachment, inner peace, self-control, and profound wisdom as he travelled all over the earth. Despite his cursed fate, Prishadhra's steadfast devotion to the Lord remained unshakeable.

One fateful day, Prishadhra encountered a raging forest fire. Without hesitation, he willingly walked into the flames, surrendering himself completely to the will of the divine. Through his unwavering faith and devotion, Prishadhra transcended the limitations of his earthly existence, ascending to the spiritual realm to attain Lord Vaasudeva.

In the end, Prishadhra's unwavering commitment to the Lord's service and his devotion led him to ultimate liberation, overcoming the confines of Vasishtha's curse and attaining eternal bliss in the divine presence of Lord Vaasudeva.

Even destiny can be altered through devotion to God.

Both the boy and Prishadhra exemplified the qualities described by Lord Krishna in the verse. Their ability to control their minds, maintain peace, and remain unaffected by worldly dualities enabled them to attain the Lord effortlessly. By cultivating these same qualities within ourselves, we too can draw closer to Krishna.

Reflect to Realize

"I want to win over others, win more trophies, win more accolades, win more achievements, and finally win over the world." This is the mindset of a man sunk and arrested by the mind's desires. For such a person, no matter what he gets, he always wants more. Therefore, he's never really successful. To attain life's real success, we need to conquer the mind. It's in this mastery that we connect with the Supersoul within. Conquering the mind does not entail giving up all its desires, but rather transcending worldly cravings by channelling them towards divine service. By directing all aspirations towards the Lord and spiritual endeavours, we gradually transform our lives into ones of profound contentment and purpose.

30

The Easy Way!

Selfless devotion is the most practical and profound way of connecting with the Divine.

Winning the favour of the Lord may seem like an insurmountable challenge to many, but according to Lord Krishna, the ease or difficulty of this task is directly related to the depth of our love and faith in serving Him. In the Bhagavad Gita, Krishna emphasizes this profound truth in a particular verse:

ananya-cetāḥ satataṁ
yo māṁ smarati nityaśaḥ
tasyāhaṁ su-labhaḥ pārtha
nitya-yuktasya yoginaḥ

"Those who always think of Me with deep devotion can easily (sulabha) attain Me, due to their constant absorption in Me." (8.14)

The use of the word *sulabha*, meaning "easy", in this verse is significant. Throughout the Bhagavad Gita, Krishna uses this term only here, highlighting the importance of *bhakti*. For those who harbor genuine and unwavering devotion towards the Lord, gaining His grace becomes effortless. This ease is a result of their constant absorption in divine thoughts and their heartfelt love for Krishna.

This constant absorption means that true devotees think of Him continuously, integrating their spiritual focus into every aspect of their lives. Genuine and unwavering faith in Krishna's love and protection enables devotees to surrender completely to Him. This faith is nurtured through regular spiritual practices, reading scriptures, and associating with other devotees. For those who possess this deep devotion and constant absorption, attaining the Lord's grace is not a strenuous task but a joyful one. Krishna reassures that for such devotees, He is easily attainable. In contrast, for those who lack genuine devotion and are not constantly absorbed in divine thoughts, the journey to attain God's favour remains arduous. Their efforts may be sporadic or driven by selfish motives, making the spiritual path seem difficult and challenging.

Let's explore the stories of two exemplary devotees who effortlessly received the Lord's divine grace.

The Deity Who Ate

Raghunandan was the son of a great devotee named Mukund. At the tender age of five, he exhibited a remarkable devotion to their family deity, Lord Gopinath (Krishna), who had been worshiped by their ancestors for generations.

One day, Mukund had to leave urgently for some work. He entrusted the responsibility of serving Lord Gopinath to his young son. "My dear child," he said, "Lord Gopinath has been worshiped by our ancestors for many, many years. Just as your mother feeds you and me every day, you should feed Gopinath today. I am going out for some important work." With these instructions, Mukund left.

Raghunandan, eager to fulfil his father's instructions, gathered all the necessary items for the offering from his mother and entered the deity room. He had observed his father performing the rituals many times. Following his father's example, he closed the curtain of the room, chanted mantras, rang the bell, and waited for Lord Gopinath to partake of the meal. To his dismay, the food remained untouched on the plate.

Disappointed and worried, Raghunandan began to cry, fearing his father would be upset that the deity had not been fed. He pleaded with tears in his eyes, "O Lord, please eat the food! Please eat!"

Moved by the innocent devotion of the boy, Lord Gopinath spoke, "My dear child, why are you crying?"

With tears streaming down his face, Raghunandan replied, "Because you are not eating the food I offered."

Lord Gopinath reassured him, "I have already eaten."

Confused, Raghunandan questioned, "When did you eat, my Lord? I haven't moved from this spot, and all the food is still on the plate. You haven't eaten. Please eat."

The Lord explained, "This is how I eat. I eat in a spiritual way, just by glancing at the food. Now the food on your plate is prasadam. You and your family can eat it."

However, young Raghunandan, not grasping the philosophy, insisted, "No, this is not eating. All the food is still here, untouched. Please eat it."

Impressed by the boy's earnest appeal, Lord Gopinath smiled. To satisfy his young devotee, He physically ate all the food with His hands, not leaving a single grain. Overjoyed,

Raghunandan brought the empty plate to his mother. His mother, puzzled and surprised, suspected that her son had eaten the food himself but chose to wait for her husband's return.

When Mukund returned, he asked Raghunandan if he had carried out his instructions. The boy replied, "Yes, father, I did as you told me."

Mukund, pleased, said, "Wonderful. Now bring some prasadam."

Raghunandan responded, "Prasadam? Gopinath ate everything I offered Him. He didn't leave anything behind."

Astonished, Mukund, knowing his son was not mischievous, was curious to understand what had transpired. He handed a laddu to Raghunandan and asked him to offer it to Gopinath. The boy, thrilled at another chance to serve the Lord, took the laddu and entered the deity room. Mukund hid nearby to observe.

As before, Raghunandan placed the laddu before Gopinath and prayed for Him to eat. When Gopinath did not immediately eat, the boy's eyes welled up with tears. Moved by his devotee's sincerity, Gopinath extended His hand, picked up the laddu, and began to eat. Mukund, witnessing this divine interaction, was overwhelmed with astonishment and joy.

Aware that Mukund was watching, Lord Gopinath ate half of the laddu, leaving the other half, as He had eaten only a short while ago.

Mukund, eyes brimming with tears, embraced his son, bathing him in the tears of affection and joy. He felt profoundly blessed to have such a pure and devoted soul as his son.

The Lord is not in need of our offerings; rather, He yearns for our love.

The Mystical Jewel

Once, there lived a man utterly consumed by greed, his thoughts and actions driven by an insatiable desire for wealth. He sought riches through any means possible. One day, he heard of a saint named Sanatan Goswami, who lived humbly in Vrindavan and was said to possess a mystical stone called the *Parasa Mani*. This legendary gem could transform anything it touched into pure gold. The allure of limitless wealth overwhelmed the greedy man, and he became determined to obtain the *Parasa Mani* for himself. "What need does a saint have for such a treasure?" he reasoned. "Surely, it would serve me better!" Driven by this thought, he set out for Vrindavan, ready to claim the miraculous gem.

With this resolve, he approached Sanatan Goswami and said, "Revered saint, I have heard that you possess a mystical stone called Parasa Mani."

Sanatan Goswami replied, "Yes, I do have it, though I do not consider it very valuable."

Eagerly, the man asked, "I wish to have it. Could you please give it to me?"

Sanatan Goswami pointed towards a filthy area nearby, where pigs were rummaging through garbage, and said, "Certainly, you may take it. It lies over there in that garbage heap."

The man was taken aback. "The Parasa Mani in garbage? In such a dirty place!" he wondered. Nonetheless, driven by greed and eagerness, he shoved the pigs aside and rummaged through the refuse until he found the Parasa Mani, its brilliance dulled by dirt. Overjoyed, he took it home.

The man soon discovered that chanting a specific mantra enabled the mystical stone to transform anything it touched into gold. With the Parasa Mani in his possession, he generated vast amounts of gold and amassed great wealth, fame, and power. Yet, despite his new-found riches, he found no satisfaction or peace. The abundance of gold and power could not bring him happiness.

Reflecting on his discontent, he thought, "Why do I feel so incomplete? I have everything I ever wanted, yet I am not happy. But that saint Sanatan Goswami seemed truly content and peaceful. He must have something far more valuable than the Parasa Mani. Otherwise, why would he keep it in the garbage and give it to me so easily? I must return to him and discover his secret treasure."

Determined, he travelled back to Vrindavan and sought out Sanatan Goswami. Upon meeting him, the man asked, "O great saint, you gave me the Parasa Mani, yet you kept it in the garbage and never used it. Do you possess something more valuable than this?"

Sanatan Goswami replied, "Indeed, I have something infinitely more valuable than that insignificant Parasa Mani."

Eagerly, the man responded, "I wish to have it. Please, give it to me."

Sanatan Goswami said, "I will give it to you, but first, you must take the Parasa Mani and throw it into the Yamuna."

The man hesitated, thinking, "If I throw this into the Yamuna, it will be lost forever. But if I am to receive something even more valuable..." With resolve, he cast the Parasa Mani into the river.

Returning to Sanatan Goswami, he said, "I have given up the most valuable possession I ever had—the Parasa Mani. Now, please give me the greatest treasure you possess."

Sanatan Goswami smiled and said, "Indeed, I shall now impart to you the most precious wealth in existence, one that grants ultimate happiness. Sit here and listen attentively: 'Hare Krishna Hare Krishna Krishna Krishna Hare Hare, Hare Rama Hare Rama Rama Rama Hare Hare.' This mahamantra is the supreme treasure. It brings me immense joy. The Parasa Mani transforms external objects into gold, but this mahamantra, the touchstone of divine names, transforms the heart into gold. By chanting this mantra, we cultivate love for the Lord and transcend this temporary material world, attaining supreme spiritual bliss and divine love."

The man, now enlightened to the true nature of wealth, began to chant the holy names of the Lord and meditate upon Him. In doing so, he found the lasting happiness and fulfilment that his worldly riches and gold could never provide.

True happiness is not within the pursuits of this material world.

Raghunandan, with his childlike innocence, anticipated the Lord to physically consume the food he offered. In response to his heartfelt plea, the Lord readily fulfilled his expectation. Similarly, Sanatan Goswami illuminated the path to genuine happiness through the simple act of chanting the Lord's names. These stories illustrate that those who approach the Lord with sincere devotion can easily attract His mercy.

Reflect to Realize

The general notion of spirituality often dictates renunciation—abandoning one's family, travels, food preferences, and friendships. This truth resonates across many spiritual paths. However, the path of *bhakti*, or devotion, offers a different perspective—it is *sulabha*, or easy to obtain. In bhakti, one can embrace all aspects of life while maintaining a central focus on connecting everything with God. For instance, we can nurture spiritual relationships grounded in Krishna consciousness, embark on journeys to holy pilgrimage sites, or savour food that is first offered to the Lord. The essence lies in connecting everything to Krishna rather than rejecting everything outright. In the midst of the tempting distractions of Kali Yuga, the age of quarrel and hypocrisy, the path of *bhakti* provides a beacon of hope, offering us the highest blessing and guiding us towards spiritual elevation.

Section IV: Bhakti–Devotion

Can we overcome our troubles by worshipping God? Is attaining relief from misery the only reason to approach the Lord? What's the best gift we can offer to Lord Krishna? How does the Lord bless us for our worship? What if we make mistakes; does He punish us or protect us?

Knowing the answers to these questions is essential for deepening our relationship with the Lord. This section presents ten jewel-like verses from the Gita as spoken by Lord Krishna, highlighting the purpose and power of bhakti, alongside twenty inspiring stories of individuals who embodied the spirit of bhakti, the ultimate teaching of the Gita.

31

The Best Gift for God

A genuine expression of love is greater than the grandeur of proud gifts.

How can one please God? It's surprisingly simple. All it takes is love.

In truth, everything we possess is a gift of God. Yet, when we lovingly and selflessly offer Him even a small gift as a token of our gratitude, He accepts it joyfully. The value of an offering is not measured by its material worth but by the sincerity and love with which it is given. Whether rich or poor, anyone can deeply touch Krishna's heart with these simple offerings, provided there is love, the essence of true worship.

In the Bhagavad Gita, Lord Krishna beautifully declares,

patraṁ puṣpaṁ phalaṁ toyaṁ
yo me bhaktyā prayacchati
tad ahaṁ bhakty-upahṛtam
aśnāmi prayatātmanaḥ

"I happily accept a leaf, a flower, a fruit, or even a little water if it is offered to Me with love and devotion." (9.26)

This verse encapsulates the essence of true worship and the simplicity with which one can connect with the divine.

Lord Krishna's acceptance of even the most modest offerings signifies His boundless kindness and accessibility. It emphasizes that divine love and devotion transcend material wealth and status. A humble leaf, a beautiful flower, a ripe fruit, or a drop of water becomes precious when offered with sincere devotion without any expectation. True worship lies in the intention, not in its grandeur. Such an attitude of selflessness truly nourishes our heart.

Moreover, this verse reassures devotees that they do not need to possess great wealth or perform elaborate rituals to please God. Of course, if one is wealthy, one can certainly make elaborate offerings, but what matters more is the purity of love in their hearts. This makes the path of bhakti accessible to everyone, regardless of their socio-economic background. It is a reminder that God's grace is available to all who approach Him with a genuine heart.

Let's live a life of love, humility, and gratitude, continually offering our hearts to God in every action, thought, and prayer. The forthcoming stories will vividly illustrate this principle.

The Fruit Seller's Divine Bounty

One day, an aborigine woman came to the village of Vrindavan, carrying a basket of fresh fruits. She called out, "Juicy fruits for sale! Come and get them!" As she wandered through the village, her footsteps brought her to the grand palace of King

Nanda. Inside, little Krishna, the cherished son of Mother Yashoda and King Nanda, heard her melodic call. Curious and delighted, Krishna's eyes sparkled with excitement—He wanted some fruit too.

In those days, it was customary to barter foodgrains for goods. Observant and quick to learn, Krishna had seen the adults do this many times. Mimicking them, He scooped up a handful of grains from home and eagerly ran towards the fruit seller. But by the time He arrived, most of the grains had slipped from His tiny fingers.

The fruit seller, enchanted by Krishna's endearing innocence, hardly noticed the handful of grains He offered in exchange. Mesmerized by His sweet demeanour, she joyfully filled His tiny hands with as many fruits as they could hold. Oblivious to His divine identity, her only desire was to bask in the delight of His radiant smile as He received the fruits.

Moved by her generosity and pure heart, Lord Krishna bestowed a miraculous blessing upon her. In an instant, her humble basket transformed, overflowing with priceless jewels and glittering gold—a divine reward for her selfless love. Yet, amidst the new-found riches, it was Krishna's smile that remained her greatest treasure, filling her heart with unparalleled joy.

Selfless service attracts God's abundant grace.

Peels for a Feast

Once, when Lord Krishna visited Hastinapur. Duryodhana, the cunning son of King Dhritarashtra, greeted Krishna with folded palms. "We are honoured, O Govinda," he said. "Please accept my invitation to dine with us. Stay in the palace of my brother Duhshasana, which is superior even to mine."

Although Duryodhana was a wealthy prince capable of offering a magnificent feast, his heart bore no love for Lord Krishna. He had hatred towards Him, mainly because Krishna always supported the virtuous Pandavas, whom Duryodhana had envied since childhood.

Aware of Duryodhana's true feelings, Krishna declined the invitation. "O prince, I will not dine with you, nor will I stay in Duhshasana's palace."

Duryodhana, though burning with anger, maintained a smile and asked, "Why do You refuse our invitation, Krishna? Are we not as dear to You as the Pandavas?"

Krishna responded, "One should only accept food offered by someone if there is love between them, or if one is in great need due to hunger. You hold no love for Me, nor am I in need of your feast. Your envy of the noble Pandavas reveals your character. Whoever despises the virtuous indirectly despises Me as well. The food you offer is tainted by your envy. Therefore, I choose to stay with Vidura."

Vidura, a devotee of Lord Krishna, was the paternal uncle to both the Pandavas and the Kauravas. He had always protected the Pandavas. Recognizing his pure heart, Krishna opted to stay and eat at Vidura's simpler home. Vidura was delighted to host Krishna. Despite the modesty of his house, he offered all he could. Vidura seated Krishna on a chair while he himself sat on the floor.

Overwhelmed with love and admiration, Vidura offered Krishna a peeled banana. So absorbed was he in Krishna's divine presence that he mistakenly handed Him the peeled skin instead of the fruit. Lord Krishna accepted the peel and ate it without hesitation or change in expression, delighting in the affection it was offered with.

Moments later, when Vidura noticed his mistake, he was embarrassed. However, Krishna was filled with joy, not for the banana, but for the pure love with which it was offered.

Even simple offerings win the Lord's heart if there is love. But, even gorgeous offerings do not impress Him if love is absent.

The contrast between the fruit seller's juicy fruits and Vidura's humble banana peels beautifully illustrates the power of selfless love to touch Krishna's heart. Despite the disparity in their offerings, both were infused with genuine devotion, earning Krishna's affection. In our own lives, whether we have samosas, rasgullas, khichri, or karela sabji, the key lies in offering them with pure love to Krishna. Just as He joyfully accepted the offerings in the stories, He eagerly accepts whatever we lovingly present to Him. And in His boundless grace, He leaves behind His prasad as a token of His blessing, enriching our lives with spiritual nourishment and divine favour. So, each offering, no matter how simple, becomes a profound expression of our devotion and a channel for receiving Krishna's divine grace.

Reflect to Realize

The essence of all scriptures lies in pleasing God. So, from now on, let's infuse our rituals with the spirit of devotion. Whether we're chanting simple spiritual mantras or performing elaborate fire sacrifices, let's remember that the secret ingredient is to please God. By working in the spirit of selfless devotion, we'll find how we aren't performing mere mechanical acts but rather entering a state of deeper satisfaction in our own life. Therefore, let's convert rituals into spiritual acts by cultivating the spirit of bhakti.

32

The Four Types of Spiritualists

Regardless of our motives, the Lord responds to our earnest appeals.

Have you ever prayed to the Lord for promotions, pay hikes, or a good job? Or perhaps for a speedy recovery from illness? It's only natural! Life is full of challenges, and in our moments of need, turning to a higher power for assistance and comfort is a common human instinct. Different devotees approach the Lord with various requests, each driven by their unique circumstances and desires. Not everyone can worship Him selflessly, as suggested in the previous verse, and that's perfectly understandable.

In this verse, Lord Krishna describes four types of people who approach Him.

catur-vidhā bhajante māṁ
janāḥ su-kṛtino 'rjuna
ārto jijñāsur arthārthī
jñānī ca bharatarṣabha

"Four kinds of pious people worship Me—the distressed, the inquisitive, the wealth seeker, and the knowledgeable." (7.16)

1. The distressed (*aarta*) turn to Krishna in times of suffering and pain, seeking relief and solace.
2. The curious (*jijnasu*) are those who are eager to understand the mysteries of life and the nature of the divine.
3. The seekers of wealth (*arthaarthi*) approach Krishna with the hope of attaining material success, prosperity, his positions and privileges.
4. Those pursuing knowledge (*jnaani*) worship Him in their quest for spiritual enlightenment and a deeper understanding of the ultimate truth.

Do you find yourself fitting into one of these categories? Or do you worship Krishna without any expectations, purely out of love and devotion? While worshiping selflessly, without any desire for personal gain, is indeed the ideal approach, there's no harm in seeking His assistance to fulfil certain wishes. Lord Krishna Himself acknowledges and accepts these diverse motivations for worship. He understands the human condition and is compassionate towards all who seek Him, regardless of their reasons. Those who sincerely approach the Lord with various motivations can eventually become pure in their purposes and start worshiping Him selflessly.

Whatever our purpose of worship may be, seeking Krishna's refuge assures us of His care and protection. He responds to the devotion of His followers, guiding them on their spiritual journey and providing support in times of need. By turning to Krishna, we can find not only the fulfilment of our immediate desires but also the strength and wisdom to navigate the challenges of life with grace and confidence. Let's explore the stories of a few characters who approached the Lord in the midst of distress and in the want of wealth.

In the Jaws of Desperation

In a dense forest on the higher planets of this universe, there resided a majestic elephant named Gajendra, who ruled over the vast expanse as its king. With a playful spirit, he and his friends ventured into a serene lake nestled within the beautiful Trikuta mountain region. Amidst the cool waters, Gajendra revelled in joy alongside his wives and children, playfully showering them with splashes from his trunk.

However, amidst this idyllic scene, tragedy struck unexpectedly. An enraged crocodile seized Gajendra's leg, capturing him in its powerful grip. Despite Gajendra's immense strength and efforts to get free, his land-dwelling nature rendered him powerless against the aquatic creature. Meanwhile, his fellow elephants could only lament on the shore but couldn't do much practically.

Believe it or not, for a millennium, Gajendra and the crocodile engaged in a relentless fight. Even the heavenly devas were astonished to see their battle. Gradually, Gajendra's vigour reduced. Meanwhile, the crocodile only grew stronger because it was in its natural state of being in water.

In his moment of desperation, Gajendra recalled a prayer he had learned in a past life. With heartfelt devotion, he turned to the Lord, seeking deliverance from his perilous plight. He cried out, "O Lord, compassionate Father! You are aware of everyone's circumstances and possess the power to rescue us from all dangers. Please save me from the clutches of this crocodile."

In a wondrous display of divine intervention, Lord Vishnu swiftly responded to Gajendra's request. Riding upon His divine bird carrier Garuda, the Lord descended from His spiritual abode Vaikuntha. Despite experiencing lots of pain from the crocodile's relentless assault, Gajendra managed to pluck a nearby lotus with his trunk and offered it to the fast-approaching Lord Vishnu with sincere devotion.

With a swift stroke of His Sudarshan Chakra (the disc weapon), Lord Vishnu severed the crocodile's head and tenderly lifted Gajendra from the treacherous waters. Through the divine touch of the Lord, Gajendra was transformed into a celestial being, adorned with four divine arms similar to the Lord's own form. Thus liberated, Gajendra ascended to Vaikuntha where he dwelled eternally in divine bliss.

The Lord pulls us out of the ocean of troubles by responding to our heartfelt prayers.

The Right to Sit

In the dynasty of Svayambhuva Manu, there once lived a great prince named Dhruva. Once, when he was five years old, his envious stepmother barred him from sitting on his own father's lap! Young Dhruva wanted to take revenge against her. Fuelled by disappointment and anger, he harboured an ambitious desire—to attain a position surpassing not only his father's, but even his great-grandfather Brahma's.

Driven by this desire, young Dhruva decided to embark alone into the forest to worship Lord Vishnu and fulfil his wish. Along the way, he encountered the great sage Narada Muni, a devoted disciple of Vishnu. Narada cautioned Dhruva, advising him to wait until he was older to undertake such a challenging endeavour. The forest was filled with great dangers for the little child.

However, undeterred by his young age, Dhruva decided to continue his adventure. His resolve impressed Narada. Narada then accepted Dhruva as a disciple and directed him to the forest named Madhuvan, on the banks of the Yamuna. There he instructed him to chant the mantra *"om namo bhagavate vaasudevaya."*

In Madhuvan, Dhruva immersed himself in worship. He sustained on meagre foods—berries, dry grass, leaves, and eventually, air—over six months of unwavering devotion. By the fifth month, he stood steadfast on one foot, his mind fixed on Lord Vishnu's form without interruption.

Pleased by Dhruva's unwavering determination, Lord Vishnu descended to Madhuvan on his divine mount, Garuda, to bless his devoted young worshipper. Overwhelmed with joy, Dhruva offered obeisances and heartfelt prayers to the Lord.

Lord Vishnu, moved by Dhruva's devotion, bestowed upon him a divine boon. By the Lord's mercy, Dhruva would rule over his father's kingdom for 36,000 years and eventually would become the king of a celestial abode named Dhruvaloka. Filled with gratitude and humility, Dhruva renounced his earlier revengeful thoughts. He realized that there was no point in having a revengeful attitude. Thus, he returned to his father's palace.

Upon Dhruva's return, King Uttanapada and his queen Suruchi, transformed by the events that had happened so far, welcomed him with open arms. Dhruva, now matured, ascended to the throne, ruling the kingdom justly before departing to Dhruvaloka aboard a resplendent chariot.

With determination combined with trust on God, success is assured.

Gajendra sought the Lord's intervention when he found himself ensnared in distress, while Dhruva turned to prayer when consumed by the desire for material position and validation. Despite the contrast in their circumstances, both found solace in Lord Vishnu's divine grace.

It's a profound reminder that regardless of our motives, whether driven by dire need or ambitious aspirations, when we earnestly reach out to the Lord with hearts overflowing with love, He unfailingly responds with boundless affection. Such is the nature of His divine benevolence.

Reflect to Realize

Imagine a prisoner making a peculiar request to the jailor, asking for comfortable cushions or pillows to enhance their sleep within the confines of their cell. Does the plea sound odd? After all, the ultimate desire for any prisoner would logically be freedom from incarceration. In a similar vein, when we beseech God, the Supreme Liberator, for transient material comforts instead of seeking eternal life in His association, we inadvertently prolong our stay within the cycle of material existence.

Just as the prisoner's focus should rightly be on securing freedom from imprisonment, our primary aspiration should be attaining liberation from the bonds of material illusion. Rather than constantly fixating on fleeting material desires, let's shift our focus towards seeking the eternal loving relationship of the Lord, by redirecting our desires and prayers towards spiritual elevation.

33

Devotion Destroys Difficulties

Challenges are an inevitable part of life, yet the way we approach them makes a difference.

Do spiritualists encounter difficulties? Absolutely! Life's challenges spare no one, not even those who have unwavering faith. But who shields them in their hour of need? Just as parents safeguard their children in times of trouble, so does Lord Krishna, the Supreme Parent of all living beings, lovingly shield His devotees from diverse adversities.

In the following Gita verse, Lord Krishna assures,

mac-cittaḥ sarva-durgāṇi
mat-prasādāt tariṣyasi
atha cet tvam ahaṅkārān
na śroṣyasi vinaṅkṣyasi

"By being conscious of Me, you can pass over all the obstacles of material life by My grace. But by acting in an opposite way due to false ego, you will be lost." (18.58)

This assurance is profound and comforting. Just as a loving father reassures his child safety from fears, Lord Krishna, our Supreme Father, is lovingly promising us His divine protection when we take His shelter. This highlights the special bond between the devotee and the divine. When we face trials and tribulations, turning to Krishna provides us with the strength and resilience to overcome them. His grace acts as a protective shield, offering solace and guidance.

Moreover, Krishna's assurance serves as a reminder of the importance of humility and devotion. Those who are arrogant and dismissive of the divine teachings often find themselves struggling alone, bereft of the higher support that comes so naturally to the humble devotee. This doesn't mean that devotees are exempt from hardships, but rather, they have the divine companionship of Krishna to help navigate through their difficulties, which enhances a loving bond between each other.

This verse encourages us to cultivate a sense of surrender and trust in Lord Krishna. By doing so, we open ourselves to receiving His grace and protection. It also serves as a call to reflect on our own attitudes and behaviours. Are we living with humility and devotion, or are we allowing ego and arrogance to distance us from divine guidance?

By embracing devotion and humility, and by seeking refuge in Krishna, we can transcend the adversities of this world and find peace and fulfilment in His divine grace. Now, immerse yourself in the sweet tales of devotees who found refuge in the Lord during their most trying times.

The Pot of Eternal Plenty

During their exile in the forest, Yudhishthira, the eldest of the Pandavas, faced a challenge. Earlier while staying in his kingdom, he would perform abundant charity. But without any resources of livelihood, how would he continue his daily charity to the brahmanas in such an austere environment? To seek a solution, he decided to please the Sun-God and seek his help. Standing in the purifying waters of the Ganga, he performed austerities.

In response to his earnest prayers, the resplendent Sun-God appeared before Yudhishthira. "O king, I am pleased with your prayers," spoke the Sun-God. "I will arrange for your food during the twelve years of your exile. Here is a mystic vessel called Akshaya-patra. Ask your wife, Draupadi, to place the meal she has cooked in this vessel. That food will not reduce in quantity until the time she eats herself. You can thus feed any number of people using this vessel and will regain your kingdom after your exile."

Gratefully accepting the Akshaya-patra, Yudhishthira emerged from the river and handed the mystical vessel to Draupadi. She immediately cooked a meal and placed it in the Akshaya-patra. She offered the food to her beloved Lord Krishna with appropriate prayers, and then served the brahmanas.

To her surprise, she saw that the food never reduced in the vessel. As soon as a portion was taken out, it immediately filled with more food. She served her husbands, and she took her meal last of all. Then the Akshaya-patra finally became empty.

One day, after Draupadi had eaten her meal, sage Durvasa came to the Pandava's camp, along with his ten thousand disciples. Seeing the sage, all the Pandavas stood up in respect, with joined palms. They offered him a seat and bowed to his feet.

"I am here with my ten thousand disciples. We have been walking all day and are hungry. Please arrange for our food. Meanwhile, we'll take our bath in the river and come back," Durvasa requested and left with his disciples.

Now the Pandavas and Draupadi were in deep anxiety. How could they feed so many people? Draupadi had already eaten, and the mystical vessel would not yield more until the next day.

Draupadi then prayed to Lord Krishna, "O Lord of the universe, and destroyer of difficulties, you are all-powerful. Please help us. As you have protected me from Duhshasana earlier, please save me now from this difficult situation too."

At that time, Lord Krishna was in Dwarka, with his queen Rukmini. Yet, He heard his devotee Draupadi's prayers. He immediately left His palace, and in a moment appeared before Draupadi.

Seeing him, Draupadi had tears in her eyes, "O Govinda, we are fearful of Durvasa's curse. Please help us!"

Krishna smiled and said, "I will help you. But first give me something to eat. I am very hungry."

Ashamed, Draupadi replied, "My lord, the Akshaya-patra remains full until I have eaten. I have just taken my meal and I don't have any food."

Krishna replied, "Fine, get the Akshaya-patra and show me. There must be something."

Draupadi brought the vessel and Krishna examined it closely. In one corner He found a particle of rice and vegetable. He ate it, and turned to Sahadeva and said, "Go quickly and bring Durvasa and his disciples for the meal." The Pandavas didn't see any food there, but they had full faith in Krishna's power.

Sahadeva went to the river to call Durvasa. At the river, Durvasa suddenly felt as if he had just consumed a big meal. Even his disciples appeared full and were rubbing their bellies and belching. None of them felt like eating anything!

Durvasa said to his disciples, "We have unnecessarily made Yudhishthira prepare a meal for ten thousand people. Now the Pandavas may be angry with us. They are very powerful because they are devoted to Lord Krishna. Let us run away from here quickly before they see us." Without another word they fled in all directions.

Sahadeva found no one at the river, except some water pots and pieces of cloth lying around. As he looked around for them, some brahmanas informed him that Durvasa and his disciples had suddenly run away from there. Sahadeva went back and informed Yudhishthira.

Yudhishthira was worried, "The ascetics might come back during the night and demand their meal!"

Krishna smiled. "You need not fear. They are afraid of your power. They won't come back. Let me now go back to Dwarka."

Yudhishthira thanked Krishna, "O Lord, as persons drowning in a vast ocean are saved by a boat, so we have been saved by You always."

Krishna left and the Pandavas thanked their wife Draupadi for her presence of mind in praying to Krishna in difficulty. Thinking of their dear Lord and friend they rested for the night.

The Lord is available and accessible for His devotees whenever they are in need.

The Narayana Missile

Millennia ago, King Dhruva ruled over big portions of the planet. Amidst his rule, tragedy struck as his younger stepbrother, Uttama, was killed by a fierce Yaksha's assault in the Himalayas.

Overwhelmed by grief and wrath, Dhruva embarked on a lone adventure towards Alakapuri, the Yaksha's kingdom. Signalling his intent with the resounding blast of his conch shell, Dhruva was very angry. Everyone got scared seeing Dhruva's resolve.

A tumultuous fight began as Dhruva faced an onslaught of Yaksha warriors. He was outnumbered by them, yet he didn't lose his determination. Arrows flew like lightning, piercing the air. However, Dhruva remained like a mountain amidst heavy rains.

With every onslaught of Yaksha weapons, Dhruva's resolve only grew stronger. He appeared similar to a mountain cleansed by torrential rains, emerging brighter than before. Though surrounded by an army of enemies, he remained determined, untouched by fear or fatigue.

In a display of unmatched strength, Dhruva scattered the Yaksha's army. Witnessing their forces shattered, the Yaksha ranks began fleeing like defeated elephants before a lion.

Despite their retreat, Dhruva remained aware. He remained wary of the Yakshas' cunning acts.

As doubts clouded his mind, ominous signs emerged. A storm of blood and pus fell upon Dhruva. Illusions covered him, sapping his strength and resolve.

Amidst this situation, suddenly wise sages appeared and offered their counsel and solace to him. They urged Dhruva to invoke Lord Vishnu's protection. They directed him to wield the divine Narayanastra weapon.

With unwavering faith, Dhruva sought refuge in meditation. He invoked the power of Narayana through his bow and chanted the Lord's names. Then he shot it. In a blaze of golden arrows and celestial swan feathers, the Narayanastra swept away the Yaksha's illusions, securing Dhruva's victory in the face of adversity.

By taking shelter of God, all illusions and confusions are destroyed.

For the Pandavas, Krishna miraculously filled the bellies of Sage Durvasa and his ten thousand disciples without physically offering any food. Similarly, when Dhruva invoked the name of Narayana, the illusions woven by the Yakshas were effortlessly dispelled. These incidents serve as profound reminders of the boundless grace and intervention of the divine in the lives of devotees.

Indeed, the Lord stands ever ready to perform such miracles for each of us as well! All it requires is unwavering trust and steadfast devotion in Him. As we surrender ourselves completely to His divine will, His omnipotent love and compassion guide us through life's trials and tribulations, illuminating our path with divine grace.

Reflect to Realize

Our ego often leads us to see ourselves as the ultimate controllers and enjoyers. To realize our true identity as servants of God, we should be humble and grateful. After achieving something noteworthy, we can remind ourselves that it is ultimately the grace of the Lord that empowered us. Additionally, engaging in selfless service and devotion helps diminish the ego's hold on us, allowing us to align with our spiritual purpose as humble servants of God.

34

The Saviour of the Sincere

Placing trust in the Divine, let's discover a profound sense of security and peace that transcends fear.

In this world, dangers lurk at every corner. Even the most genuine people are sometimes attacked by the envious, who try to harm them with selfish motives. But can anyone truly harm or vanquish the devotees under the protective gaze of Lord Krishna?

In the following Gita verse, Lord Krishna proclaims,

teṣām ahaṁ samuddhartā
mṛtyu-saṁsāra-sāgarāt
bhavāmi na cirāt pārtha
mayy āveśita-cetasām

"For those who are fully devoted to Me, I become their saviour, rescuing them from the cycle of birth and death." (12.7)

Time and again, Lord Krishna personally intervenes to safeguard His devotees from dangerous situations. Whether it is through His direct intervention or by dispatching His divine associates, Krishna ensures the protection of those who surrender to Him. Ultimately, He liberates them from the cycle of birth and death, ushering them into the eternal realm of spiritual bliss.

This divine assurance offers solace to devotees, knowing that their unwavering faith and devotion do not go unnoticed. Through devotional service, devotees can cultivate a deep, personal relationship with Krishna, one that transcends the material plane. The rewards of such devotion are not only immediate protection and guidance but also the ultimate liberation from the cycles of worldly existence. In this divine realm, they experience eternal bliss and happiness with the Supreme. Thus, Krishna's promise is not just a pledge of safety in this life but a guarantee of eternal spiritual fulfilment.

Understanding this, let us try to seek the Lord's shelter with devotion and place our trust in Him. His grace shields us from the evils of the world and guide us toward eternal happiness. Herein lie the tales of two souls whom the Lord graciously spared from the clutches of death.

Protected Before Birth

After the Kurukshetra war, as the Pandavas grappled with the loss of their dear ones, Lord Krishna remained a steadfast source of solace and support. His presence in Hastinapur provided a beacon of hope amidst the darkness of their grief. However, as time passed by, Krishna had to leave for Dwarka. But just on the day of his departure an emergency arose!

Uttara, the wife of Abhimanyu, found herself in danger as a fiery arrow flew towards her. That arrow was being directed at the child in her womb. Despite the presence of Arjuna, Bhima, and Yudhishthira at that place, Uttara spontaneously ran towards Krishna to seek His shelter. With an earnest prayer, she prayed to Krishna to shield her unborn child from harm. She was willing to give up her own life in exchange.

Krishna, ever compassionate and swift to respond to the call of His devotees, instantly intervened. Manifesting Himself in a tiny four-handed form within Uttara's womb, He was adorned with regal splendour. Within the womb, Krishna neutralized the deadly brahmastra aimed at the unborn child by heinous Asvatthama, a friend of evil Duryodhana, who desired to kill the last descendant of the Pandavas. With His divine touch, Lord Krishna dispelled the looming threat, leaving Uttara and her child completely protected.

Subsequently, Uttara gave birth to an illustrious child, the result of the Lord's miraculous intervention. The blessed child would curiously examine people seeking out the divine Lord whom he had seen in his mother's womb. Therefore, he earned the named "Parikshit," the discerning seeker. The story of Uttara and Parikshit stands as a testament to the boundless affection and protective benevolence of Lord Krishna towards His devotees.

The Lord's affection for His devotees is one of His sweetest qualities.

Goddess Kali's Fierce Protection

The story of Jada Bharat is a powerful example of unwavering faith and divine protection. Long ago, Jada Bharat, a devotee of Lord Vishnu, once found himself in a dangerous situation when a group of dacoits kidnapped him and decided to offer him as a human sacrifice to the fierce Goddess Kali.

While he was captured and bound by the dacoits, Jada Bharat remained calm and steadfast in his faith. He accepted his fate without fear. Then as the ritual reached its peak and the sacrificial sword was about to strike Bharata's head, something extraordinary happened. Goddess Kali, enraged by the misuse of her name for such a heinous act, actually manifested out of the deity in a blaze of fury.

With righteous anger, she swiftly defeated the dacoits, sparing Jada Bharat from harm. Her divine wrath killed the enemies, proving the victory of good over evil. In the aftermath, Jada Bharat emerged unharmed, a living testament to the protective power of his unwavering faith in Lord Vishnu. Goddess Kali saw that Jada Bharat was the Lord's devotee, therefore she protected him.

The Lord always arranges for the protection of His devotees.

This tale of Jada Bharat reminds us of the profound protection that the divine extends to those who are devoted. It highlights the incredible strength of faith, even in the face of extreme adversity, and reassures us that the divine always watches over and protects His true devotees.

Certainly, fear is a common part of life, whether it's the darkness of a room, the tension of a horror movie, or the anxiety of a surprise interview. Yet, stories like those of Uttara and Jada Bharata remind us that we need not face our fears alone. These devotees show us the path to seek refuge in Lord Krishna, the ultimate protector. They teach us that Krishna has the power to shield us from all dangers, even the most daunting ones, including the fear of death itself. When we place our trust in Him, we discover a profound sense of security and peace that transcends any fear we may encounter.

Reflect to Realize

Lord Krishna promises liberation for those who invest their consciousness in Him (*mayy aveshita-cetasam*). It's common to confine devotion to specific times or places, such as a temple hall or morning meditation sessions. However, this verse urges us to transcend such limitations. Alongside designated spiritual practices, we're called to integrate spirituality into every aspect of our lives. Rather than pursuing the fleeting pleasures of this world, we're encouraged to immerse ourselves in thoughts of the Divine.

35

Help for God Lovers

Temple deities are not mere stone statues but are the most accessible forms of the Lord.

The Lord's compassion manifests in various forms, one of which is His divine presence as the deity in temples. The deity in the temple, installed in accordance with the scriptural injunctions, is a direct manifestation of the Lord, and is not different from Him. Since our material eyes can't see His spiritual form, He graciously appears in forms made of stone, metal, clay, and other materials. Thus, the Lord gives us an opportunity to see Him as the deity, serve Him to our heart's content, connect with Him spiritually through worship (*archana*), finding solace and guidance in their prayers. When worshippers bow before the deity, they are engaging in a direct and personal communion with Krishna, not just venerating an image. Through these sacred forms, devotees receive protection and blessings in return for their devotion.

In the Bhagavad Gita, Lord Krishna assures,

teṣāṁ satata-yuktānāṁ
bhajatāṁ prīti-pūrvakam
dadāmi buddhi-yogaṁ taṁ
yena mām upayānti te

"For those who are constantly devoted to Me and worship Me with love, I give the understanding by which they can come to Me." (10.10)

This promise demonstrates Lord Krishna's unwavering commitment to support and uplift those who seek His refuge. When a devotee worships the Lord who made Himself accessible to us in the form of a Deity in the temple, that fosters a deep sense of closeness and intimacy with the Lord, individually and communally.

Furthermore, the temple becomes a place of peace and a beacon of hope for the faithful. It is a place where the burdens of the world can be set aside, and the soul can find respite in the divine presence. The deity's compassionate glances envelops the devotees, providing them with strength and guidance to navigate life's challenges.

Now, let's delve into some inspiring tales of how Lord Krishna, in His deity forms, extended His divine assistance to devotees facing adversity. It's time for some captivating stories of divine intervention!

Guruvayur—The Divine Defender

In the peaceful landscapes of Kerala lies the enchanting Guruvayur temple, home to the beloved deity Guruvayurappan, a manifestation of Lord Krishna. One of Guruvayurappan's devoted followers was Poonthanam, who often made long journeys on foot to visit the temple.

One fateful day, while on his way to the temple, Poonthanam was ambushed by ruthless robbers. They took almost everything he had. He was desperately clutching a small bag, which contained his most treasured possession, the Srimad Bhagavatam. Poonthanam was devastated when the robbers tried to take that too. In his desperation, he cried out to Lord Krishna for help.

Miraculously, a powerful soldier on a majestic horse appeared out of nowhere. He swiftly drove off the robbers and retrieved Poonthanam's belongings. Overwhelmed with gratitude, Poonthanam held onto his beloved Srimad Bhagavatam, tears of relief streaming down his face.

Wanting to show his appreciation, Poonthanam offered the soldier a ring and asked for his name. The soldier revealed himself as a minister serving the king, and departed.

That night, the priest of Guruvayur temple had a divine dream. Lord Krishna appeared in his dream and instructed him to give the ring to Poonthanam when he comes to the temple. As dawn broke, the priest noticed a ring on the deity's finger, confirming the divine message.

When Poonthanam arrived at the temple, the priest, recognizing his devotion, presented him with the ring, declaring it a personal gift from Lord Guruvayurappan. Overwhelmed with emotion, Poonthanam realized that it was the Lord who came the previous day to save him from the dacoits. The ring on the deity's finger was a testament to the Lord's benevolence, filling Poonthanam with profound gratitude.

The Lord cannot see His devotee in distress. He saves them at all costs.

A Sublime Witness

In the peaceful town of Vidyanagara in Southern India, two brahmanas decided to go on a sacred pilgrimage. They visited many holy sites, like Gaya, Mathura, and Vrindavan, finally arriving at the beautiful temple of Lord Gopala. Throughout their journey, the young brahmana took great care of his elder companion, earning his admiration and gratitude.

Impressed by the young brahmana's devotion and selfless service, the elder brahmana felt the need to show his appreciation. He decided to offer his daughter's hand in marriage to the young man, despite the young brahmana's poor background. When he proposed this, the young brahmana humbly declined, feeling unworthy.

But the elder brahmana was determined. He made a solemn vow before the deity of Lord Gopala to keep his promise. However, when he returned home, his family strongly opposed the marriage, arguing that the young brahmana was poor and uneducated. The old brahmana prayed fervently to Lord Gopala for a solution.

Soon, the young brahmana visited the elder's home to ask for his daughter's hand. When he arrived, the elder brahmana's son accused him of cheating his father during the journey and stealing money, claiming he was now trying to marry his sister. The villagers got involved, doubting the young brahmana's integrity simply because he was poor.

Determined to prove his honesty, the young brahmana turned to the Lord for justice. He decided to go to the temple and ask Lord Gopala to witness the promise made by the elder brahmana. With unwavering faith, he journeyed to Vrindavan and pleaded with the deity of Gopala to bear witness to the promise. Moved by the young brahmana's sincerity, Lord

Gopala agreed to accompany him to the village. Despite being in the deity form, He decided to walk with the young brahmana to the village.

In an extraordinary display of divine grace, Lord Gopala manifested Himself and confirmed the elder brahmana's promise to the villagers. Everyone was filled with awe and reverence at the divine intervention.

Acknowledging the young brahmana's devotion, Lord Gopala blessed them and also granted his wish for His temple to be established in Vidyanagara. The deity became known as "Sakshi-Gopala", or "Gopala, the witness", forever enshrining His presence in the hearts of devotees.

Firm faith in the Lord is the key to His grace.

The Lord is perpetually vigilant, poised to shield us from harm, much like His swift intervention to save Poonthanam from the clutches of bandits. His benevolent nature knows no bounds, as evidenced by His unwavering journey to the distant village of the young brahmana, transcending physical and metaphysical barriers out of pure compassion. When we devote ourselves to His service with genuine love, we invite His endless grace and protection into our lives. When we reach out to Him with sincere affection, He responds with boundless love, creating a divine connection that knows no limits.

Reflect to Realize

In the aforementioned series of stories, we discovered the profound understanding that the deity in the temple is not distinct from the Lord Himself. Nevertheless, at times, the sceptical mind within us may lead us to perceive the deity as mere stone. Here's an exercise to counteract such thoughts: Each time you visit the deity, address Him by His name and converse with Him as you would with any other person. While you may not receive a verbal response, you will undoubtedly receive a heartfelt one that fills your heart with satisfaction.

36

What if a Devotee Makes a Mistake?

What happens when spiritualists make mistakes? Are they condemned as sinners by God? Does Lord Krishna abandon or severely punish them? He answers this question in the following verse:

kṣipraṁ bhavati dharmātmā
śaśvac-chāntiṁ nigacchati
kaunteya pratijānīhi
na me bhaktaḥ praṇaśyati

"Even if My devotees commit sins accidentally or unintentionally, if they worship Me sincerely, I consider them saintly. They will soon become virtuous and attain lasting peace. O Arjuna, boldly declare that My devotees never perish." (9.31)

Genuine devotees do not intentionally commit sins. However, sometimes, they may inadvertently make mistakes. Yet, if they sincerely repent, Lord Krishna, in His infinite kindness, forgives them and guides them back to the right path. Thus, there is boundless hope for devotees who cultivate bhakti.

The compassionate Lord understands the human condition, and recognizes that even the most devoted individuals can falter at times, accidentally and not deliberately. However, if they are sincere, they genuinely repent for their mistakes, and turn to Krishna with a humble heart, seeking His forgiveness. The Lord does not condemn them but rather embraces them with open arms. Through sincere worship and a heartfelt connection with Krishna, devotees are not only forgiven but are also uplifted and guided towards a path of virtue.

This process of transformation happens by the boundless grace of Krishna, who ensures that His devotees are never lost, no matter how many times they stumble. But if a devotee takes undue advantage of the Lord's accommodating nature and deliberately commits mistakes, the Lord does the needful to teach them a lesson, in the mood of rectifying them. The purpose of the Lord's punishment is reformation and not rejection.

The assurance that "My devotees never perish" offers profound solace and encouragement to devotees. It signifies that the relationship between the devotee and the Lord is eternal and unbreakable. Krishna's commitment to His devotees is unwavering, providing them with a sense of security and hope. Here are some exciting episodes that exemplify Krishna's promise.

King Indradyumna Becomes Gajendra

The illustrious ruler Indradyumna governed the prosperous Pandya-desa in southern India. He was a great devotee of Lord Krishna. After years of diligent service, he retired to the quiet Malaya hills. There he built a hermitage and embraced the ascetic life, adorned with matted locks and immersed in *tapasya*. Deep in meditation, he cultivated an intense love for his beloved Lord Hari.

During his meditation, the revered sage Agastya visited, but Indradyumna, engrossed in worship, didn't realize the sage's presence. Agastya, feeling insulted, uttered a curse, predicting that Indradyumna would be reborn as a less intelligent elephant. Accepting his fate as the will of Lord Hari, Indradyumna embraced the curse with humility. Unknown to him, that life as an elephant would be his last one in the material world.

In his subsequent life as Gajendra, the king of elephants, Indradyumna recalled his devotion that he had practised in his previous life. Once, when a crocodile caught his leg, he fervently prayed to Lord Hari, who swiftly rescued him. The Lord then granted him liberation from the cycle of birth and rebirth. Thus, Sage Agastya's seemingly harsh curse ultimately led Indradyumna to eternal proximity with Lord Hari in Vaikuntha, transcending mortal limitations and finding everlasting bliss.

Devotion to the Lord turns even curses into blessings.

The Curse That Liberated

There once lived a great king named Chitraketu. By the grace of his guru Narada Muni, he got the darshan of Lord Vishnu. This filled his heart with boundless love and joy. Blessed with a divine flying machine, he travelled the skies, constantly singing praises of the Lord.

One day, while flying in the air, Chitraketu saw Lord Shiva sitting in the midst of sages with Parvati seated on her lap. Impelled by a subtle pride, he voiced his astonishment. He felt, "Even an ordinary man embraces his wife when they are alone, but what is Lord Shiva doing in public?" Chitraketu only corrected Lord Shiva so that people don't misunderstand his exalted position and belittle him for his apparently unconventional behaviour. But Chitraketu inadvertently caused an offence to Lord Shiva.

Understanding his underlying intention, Lord Shiva smiled. However, Parvati, angered by Chitraketu's impudence, and pronounced a curse upon him, "May you become a demon in your next life, so that you wouldn't disrespect exalted personalities like this."

Accepting Parvati's chastisement with humility, Chitraketu bowed before her, seeking forgiveness, addressing her as a mother. Meanwhile, Lord Shiva, acknowledged the greatness of Lord Vishnu's devotees. He was impressed seeing Chitraketu's unwavering humility and fearlessness from any curse.

Reborn as demon Vritrasura, Chitraketu retained his devotion to Lord Vishnu. Despite his demonic form, he remained steadfast in his devotion and was eventually liberated in a battle with Indra. Ultimately, the Lord removed the tinge of pride in Chitraketu through Parvati's curse, and brought him to Vaikuntha, his eternal abode.

A devotee is safe in all circumstances by the Lord's loving grace.

Both King Indradyumna and King Chitraketu found themselves ensnared by unintentional offences. While Indradyumna inadvertently overlooked offering a warm welcome to Sage Agastya, Chitraketu's attempt to publicly correct Lord Shiva led to their respective curses. Despite their missteps, Lord Hari (Vishnu) intervened and rescued them from their downtrodden conditions and ultimately led them to His divine abode. Just as Lord Hari (Vishnu) extended His grace to Indradyumna and Chitraketu, we can be blessed similarly, if we wholeheartedly worship Hari, seeking refuge in His divine love and guidance.

Reflect to Realize

The Lord extends His forgiveness for the accidental errors and minor shortcomings of His devotees. However, this does not grant a licence to deliberately commit mistakes and seek forgiveness afterward. His promise of protection applies to unintentional slips, not to deliberate transgressions. True forgiveness requires sincere repentance and a commitment to improvement. Let us, therefore, strive to walk the spiritual path with sincerity and honesty, avoiding intentional wrongdoings.

37

Dedicated Service

Bhakti is not just an emotion, but a dedicated action performed with sincere intention.

Who is a mahatma? Is it someone who possesses great strength, beauty, or wealth? The word "mahatma" literally translates to a "great soul." But what truly defines greatness of a person? Let's turn to Lord Krishna Himself for insight.

In this verse, Krishna reveals,

mahātmānas tu māṁ pārtha
daivīṁ prakṛtim āśritāḥ
bhajanty ananya-manaso
jñātvā bhūtādim avyayam

"Mahatmas or great souls are those who take refuge of My divine energy. Recognizing Me as the source of the entire universe and all beings within it, they constantly contemplate upon Me and serve Me with unwavering devotion." (9.13)

This definition provided by Lord Krishna elevates the concept of greatness to a spiritual plane. A mahatma is not measured by material attributes such as power, beauty, or wealth, but by their spiritual qualities and their deep connection with the divine.

A true mahatma understands the supreme reality that Krishna is the origin of everything. This profound realization shapes their thoughts, actions, and their entire existence. They see the world and all living beings as manifestations of Krishna's divine energy. This recognition creates a sense of humility, compassion, and unwavering devotion in their hearts.

Mahatmas dedicate their lives to serving Krishna with complete faith and commitment. Their devotion is not a part-time endeavour but a continuous, wholehearted dedication. They engage in various forms of devotional service (bhakti), such as chanting the Lord's name, and spreading His teachings. This constant engagement in Krishna consciousness not only purifies their hearts but also strengthens their bond with the Supreme.

Moreover, the devotion of a mahatma transcends personal gain or recognition. Their service is motivated solely by love and devotion to Krishna, without any desire for material rewards. This selfless devotion is what truly sets them apart as great souls.

Now, let's delve into the story of a mahatma who exemplified this profound devotion, serving Lord Krishna wholeheartedly and thereby receiving His special grace and blessings.

Unearthing Lord Gopala

Madhavendra Puri, a great mendicant, once reverently circumambulated the holy Govardhan Hill at Vrindavan, the holy land where Lord Krishna lived. He experienced immense joy at the sacred place. He sat beneath a tree to meditate on the

Lord. Sustained solely by the grace of God, he never begged for food but accepted whatever sustenance came his way.

As Madhavendra Puri sat chanting the names of Lord Krishna, a young cowherd approached him. The boy smiled warmly and offered him a pot, saying, "O Sadhu, please accept this milk. You seem to be hungry."

Puri, intrigued, asked, "Who are you, my dear boy? How did you know that I am hungry?"

The boy replied, "I am a cowherd from this village. No one should be hungry here. The women who came here to fetch water have sent this milk for you. Now, I must go to milk the cows, but I shall return to collect this milk pot." Saying that, the boy left.

Madhavendra Puri was captivated by the boy's sweet and caring nature. He drank the milk and washed the pot and waited for the boy's return. However, the boy didn't come back. Puri continued his devotional chants until sleep finally overcame him, bringing a divine vision of the same boy.

In his dream, the boy revealed himself as Lord Krishna and took Puri to a bush in the jungle, and said, "I reside in this bush, enduring cold, rain, wind, and heat. Please get the villagers to take me out, build a temple on top of that hill, and consecrate Me there. When some invaders attacked this village, the priest who was serving Me hid Me in this bush and fled to save his life. For many days, I have been waiting for you."

Overwhelmed by the revelation, Puri awoke with tears in his eyes, regretting that he had not recognized his beloved Lord earlier. Driven by devotion, he immediately gathered the villagers and shared his vision.

The villagers, inspired by Puri's words, cleared the path through the jungle and found the Deity of Lord Gopala hidden amidst the foliage. They fashioned a large stone throne and placed Lord Gopala upon it.

The villagers called for brahmana priests and began singing and dancing in celebration. They brought milk, curd, ghee, sweets, various foods, Tulasi leaves, flowers, garments, and 900 pots of water from Govinda-kund, a sacred lake in Vrindavan. Madhavendra Puri commenced the *abhishek* (bathing) of Lord Gopala with pancha-gavya (milk, curd, ghee, cow urine, and cow dung) and panchamrita (milk, curd, ghee, honey, and sugar). Gopala was then dressed in new garments, and Madhavendra Puri offered all the food items to the Lord. The Lord, who had been hungry for many days, accepted the offerings. Madhavendra Puri witnessed the divine act of the Lord eating the offerings, who also left prasadam for His devotees.

The entire festival and installation of Lord Gopala were arranged in just one day, by the grace of the Lord Himself. News of Lord Gopala's appearance atop Govardhan Hill spread quickly, attracting people from neighbouring villages. They came and performed the Annakut ceremony, offering huge quantities of food to the Lord day after day. Wealthy businessmen from Mathura brought various presents, and one rich man constructed a beautiful temple for the Lord. Every family in Vrindavan contributed one cow, resulting in thousands of cows serving Lord Gopala daily. In this way, all the devotees used their wealth and hearts to serve their beloved Lord.

By the Lord's grace, the impossible becomes possible.

The Sandalwood Quest

One day, after Sri Madhavendra Puri had established the deity of Lord Gopala in Vrindavan, the Lord appeared to him in a dream and said, "Dear Madhavendra, please bring sandalwood from the Malaya Mountain region and smear the pulp over My body. My body still burns with the heat it had to bear when I was left alone in the forest. No one else except you can do it."

Madhavendra Puri awoke, feeling grateful for another opportunity to serve Lord Gopala. He made all the necessary arrangements for the regular worship of Lord Gopala and began his long journey towards Jagannath Puri to obtain the sandalwood. With no chariot or vehicle, he set out on foot.

As he travelled through Bengal, he reached a village called Remuna, where he visited a beautiful temple of Lord Gopinath, another deity of Lord Krishna. Upon seeing Lord Gopinath, Madhavendra Puri was filled with spiritual joy, singing and dancing in ecstasy, and then tasted the prasadam. After this uplifting visit, he continued his journey on foot to Jagannath Puri.

Upon reaching Jagannath Puri, Madhavendra Puri shared the story of Lord Gopala's appearance and His instruction to bring sandalwood. His reputation as a great devotee of Krishna was well-known in Jagannath Puri, and the devotees there were eager to help. They offered him one maund (about 37 kilos) of sandalwood and camphor, along with two assistants to help carry the load and cover travel expenses.

Madhavendra Puri started back towards Vrindavan with the sandalwood. On the way, he once again reached Remuna and stayed at the Gopinath temple. The priests welcomed him warmly and offered him prasadam.

That night, Lord Gopala appeared in Madhavendra Puri's dream once more and said, "Dear Madhavendra, I have already received all the sandalwood and camphor I need. Now, just grind them together and smear the pulp on Lord Gopinath's body daily until it is all used up. The temperature of My body will come down, as there is no difference between His body and Mine."

Upon waking, Madhavendra Puri called the priests of Gopinath and recounted his dream. The devotees enthusiastically participated in grinding the sandalwood and camphor, and the paste was applied daily to Lord Gopinath. Madhavendra Puri stayed in Remuna until all the sandalwood was used up.

Madhavendra Puri felt immensely blessed to receive direct instructions from Lord Krishna multiple times in his dreams. Though he was happy to carry the heavy loads of sandalwood for Lord Gopala out of intense love, the Lord, not wanting to burden His devotee, instructed him to apply the sandalwood paste to Lord Gopinath at Remuna instead of undertaking the strenuous journey back to Vrindavan.

The Lord's care and compassion for His dedicated devotees are boundless.

The depth of our love for God is revealed in the extent of our dedication to His service. A true devotee displays unwavering willingness to make any sacrifice for the Lord's satisfaction. Mahatmas, exemplified by devoted souls like Madhavendra Puri, wholeheartedly embrace challenges and hardships in their relentless pursuit of serving the divine. Their actions speak volumes about their profound love and devotion for the Lord.

Reflect to Realize

In this verse, Lord Krishna advises turning to His divine counterpart, the divine mother (*daivi prakriti*). By seeking refuge in Srimati Radharani or Mother Lakshmi, our loving mother will happily cleanse us of all our *anarthas* and make us ready to enter Krishna's loving embrace. When we approach the Lord's feminine potency first, He will be more eager to accept us.

38

Constant Devotion

Consistent effort to come closer to God enlivens more than intermittent spiritual experiences.

God is certainly pleased when we offer Him opulent dishes, but His true delight lies in something deeper. In this verse, Lord Krishna reveals,

satataṁ kīrtayanto māṁ
yatantaś ca dṛḍha-vratāḥ
namasyantaś ca māṁ bhaktyā
nitya-yuktā upāsate

"My devotees demonstrate their love for Me through unwavering chanting of My names and glories. They bow before Me with steadfast devotion and worship Me unceasingly." (9.14)

Chanting Krishna's names and glories is a powerful way to practise bhakti. When devotees chant His holy names, they fill themselves with divine vibrations that purify their hearts and minds, bringing them closer to the Lord. This repetition acts as a spiritual anchor, helping devotees stay connected to Krishna amidst life's distractions and challenges.

Bowing before Krishna with unwavering devotion is a profound expression of humility and reverence. It's more than just a physical act; it signifies surrendering one's ego, desires, and will to Krishna's will. This inner submission shows a deep respect for His supreme position.

True devotion is unceasing. It's not limited to specific rituals or times of the day but is a continuous, ever-present dedication. Whether through singing His praises, meditating on His form, or performing selfless service, true devotees keep Krishna at the centre of their lives at all times.

Chanting Krishna's names keeps the mind focused on the divine, reducing negative thoughts, fosters a sense of inner peace, brings clarity, helps overcome challenges, and strengthens our bonding with Krishna. This relationship is based on love, trust, and affection, where Krishna is not a distant deity but a loving, responsive presence in the life of the devotee.

But how do we cultivate such profound love for Krishna? One effective method is to learn from the stories of devoted souls who have achieved it. So, here are a couple of inspiring tales for you!

The Hunter Who Chanted

"All the animals have fled because of you! O sadhu, why did you come this way?" The hunter asked Sage Narada Muni in frustration. He appeared quite fierce, with a blackish body and reddish eyes, holding a bow and arrows.

Narada replied, "I have a doubt. I saw a deer, a boar, and a rabbit lying half-dead as I was coming here. They were howling in pain. Did you shoot them with arrows?"

The hunter replied, "Yes!"

Sage Narada asked, "Why did you just injure the animals and make them suffer? Why did you not kill them completely and ease their pain?"

The hunter replied, "My name is Mrigari, the enemy of animals! My father taught me to kill them this way. When I see half-dead animals cry out in pain, I feel great joy."

"I have one thing to beg of you," requested Narada.

Mrigari said, "I can give you a deerskin or even a tiger skin – if that is what you want. I do not have anything more to give."

Narada said, "I do not want any skins. I beg you to kill animals only when you need to, and that too completely. Do not leave them half-dead."

Mrigari said, "Why? What's wrong with doing that?"

Narada explained, "By leaving the animals half-dead and intentionally giving them unnecessary pain, you will incur great sin. Those animals whom you killed will kill you one after the other in your future lives."

Ignorant Mrigari didn't know this. Narada Muni's divine demeanour, concern, and wise words made him think. He became somewhat afraid and asked, "How can I be freed from the sin? Please tell me."

"First, break your bow. Then I shall tell you what is to be done," said Narada.

"If I break my bow, how shall I maintain myself?" asked the hunter, perplexed.

"Do not worry. I shall supply all the food you need every day," assured Narada.

Thus reassured, Mrigari broke his bow and fell at Narada's feet. Narada raised him and advised him, "Go home and distribute all your wealth to the brahmanas. Leave your home with your wife and construct a small cottage on the bank of the river. Grow a Tulasi plant in front of your home. Water the Tulasi daily and circumambulate it while chanting the mantra – *'Hare Krishna Hare Krishna, Krishna Krishna Hare Hare, Hare Rama Hare Rama, Rama Rama Hare Hare.'* Every day, I shall send sufficient food for you both."

Then, powerful Narada Muni healed the wounded deer, boar, and rabbit. The three animals got up and swiftly fled from there. Mrigari was struck with wonder. He bowed down to the sage and returned home. He followed the instructions of Narada Muni, his guru.

The news of Mrigari's transformation into a devotee spread across the village. Because he stopped hunting animals and started chanting the Lord's holy names constantly, all the villagers brought alms for him. In one day, he received enough food for ten or twenty people, but he and his wife would accept only as much as they could eat.

One day, Narada Muni came to Mrigari's home, along with his friend Parvata Muni. Mrigari saw them from a distance and eagerly ran towards his guru. But he could not bow down immediately because he saw some ants around his feet. He cleared them away with a cloth and then fell flat at their feet.

Narada Muni became happy and said, "This behaviour is not at all astonishing. A man in bhakti is automatically non-violent."

Mrigari then took Narada Muni and Parvata Muni into his house and offered them seats. He washed their feet with great devotion. When Mrigari chanted the holy names of God before his guru, tears of love fell from his eyes. He started dancing, waving his garments up and down. Seeing his love, Parvata Muni told Narada, "By your mercy, a cruel hunter has become attached to Lord Krishna."

Bhakti is born in the association of sincere devotees.

Pre-birth Bhakti Lessons

Hiranyakashipu, the king of demons, reigned with unparalleled cruelty and power. Even the gods in heaven trembled upon hearing his name. His brother Hiranyaksha's demise at the hands of Lord Varaha, an incarnation of Lord Vishnu, fuelled Hiranyakashipu's thirst for revenge. Determined to attain immortality and control over the gods, he embarked on rigorous austerities in the forest to appease Lord Brahma and secure divine boons.

During Hiranyakashipu's absence, the heavenly devatas seized the opportunity to attack his city. Witnessing the slaughter of their city, other demons fled to safeguard their lives, leaving Hiranyakashipu's palace vulnerable to plunder. Amidst the chaos, the queen, Kayadhu, pregnant with Hiranyakashipu's child, was captured by Indra, king of the gods. As she wept in distress, similar to a helpless bird caught by a predator, Narada Muni, the celestial sage, intervened.

Halting Indra's actions, Narada exclaimed, "This woman is innocent. She is the faithful wife of another man. It is unjust to subject her to such ruthless treatment. Release her immediately."

Indra, disclosing his intentions, responded, "She carries the seed of another demon, a potential threat to us. We shall retain her until her child is born, then deal with the offspring."

However, Sage Narada, blessed with divine insight, proclaimed, "The child within her is blameless. In fact, he shall emerge as a great devotee of Lord Vishnu." Convinced by Narada's words, the gods respectfully left Kayadhu and offered respects to the devotee living within her.

Then, Narada took Kayadhu to his hermitage and ensured her safety. Narada advised her to wait there till her husband's return. Kayadhu agreed to stay there and served Narada devotedly. While living in the ashram, compassionate Narada imparted to her the path of devotion to Lord Vishnu. Although Kayadhu's thoughts often wandered to her husband, her unborn child, Prahlada, absorbed Narada's teachings with profound attentiveness. In spite of being within the womb he eagerly heard Narada's teachings. Thus, even before his birth, Prahlada developed an unwavering devotion to Lord Vishnu.

Soon upon his birth, Prahlada constantly invoked the Lord's name and immersed himself in devotional meditation. Despite his father's hate towards Vishnu, Prahlada continued worshipping the Lord. He even imparted these devotional teachings to his friends. Thus, he created a wonderful atmosphere for himself and others.

By a devotee's blessings, one can become a devotee and constantly praise the Lord.

From the remarkable transformation of stonehearted individuals like Mrigari into staunch worshipers, to the nurturing of devotion within unborn children like Prahlada, the potency of bhakti is truly wondrous. It is through the constant repetition of the Lord's divine names that our hearts become suffused with love for Him. And as this love blossoms within us, thoughts of the Lord naturally occupy our minds, prompting us to speak of Him incessantly. Thus, the practice of continuous chanting serves as a means to cultivate and express our profound affection for the Divine.

Reflect to Realize

When Krishna says "*satatam kirtayanto mam*," it means that we should continuously chant His name. Spiritual seekers keep a minimum quota of chanting the Lord's names daily. Further, whether walking, working, or travelling, we can softly repeat the Lord's names. This chanting is a means to develop love for God. It doesn't distract us from our daily tasks, but actually helps us refocus. Acting as a mantra, it aids in controlling the mind and brings peace and love into the heart. To truly understand its benefits, try it out for yourself. As they say, the proof of the pudding is in the eating.

39

Firm Faith

Faith is the beginning and the driving force in the spiritual path.

Who do you think is the greatest yogi? Is it the one who can rise in the air sitting cross-legged with closed eyes? Or is it the one who can survive on little or no food and drink for years? These feats may seem impressive, but as Lord Krishna reveals in this verse, the greatest yogi is not defined by such extraordinary material abilities.

yoginām api sarveṣāṁ
mad-gatenāntar-ātmanā
śraddhāvān bhajate yo māṁ
sa me yukta-tamo mataḥ

"Of all yogis, the one who faithfully thinks of Me and constantly serves Me is the best." (6.47)

The essence of yoga is connection with the divine, and this connection is most perfectly achieved through bhakti, or loving devotion. A bhakti-yogi dedicates one's entire being to Krishna, constantly meditating on His glories and engaging in acts of worship and service. Such an inner state of sincere devotion is greater than external accomplishments.

The greatness of bhakti-yogis lies in their unwavering focus on Lord Krishna. Whether they are chanting His holy names, reading scriptures, performing worship, or offering selfless service, their hearts remain centred on the Lord. This continuous remembrance and devotion create a deep, personal connection with Krishna that transcends the material realm.

Bhakti-yoga is most accessible to everyone, regardless of one's social, financial or physical status or capabilities. It is not about what one can do with the body, but how one can cultivate the heart's devotion. This form of yoga emphasizes the importance of sincere love, humility, and a genuine desire to serve the Lord. It is through these qualities that a devotee attains the highest state of yoga.

Moreover, this verse highlights the inclusive nature of bhakti-yoga. Unlike other paths that may require rigorous physical discipline or strict ascetic practices, bhakti-yoga welcomes all who are willing to devote themselves to Krishna with a pure heart. It is a path of grace, where the Lord reciprocates the love and devotion of His followers, guiding them towards spiritual fulfilment.

The path of bhakti-yoga also brings immense joy and satisfaction to the practitioner. As they deepen their relationship with Krishna, they experience profound contentment. The challenges and tribulations of the world become easier to bear, as the *bhakti-yogi* finds strength and solace in their devotion.

The greatest yogi is one who transcends the superficial aspects of yoga and focuses on cultivating a loving relationship with the divine. By constantly thinking of the Lord and faithfully serving Him, a bhakti-yogi achieves the highest state of spiritual realization and union with the Supreme. So, let's find out more about such great yogis by reading their exciting stories.

Sudarshan Chases Durvasa

King Ambarish was a great emperor and a devout follower of Lord Vishnu. Once, he observed the Ekadashi and worshipped the Lord. As he was about to complete his vow and break his fast, the sage Durvasa Muni appeared unannounced. King Ambarish welcomed the sage and requested him to join him for a meal. Durvasa agreed but went to the Yamuna to perform his rituals before eating.

In the meantime, the appropriate time to break the Ekadashi fast was passing. Ambarish consulted the brahmanas and decided to break his fast by just drinking water, which could be accepted as both eating and not eating. However, Durvasa, using his mystic powers, understood that Ambarish had drunk water. Durvasa, a proud brahmana and mystic, felt offended. He plucked a bunch of his hair and created a fiery demon to punish Ambarish.

The blazing demon rushed towards Ambarish to kill him, but the king stood calmly with folded hands, meditating on Lord Vishnu. Suddenly, Lord Vishnu's Sudarshan Chakra appeared and incinerated the demon instantly. Then, the Sudarshan Chakra started chasing Durvasa.

Durvasa, now terrified, ran away with the Sudarshan Chakra behind him in relentless pursuit. He sought refuge in Brahmaloka from Lord Brahma, but Brahma said, "I cannot protect you." He then went to Kailasha to beg Lord Shiva for protection, but Shiva too said, "I cannot save you from Lord Vishnu's Sudarshan Chakra."

Finally, Durvasa went to Vaikuntha and fell at the feet of Lord Vishnu, begging for forgiveness and protection. Lord Vishnu replied, "O sage, I cannot protect you. I am bound by My love for My devotees. My devotees are always within My heart, and I am always in their hearts. You can be saved only by pleasing Ambarish."

Humbled and desperate, Durvasa approached King Ambarish and fell at his feet. Ambarish, embarrassed to see the great sage at his feet, prayed to the Sudarshan Chakra to spare Durvasa. The Sudarshan Chakra, honouring Ambarish's request, relented.

Durvasa had been fleeing for an entire year, and finally, relieved of the danger, he praised Ambarish's unwavering devotion and remarkable tolerance. Ambarish, who had also abstained from eating for the whole year, humbly invited Durvasa to join him for a meal. With gratitude, Durvasa accepted, and together they sat down to share their food.

Offending a devotee wounds the heart of God more than anything else.

The Cure to Krishna's Headache

"My head is severely aching. I am in great pain!" said Krishna. All his queens and family members in the palace of Dwarka were worried. In fact, the entire city of Dwarka was shocked by the news of Krishna's headache.

Krishna was lying on his cosy couch without movement. Many doctors came and went, but no one could cure his headache with any of their medicines. Then Krishna himself suggested the remedy, "If the dust from the feet of my devotees is placed on my head, I will be relieved from this headache."

This astonished everyone. How could they put the dust from their feet on the head of God? But at the same time, how could devotees see their beloved Lord in pain? They were in deep anxiety and confusion, unable to figure out what to do.

At that moment, the great sage Narada Muni arrived, playing his veena. His presence filled everyone with a sense of hope. They quickly informed Narada Muni about Lord Krishna's severe headache and the suggested cure. Narada, surprised, replied, "How is this possible? This is something I have never heard of!"

Someone even asked Narada Muni, "O sage, you are a great devotee of Krishna. Can you please give the dust from your feet?" Narada replied, "Oh, how can I do that? Placing the dust of my feet on my Lord's head is such a great sin. If I do so, I will surely go to hell!" Everyone else feared the same.

Narada Muni asked Krishna's queens respectfully, "You all are Lord Krishna's dear wives. You are certainly great devotees. Can you please give the dust from your feet to cure His headache."

The queens replied, "Impossible. We can't do that. If our dust is placed on the head of the Lord, we will go to hell." All the queens of Krishna backed off in quick succession.

Narada even approached Lord Brahma in Brahmaloka, Lord Shiva in Kailasha, and Indra in Swarga. No one agreed to give their dust to be put on Lord Krishna's head. Some people even dismissed the request saying, "How can the Lord have any pain?"

Finally, Narada Muni entered the village of Vrindavan, where Krishna had spent his childhood. Narada saw the gopis, the cowherd girls. Among them was the golden-complexioned goddess, Srimati Radharani, the foremost of the gopis. Seeing the sage, the gopis bowed low in respect.

Narada informed them urgently, "Your dear Lord Krishna is suffering from a severe headache."

Hearing this, the gopis' faces became pale. They were almost about to faint. Gaining some composure, they anxiously asked, "There must be some cure?"

Narada replied, "Yes, the cure is suggested by Krishna himself. Only by placing the dust from the feet of a devotee of Krishna on his forehead will he be relieved of the pain."

The gopis were relieved of all anxiety. There was a joyful smile on their lotus-like faces. They replied excitedly, "Oh! Is that all? Please take the dust from our feet immediately!"

They bent to the ground, picked up a few handfuls of dust scattered around their delicate feet, placed the dust in a pot, and gave it to Narada Muni. "Please take this, and cure the headache of our beloved Krishna."

Narada received the pot with relief but looked doubtful. He said to the gopis, "Do you know the result of keeping the dust from your feet on the Lord's head? You will go to hell."

The gopis were confused, "You said Krishna will be relieved from a headache with this dust. Right? Why are you hesitating now? Please go fast. Our Lord is suffering."

Narada was surprised at the devotion and determination of the gopis. He asked them, "Aren't you afraid of going to hell?"

The gopis said, "That doesn't matter. We can stay forever in hell if this dust can relieve Krishna's headache even for a moment."

Narada's heart was touched by the love of the gopis. He happily took the pot to Krishna and placed the dust from the gopis' feet on his forehead. Krishna was instantly cured.

Of course, the gopis never went to hell. In fact, Krishna's headache wasn't real. He was just pretending to suffer from a headache to reveal the extent of the gopis' love for Him.

A true devotee cares for the Lord's happiness more than their own troubles.

Through the episodes of King Ambarish and the gopis, the Lord makes it clear that those who think of Him with love are very dear to Him. They are the best yogis, surpassing even those who perform extraordinary feats of mysticism. King Ambarish's steadfast devotion and the gopis' unwavering love demonstrate that the essence of yoga lies in pure devotion and selfless love for the Supreme.

Reflect to Realize

In moments when we are unable to engage in physical acts of devotion, the power of *smaranam*, or remembering the Lord, becomes invaluable. In this verse, Krishna inspires us to think of Him within our minds. We can offer a flower shower, perform aarati, cook for the Lord, or sing for Him—all within the sanctuary of our hearts. Isn't it magnificent?

40

Complete Surrender

Loving bond with God sets us free from all sins, obligations, longings and the world itself.

We all bear distinct responsibilities in life, in accordance to our diverse identities as students, teachers, professionals, and so on. Yet, amidst our varied identities, there exists one singular identity shared by all—a child of God. That is our eternal spiritual identity, and the associated activity with that identity is loving service to the Lord.

In this profound verse of the Bhagavad Gita, Lord Krishna, the Supreme Father of all living beings, implores us:

sarva-dharmān parityajya
mām ekaṁ śaraṇaṁ vraja
ahaṁ tvāṁ sarva-pāpebhyo
mokṣayiṣyāmi mā śucaḥ

"Abandon all varieties of duties and just surrender unto Me. I shall deliver you from all sinful reactions. Do not fear." (18.66)

This verse encapsulates the essence of Lord Krishna's teachings, bhakti. Bhakti integrates all dharmas, and all dharmas culminate in bhakti. Here, Lord Krishna's focus is not on *rejecting* dharma, but *raising* dharma to its ultimate summit of loving God. Such a declaration is a powerful reminder of the unconditional love and protection that Krishna offers to all who turn to Him with sincerity and devotion.

The verse encourages us to prioritize our spiritual connection with God above everything else. While our worldly roles and responsibilities are important, they should never overshadow our primary duty to cultivate a relationship with the Lord. By seeking refuge in Krishna, we align ourselves with His divine will and open our hearts to His grace.

This message resonates deeply with devotees, offering reassurance and hope. It highlights how accessible the Lord is—no matter our past actions, we are always welcome in Krishna's embrace. This inclusive call to seek refuge in the Lord has historically inspired not just saints and sages but also those who strayed from righteousness to find solace in His loving protection.

Krishna's compassionate assurance, "Do not fear," is a call to embrace faith over doubt and love over fear. It encourages us to trust in His divine plan and to let go of anxieties that hinder our spiritual progress. By surrendering to Krishna, we allow ourselves to be enveloped by His infinite love and mercy, which empowers us to face life's challenges with courage and resilience.

What unfolds next are two stories of devotees who surrendered to the Lord and achieved great bliss.

Three Steps of Land

Bali, a powerful king among the demons, became the ruler of all three worlds after defeating the devas, and seizing control of the heavens. While the devas were left homeless, Bali presided over the world with unchallenged authority.

Once, King Bali conducted a sacrifice on the northern bank of the Narmada, guided by his guru, Shukracharya, and attended by numerous brahmana priests. In the ceremony, King Bali encountered a radiant brahmana boy named Vamana, an incarnation of Lord Vishnu. Dressed in deerskin and a simple straw belt, Vamana held a begging bowl, a water pot, an umbrella, and beads. His divine presence captivated everyone.

Moved by affection, Bali welcomed the charming brahmana and said, "Dear brahmana, what is the reason for your arrival here? I shall offer you anything you desire."

In response, Lord Vamana praised Bali's generosity and requested only three paces of land, measured by his own steps. Puzzled by the boy's modesty, Bali felt that the boy was unintelligent to ask so little from such a great king. He told the boy to ask for more.

However, Lord Vamana explained, "O King, satisfaction lies not in having vast possessions but in accepting destiny and honest endeavour. Even the entire world cannot satisfy one who is not content with whatever he has obtained by one's genuine efforts and destiny."

King Bali smiled and told Vamana, "All right, take whatever you like." Then, Bali took up his water pot in order to make an oath.

Just then Bali's guru Shukracharya warned him, "Dear King, this brahmana boy is actually Lord Vishnu. He is here to take away your kingdom in the guise of charity and give it to the devas. Do not fall for this trick. Take back your promise."

But Bali remained resolute in his commitment to truth and virtue, being the grandson of the great devotee Prahlada. Rejecting the advice to retract his promise, Bali offered his charity to Vamana. This led to a divine spectacle. Vamana expanded Himself so much that His first step covered the entire earth and His second step covered the entire heavenly regions leaving no place for the third step. At that time, lord Brahma washed Vamana's upraised foot, and that sacred water formed the holy Ganga, purifying everything it touched.

Lord Vamana then reduced to His size to that of a normal boy. The devas and the sages worshipped him. The demons tried to attack Him, but Bali stopped them.

Then Lord Vamana accused Bali, "O King, being proud of your wealth, you had promised me three steps of land, but I occupied the entire universe with just two steps. Where shall I keep my third step? You couldn't fulfil your promise, so you should go to hell."

Even though the Lord apparently tricked Bali and intentionally made him break his promise, Bali didn't get offended. Instead, he said, "O Lord, please place your third footstep on my head. I completely surrender unto You." Thus, Bali offered himself to the Lord, after having offered all his property. He considered it to be his great fortune.

This episode displayed Bali's truthfulness, dedication, devotion and surrender to the Lord. Generally, men become famous when they gain wealth, but Bali became famous by losing his wealth!

Highly pleased with him, Lord Vamana said, "Dear Bali, you will become the king of heaven (Indra) in the next *manvantara*. Until then you may live on the Sutala planet, which is more prosperous than heaven. I shall personally guard your palace as a doorkeeper." Bali was overwhelmed by the Lord's unlimited kindness. He thanked him profusely and went to Sutala.

The Lord offers Himself to those devotees who offer themselves to Him.

Vibhishana Takes Shelter of Lord Rama

Ravana, the king of demons, committed the grievous act of abducting Mother Sita, the beloved consort of Lord Rama, and held her captive in his luxurious kingdom of Lanka. Unlike the prideful Ravana, his younger brother Vibhishana was known for his saintliness and virtue.

Vibhishana repeatedly advised Ravana to submit Mother Sita back to Lord Rama. But the ego-driven king obstinately ignored his brother's wise words and even rebuked him. Vibhishana, deeply wounded by his brother's insults, chose to leave his side and even his kingdom. Crossing the ocean, he sought the shelter of Lord Rama, the epitome of righteousness.

As Vibhishana approached the assembly of Lord Rama, the Vanaras became cautious. Sugriva, the king of the Vanaras, thought that Vibhishana was after all a part of the enemy's camp. He wasn't inclined to welcome Vibhishana. But Hanuman, known for his wisdom, saw no deceit or malice in Vibhishana's character. Sugriva expressed his doubts and concerns to Lord Rama. He feared that Vibhishan might cheat them. Despite scepticism from other Vanara leaders, Hanuman advocated for Vibhishana's acceptance and affirmed his sincerity.

Lord Rama, weighing the opinions carefully, recognized Vibhishana's genuine heart. Rama then proclaimed, "Even an enemy who seeks My refuge with folded hands will be protected by Me by all means. Moreover, it is my solemn vow that if anyone surrenders himself to Me, even once, saying, 'O Lord, I am Yours,' I award that person freedom from all fear. Not just Vibhishana, even if Ravana were to come here to surrender unto me, I would forgive him and protect him." Sugriva was moved by the Lord's compassion, and accepted Vibhishana's presence in the camp.

The Lord never refuses to accept a person who sincerely seeks His shelter.

The stories of King Bali and Vibhishana serve as poignant reminders that nature of birth does not bar one from seeking divine protection. Despite their demoniac lineage, both Bali and Vibhishana exhibited unwavering faith and surrendered themselves to the Supreme Lord. Their stories illustrate the timeless promise of Lord Krishna, who pledges complete safeguarding to all who earnestly seek His refuge.

Reflect to Realize

"Surrendering to the Lord"—Lord Krishna's conclusive teaching of the Gita—goes beyond just physical acts; it means giving our entire being—body, mind, and words—to God. It involves shifting our focus from self-gratification to pleasing God, aligning our thoughts and actions with His will. This state of surrender is like the trust and dependence a child has on a loving parent. It means recognizing our limitations, trusting in the Lord's guidance, and knowing that our ultimate welfare is in His hands. Surrendering to the Lord is a transformative journey that frees us from ego and worldly anxieties. It brings peace, joy, and fulfilment as we find comfort in the loving embrace of the Divine.

Section V: Sadguna–Virtues

How does determination help us attain our goals? By gentle speech can we make good friends? What is the benefit of being selfless, tolerant and forgiving? How to be kind and non-violent towards others? What does it mean to be humble? Can we be equal in joy and sorrow, praise and criticism, honour and dishonour? In the Bhagavad Gita, Lord Krishna kindly describes many virtues to be developed by humankind for a happy and meaningful life. This final section of the book presents simple yet authentic explanations of such great virtues, intertwined with hair-raising tales for each topic. Along with practising spiritual life by meditating on the Lord, chanting His names, worshiping Him and hearing His teachings, one should also cultivate certain virtues.

41

Determination

If you are not determined for anything,
you are distracted by everything!

What facilitates the achievement of your goals with ease, and shapes the journey of your life? It's the attribute of unwavering determination.

Determination is like the steady flame that fuels our actions, propelling us towards our goals. To the degree we love our goals, to that extent we become committed to attain them. Determination is that unwavering commitment to persevere even in the face of challenges. Just as a mighty river carves its path through rugged terrain, determination carves a path towards our goals, overcoming obstacles with resilience.

In the tapestry of life, determination weaves the threads of perseverance and one-pointed focus. It empowers us to stay grounded in our purpose, leading us towards growth and accomplishment, and ultimately, to inner fulfilment, as Lord Krishna described in the following verse.

vyavasāyātmikā buddhir
ekeha kuru-nandana
bahu-śākhā hy anantāś ca
buddhayo 'vyavasāyinām

"Those who are determined remain fully focused on their objectives with a one-pointed vision. Conversely, those who lack determination become scattered in their pursuits due to distracted mindsets." (2.41)

Determined individuals navigate obstacles, accepting what aids their goals and discarding what doesn't. This firm resolve attracts support from higher powers that assist them to attain their goals more easily.

Here are the tales of two remarkable individuals who demonstrated unwavering determination in their pursuits, and ultimately attained success.

The Sparrow's Victory

Once upon a time, a small sparrow made her home on the shore of a majestic ocean. She diligently gathered food from the nearby forest, living a simple yet contented life. One day, she joyously laid her tiny eggs upon the soft sand, eagerly awaiting the arrival of her offspring. Each dawn, she watched with delight as the ocean's waves danced and played, their frothy crests painting intricate designs upon the water's surface.

But one fateful day, tragedy struck. A powerful wave swept in from the ocean, carrying the sparrow's precious eggs away into its depths. Heartbroken and distraught, the little sparrow cried out to the mighty ocean, pleading for the return of her cherished eggs. Yet, the vast expanse of water remained unmoved by her pleas, indifferent to her sorrow.

Determined not to succumb to despair, the courageous sparrow resolved to take matters into her own hands. With unwavering determination burning in her heart, she began a Herculean task: to dry up the ocean itself and reclaim her beloved eggs. Undeterred by the enormity of her goal, she tirelessly scooped up water with her tiny beak, spitting out the droplets at a distant place.

Though some may have scoffed at her seemingly futile endeavour, the sparrow remained focused, driven by a fierce determination that knew no bounds. Her unwavering commitment and sheer tenacity soon caught the attention of Garuda, the mighty bird carrier of Lord Vishnu.

Upon hearing of his little sister's plight, powerful Garuda descended with his massive wings casting a shadow over the shoreline. With a voice that thundered, he commanded the ocean to return the sparrow's eggs, lest he unleash his formidable power upon its waters.

Faced with the wrath of Garuda, the ocean relented, its waves gently carrying the sparrow's precious eggs back to the safety of the shore. Overwhelmed with gratitude, the little sparrow embraced her eggs, tears of joy streaming down her feathers.

At that moment, the sparrow learned a powerful lesson: that true determination, coupled with divine intervention, could overcome even the most insurmountable obstacles. And as she watched the sun set over the horizon, casting a golden glow upon the tranquil ocean, she knew that her unwavering spirit had triumphed against all odds.

Our determination attracts superior assistance.

Bhagiratha Invites River Ganga on Earth

Once, in the annals of ancient history, the illustrious Emperor Sagara embarked upon the grandeur of a horse sacrifice, his kingdom adorned with opulence and resplendence. Yet envy, a lurking spectre, found harbor in the heart of the king of the gods, who stealthily absconded with Sagara's cherished sacrificial steed. This nefarious act ignited a chain of events that would test the mettle of Sagara's lineage.

With resolve as firm as the mountains and hearts ablaze with determination, Sagara's sixty thousand sons embarked on a quest to retrieve the stolen horse. Guided by the whispering winds and the silent beckoning of destiny, their journey led them to the tranquil abode of the sage Kapila, nestled upon the sacred shores of Gangasagar.

In the midst of a tumultuous storm of accusation and suspicion, the sons of Sagara confronted the sage, their agitation contrasting sharply with his calm composure. Kapila Muni, a living embodiment of divine virtue, met their accusatory gaze with unwavering serenity. Despite their offensive demeanour, the sanctity of his honour remained unshaken. In response to their hostility, the fiery wrath of Kapila Muni reduced the impetuous sons of Sagara to ashes, their anger transformed into nothingness.

Upon learning of the tragic fate of his sons, Sagara turned to his grandson, Amsuman, charging him with the sacred duty of reclaiming the lost horse and reviving his sixty thousand fallen kin. Amsuman traversed the vast expanse of the earth until he stumbled upon the somber remnants of his uncles, their ashes a poignant testament to their ill-fated endeavour.

Sage Kapila told Amsuman, "Embark on a quest to secure the sacred Ganga, whose sanctifying waters alone possess the power to liberate Sagara's sons. Thus, with reverence in his heart and purpose in his stride, Amsuman sought the sacred river's descent to the earth.

In a lineage marked by resilience, it was Bhagiratha, the son of Dilipa, who emerged as the torch-bearer of hope. Fuelled by an unyielding resolve, Bhagiratha undertook arduous penance, beseeching the celestial realms for the descent of the sacred Ganga.

Moved by Bhagirath's unwavering devotion, Ganga-devi, the personification of the sacred river, heeded his call. Yet, her descent posed a formidable challenge, her force threatening to ravage the earth. Undeterred, Bhagiratha sought the benevolence of Lord Shiva, entreating him to cradle the mighty river's torrential flow within his matted locks.

Thus, with the cosmic dance of fate unfolding, Bhagiratha led the Ganga on her descent to earth, her purifying waters weaving a tapestry of redemption across the land. From the hallowed shores of Gangasagar to the sacred precincts of Lord Kapila's hermitage, Ganga's divine waters breathed life into the ashes of Sagara's sixty thousand sons, absolving them of their sins and guiding their souls to liberation.

In the annals of time, the saga of Sagara's lineage stands as a testament to the resilience of the human spirit and the boundless grace of the divine, where determination and devotion intertwine to shape the destiny of gods and mortals alike.

Determined effort coupled with support from great souls guarantees success.

Achieving significant goals requires unwavering determination. The sparrow's steadfast focus enabled her to gain the support of the mighty Garuda. Similarly, Bhagiratha's relentless dedication brought the Ganga to earth, purifying the ashes of his ancestors. Determined individuals seize favourable opportunities and overcome distractions, remaining steadfast even in the face of adversity. In contrast, those without determination give up and become discouraged when confronted with challenges. By nurturing determination, we unlock our highest potential and pave the way to success.

Reflect to Realize

Those who are steadfast in their resolve can navigate life's complexities with clarity. Yet, depending on the complexity of a situation, we require support from others. By acknowledging our limitations and seeking assistance when needed, we equip ourselves with the necessary strength to confront challenges effectively. When our resolve is firm, we garner support from others and higher powers. This blend of personal determination and able guidance paves the way for success, propelling us to new heights. Determination means to terminate our temptations. Guidance means to find out how to do so.

42

Spiritual Vision

True wisdom lies in acknowledging the spiritual equality amongst all living beings despite their material differences.

Striving for knowledge and wisdom is indeed a noble pursuit. But what does it truly mean to be wise?

In the timeless teachings of the Bhagavad Gita, Lord Krishna elucidates the profound attributes of wisdom. True wisdom transcends mere accumulation of knowledge and intellectual analysis. It encompasses a profound understanding of the self, the world, and the interconnectedness of all existence. An essential aspect of wisdom is the understanding that every living being, irrespective of their gender, nationality, species, and ethnicity, is a child of God.

Thus, on a spiritual plane all living beings are interconnected with God in centre. One who realizes this genuinely respects everyone.

Lord Krishna elucidates in the following verse:

vidyā-vinaya-sampanne
brāhmaṇe gavi hastini

śuni caiva śva-pāke ca
paṇḍitāḥ sama-darśinaḥ

"A wise person is humble, and regards a brahmana, a cow, an elephant, a dog, and even a dog-eater with equal vision!" (5.18)

Of course, the five types of beings that Lord Krishna mentioned in the above verse are not literally equal in all respects. But spiritually they all are equal, being the children of God. True wisdom is in acknowledging that spiritual equality among all living beings regardless of their external differences or societal hierarchies.

Our wisdom manifests in our compassion and empathy towards all living beings, recognizing the inherent dignity and worth present in every creature. This profound respect for life extends beyond superficial appearances, penetrating to the core of each being's spiritual essence. By acknowledging the inherent spiritual nature of all beings, a wise person cultivates a deep sense of interconnectedness with all of creation. Let's delve into a couple of narratives to dig deeper into this concept.

Rantideva's Food Distribution

In ancient India, there once reigned a noble king named Rantideva, renowned for his boundless kindness and philanthropy. His acts of charity were so profound that his fame extended not only across every corner of the earth but also into the heavens.

Rantideva harboured no greed for amassing wealth; he found contentment in whatever provisions the Lord bestowed upon him. Whenever guests graced his home, he wholeheartedly bestowed upon them all that he possessed, without a moment's hesitation.

Once, after fasting for forty-eight days, Rantideva was about to break his fast with a meagre offering of food made with milk and ghee. Yet, before he could partake of the food, a brahmana guest arrived. Recognizing the divine within every living being, Rantideva warmly welcomed the guest and shared his humble meal. Pleased by Rantideva's generosity, the brahmana honoured the food and departed.

Subsequently, Rantideva divided the remaining food among his family. Then, just as he was about to partake of his portion, a weak beggar arrived. Seeing him as another child of God, Rantideva willingly shared yet another portion of his meal. In Rantideva's eyes, whether brahmana or beggar, rich or poor, all were equally beloved by the divine. Then, when a guest accompanied by dogs begged him for food, Rantideva unhesitatingly offered the remainder of his food to both the guest and his dogs, displaying remarkable patience and tolerance.

Left with only a small quantity of drinking water, sufficient for only one person, Rantideva was approached by a weak and famished man on the brink of collapse. Moved by compassion, Rantideva prayed to the Lord, "I cannot bear to witness their suffering. Please relieve their distress. I willingly endure hunger, thirst, and fatigue on their behalf." Despite his own dire condition after fasting for forty-eight days, Rantideva selflessly offered his water to the desperate man, satisfying his thirst.

Unknown to Rantideva, all the people who had approached him for sustenance were celestial beings (devatas), including Lord Brahma and Lord Shiva, testing his virtue. By exhibiting such unwavering generosity and compassion, Rantideva passed their test with flying colours. In recognition of his exemplary character, Brahma and Shiva revealed their divine forms, bestowing blessings upon the benevolent king.

Through the noble example of Rantideva, we learn the profound lesson that all living beings are children of God and thus deserve equal love and respect.

Everyone is a child a God, despite their external differences.

Lord Shiva in Disguise

Once in Varanasi, the great saint Shankaracharya emerged from the sacred waters of the Ganga after performing his rituals. On his way back, he encountered a man of the lowest caste, a chandala, accompanied by four unclean dogs.

With the natural purity of a brahmana, Shankaracharya instinctively urged the man to move aside. However, the chandala stood his ground and posed a profound question to the revered sage: "Why do you ask me to move away, O great Brahmin? Is there truly any difference between you and me? Regardless of our external distinctions, are we not both souls, spiritual beings at our core?"

Shankaracharya was taken aback by the chandala's insight and wisdom. Recognizing the depth of the man's understanding of the soul's true nature, Acharya Shankara realized his mistake in disrespecting him. With humility and reverence, Shankara bowed before the chandala, acknowledging him as his guru.

In that sacred moment, the chandala vanished, revealing in his place none other than Lord Shiva himself. The divine presence of the Lord bestowed his blessings upon Shankaracharya, illuminating the profound truth that the soul transcends all material designations and distinctions.

Inside everyone's body is the spirit soul, the real person.

The stories of Rantideva and Shankara teach us to treat everyone with respect. We should give up qualities like pride, envy and hatred and inculcate the culture of honouring others focusing on their spiritual identities. Considering everyone to be God's child, we should see them equally on a spiritual plane.

Reflect to Realize

The fruit of knowledge (vidya) is humility (*vinaya*). One who is equipped with knowledge and humility sees everyone with an equal vision and genuine respect. This vision helps one relinquish pride and envy, and hatred towards others.

43

Compassion

Compassion is a gift we can offer freely to others, enriching our lives and the world around us with boundless warmth.

More than one's talents, skills, accomplishments and assets, it's the noble qualities that make a person glorious. Therefore, apart from deep philosophy, Lord Krishna, in the Gita, repeatedly emphasizes on developing virtues. In the following verse, He enumerates a few virtues to be developed for a fulfilling life.

adveṣṭā sarva-bhūtānāṁ
maitraḥ karuṇa eva ca
nirmamo nirahaṅkāraḥ
sama-duḥkha-sukhaḥ kṣamī

"Noble individuals harbour no envy towards others; they are friendly and compassionate towards all living beings. They do not perceive themselves as proprietors of this world. Free from

false ego, they remain equipoised towards happiness and distress." (12.13)

Of all the above great virtues, *compassion* has a unique role to play in human lives. Noble people embody compassion not solely within the confines of their immediate social circles but extend their compassion and care towards all living beings including animals, birds, and even the silent sentinels of nature—the trees.

Compassion enlivens both givers and receivers.

- For givers, acts of compassion offer a sense of fulfilment, elevate their sense of empathy, nurture their capacity for understanding and ultimately foster a deeper connection to the world around.
- For receivers, kindness serves as a beacon of hope, offering solace in times of distress and restoring faith in humanity and divinity.

There are three dimensions of compassion

1. *Physical:* Helping people with their bodily needs like food and health care.
2. *Emotional:* Genuinely encouraging and motivating people, and offering them the much-needed emotional support during their tough times.
3. *Spiritual:* Making people aware of their spiritual identities and their eternal connection with God, and assisting them in their spiritual progress.

A compassionate soul sometimes goes to any extent to help others. Here, we delve into the accounts of two compassionate kings who rescued a cow and a dove. Undoubtedly, it's difficult to match their level of compassion. However, we can still find inspiration in their deeds, and take our baby steps to cultivate this virtue over time, by beginning with whatever is practically possible for us.

King Shibi's Promise

Shibi, a renowned king celebrated far and wide for his boundless charity, had made a solemn vow to extend his protection to all who sought refuge under his benevolent rule.

One fateful day, as Shibi presided within the opulent confines of his palace, a scared dove sought shelter, pursued relentlessly by a menacing eagle. With nowhere else to turn, the trembling bird alighted upon the king's lap, pleading for protection from its relentless enemy.

Moved by compassion, Shibi reassured the trembling dove, vowing to shield it from the eagle. Yet, even as he pledged his unwavering protection, the powerful eagle swooped down before him, demanding the return of its prey.

The eagle then asked Shibi, "O King, that dove is my food. I have chased it till now. I am hungry, and was about to eat it. You can't hide my prey. Give it back to me."

Being a righteous king, Shibi felt that the eagle's demand was right. After all, the dove was the eagle's natural food and rightful prey. Though duty forced Shibi to acknowledge the eagle's claim, his commitment to protect the dove remained resolute. Shibi requested the eagle to search for someone else but the dove.

However, unyielding in its pursuit, the eagle refused Shibi's requests. The eagle demanded an equivalent weight of flesh from the king's own body in exchange for sparing the dove. Unmoved by the scary request, Shibi decided to honour his vow, even at the cost of his own flesh.

With knives and scales brought forth, the noble king began the painful ritual, severing portions of his own body to balance the scales against the dove's weight. Yet, with each piece of flesh added to the scale, the mystic dove unexpectedly outweighed the king's offering, defying all earthly logic.

Undeterred by the escalating pain, Shibi continued to offer his own flesh, ultimately relinquishing nearly half his body in his unwavering quest to fulfil his sacred pledge. Even as he lay ready to surrender his very life, the enigmatic dove and eagle vanished, revealing their divine guises as Agni, the fire-god, and Indra, the celestial king.

In a stunning revelation, it became clear that the trial had been orchestrated by the gods themselves, who had assumed mortal forms to test the depths of Shibi's compassion and selflessness. Moved by his unparalleled sacrifice, the heavens resounded with celestial praise, hailing Shibi's boundless generosity and unwavering commitment to the welfare of all beings.

A noble and kind-hearted person never fails to honour one's promise.

King Dilipa Serves a Cow

Once, there lived a king named Dilipa, hailing from the illustrious Raghu dynasty. He was the ancestor of Lord Rama. Once he visited his friend Indra, the king of heaven. On his way back to his kingdom on Earth, a Kamadhenu cow happened to pass by.

According to sacred tradition, reverence towards the holy cow is paramount. However, preoccupied with his haste, King Dilipa failed to extend the customary respect to Kamadhenu. Displeased by his disregard, Kamadhenu pronounced a curse upon the king, predicting that he would remain childless until he dutifully served a cow. Not knowing about the curse cast upon him (for his benefit), Dilipa continued his path.

As time passed without the blessing of progeny, King Dilipa turned to his spiritual mentor for guidance. Through introspection, the sage revealed the king's transgression towards Kamadhenu and prescribed a remedy. Dilipa was entrusted with the care of a cow named Nandini, with the instructions to serve her devoutly to earn the boon of a child.

Following his guru's directive, Dilipa carefully tended to Nandini's needs. Each day, he led her to graze in the lush forests, carefully safeguarding her from any lurking danger. During one such excursion, amidst the enchanting beauty of nature, Dilipa momentarily lost sight of Nandini. Helplessly calling out to her, he stumbled upon a heart-stopping sight: a lion poised to pounce upon his cherished cow.

Without hesitation, Dilipa immediately ran to the place and told the lion, "Please don't kill Nandini." The lion said, "My name is Kumbhodara. I have been given authority by Lord Siva to protect this area. Anyone who enters this area without my permission would be devoured by me."

Dilipa replied, "You may instead kill and eat me in order to satisfy your hunger."

The lion said, "You are a king. You are supposed to enjoy your kingdom. Why should you give up your life just for a cow?"

Dilipa answered, "Protecting Nandini is more important for me than my own life. Ideal kings do not look forward to enjoy kingdom at the cost of the life of an innocent creature."

The lion understood the sincerity of the king and disappeared. Nandini then told Dilipa that the lion was an illusion created by her to test Dilipa's sincerity.

Acknowledging Dilipa's unwavering commitment, Nandini granted him his heart's desire—the blessing of a son. Thus, through his selfless devotion to the noble cause of protecting an innocent life, King Dilipa not only earned the boon of progeny but also exemplified the timeless virtue of compassion and integrity.

True compassion means putting others' troubles before one's comforts.

King Dilipa and King Shibi are revered for their exemplary kindness and selflessness. While such acts of kindness might seem beyond our reach, they serve as powerful sources of inspiration. By reflecting on their activities, we can strive to cultivate similar virtues within our own capacity. We can start with small acts of kindness and gradually expand our capacity for compassion. Ultimately, the love one has for God is mirrored in one's kindness towards all beings, recognizing them as His children. By nurturing our spiritual connection, we can develop a deeper sense of empathy and kindness, contributing to a more compassionate world.

Reflect to Realize

Ultimately, the acts of kindness of great souls reflect their profound love for God, which manifests in their compassion towards all beings as His children. Compassion transcends boundaries of age, race, or species, serving as a universal language that unites humanity. Whether it's a kind word, a helping hand, or a simple gesture, acts of compassion have the power to uplift spirits, heal wounds, and ignite a chain reaction of positivity.

44

Non-violence

The virtue of non-violence extends far beyond the mere absence of physical harm.

The core values that a person upholds in all circumstances despite all odds, reveal his or her true glory. These values are not meant to be mere strategies to get things done but are meant to be intrinsic characteristics of our existence. They make one's life fulfilling and meaningful.

Lord Krishna delineates some beautiful virtues in the following verse from the Gita:

ahiṁsā satyam akrodhas
tyāgaḥ śāntir apaiśunam
dayā bhūteṣv aloluptvaṁ
mārdavaṁ hrīr acāpalam

"Non-violence, truthfulness, freedom from anger, detachment, peace, non-critical nature, mercy, freedom from greed, gentleness, modesty, and determination are some amazing values of a noble individual." (16.2)

The first on the list is non-violence, which holds a sacred place in the moral conscience of humanity. Found within scriptures and echoed by saints throughout time, it stands as an unwavering call to exhibit kindness towards all living beings.

Just as compassion, there are three dimensions of non-violence as well

1. *Physical:* Refraining from causing unnecessary physical harm to others either mildly or severely. However, physically punishing a criminal, depending on the extent of the crime committed, can be an act of compassion, if it's intended to and results in the reformation of the criminal.
2. *Emotional:* Even when we refrain from physical violence towards others, our words, glances and actions can inflict deep wounds upon others' emotions. This form of harm often surpasses the impact of physical violence. Refraining from doing that is emotional non-violence.
3. *Spiritual:* The suffering of people in this material world since time immemorial is primarily due to ignorance of their spiritual connection with God. A fortunate person possesses divine wisdom and is capable of enlightening them. Thus, the greatest act of non-violence lies in educating others with spiritual wisdom. Conversely, not sharing this wisdom, despite having the ability, constitutes another form of violence.

Embracing non-violence nurtures a culture of peace and harmony, fostering both inner tranquility and societal cohesion. Rejecting aggression and hostility, we need to cultivate empathy and a spirit of cooperation. Those who are non-violent are committed to resolving conflicts through dialogue and understanding, rather than resorting to aggression or force.

Let us now delve into a couple of stories that exemplify the principle of non-violence.

The Violent Yajnas

Once, there reigned a great king named Prachinabarhi, deeply immersed in the performance of numerous yajnas, or fire sacrifices. His kingdom was adorned with lush Kusha grass, beautifully cultivated for these sacred rituals. However, these ceremonies involved the sacrifice of countless animals, a practice that went unquestioned until the arrival of the sage Narada.

Moved by compassion for both the animals and the king himself, Narada decided to impart wisdom to Prachinabarhi. Addressing the monarch, Narada questioned the purpose of these yajnas, highlighting the grave karmic consequences of needlessly sacrificing innocent creatures and the futility of seeking lasting happiness through these rituals.

Prachinabarhi, humbled by his lack of understanding, begged to Narada for guidance. In response, the sage conjured a mystic vision, revealing to the king the revengeful spirits of the animals he had killed. The tableau in the sky showed how these animals were waiting for the king to be killed in order to hurt him in the same way he had hurt them.

Narada Muni then narrated a symbolic story of a mythical character called Puranjana: "King Puranjana lived in a city of nine gates. He represents a living being who dwells within a material body with nine holes (mouth, ears, eyes and so on). He would kill innocent animals in the forest by hunting. He was too attached to his wife, children, grandchildren and household comforts and didn't take interest in spiritual life. Eventually he died while thinking of his wife. Yamadutas, the messengers of Yama, the lord of death, dragged him to hell. After undergoing hellish suffering, he was again born as a woman. In this manner, if a person is too absorbed in material activities due to material desires, one has to take birth again and again in various species. The only way to stop this cycle of birth and death is to perform bhakti unto Lord Krishna, under the guidance of a guru. Bhakti is very joyful and takes us to the eternal world of God."

The real purpose of sacrifice is to worship Lord Vishnu or Krishna. Sacrifices that involve animal killing are prohibited in this age. Instead of killing innocent animals in the name of yajna, better one worships the Lord with devotion.

Narada Muni then narrated another story, "Once a deer was grazing on grass and enjoying with his wife in a serene garden filled with fragrant flowers. The deer relished the songs of the bumblebees swarming around in the garden. But, in his great joy, the deer didn't notice a hungry tiger coming in front of him. Also, a hunter was hiding behind a tree to shoot the deer with his arrows. Similarly, a materialistic person becomes absorbed in temporary enjoyment and doesn't notice the passage of time (tiger) and the Lord of death (hunter) standing behind."

Enlightened by these tales, Prachinabarhi expressed profound gratitude to Narada for rescuing him from a path leading to spiritual ruin. He renounced his attachment to elaborate yajnas and devoted himself wholeheartedly to the worship of Lord Krishna. Departing for Kapilashrama (a pilgrimage spot), he immersed himself in constant devotion to the Lord, ultimately attaining the spiritual world.

The timely intervention of great souls in our lives helps us refrain from unnecessary violence.

The Non-violent Attack

Once, there lived a venomous snake renowned for its aggressive nature. Its mere presence struck fear into the hearts of all who dared to enter near its domain, for it would strike out at any who crossed its path.

One auspicious day, the great sage Narada chanced upon the area where the serpent lived. Engrossed in his melodious songs to the Supreme Lord, Narayana, and the enchanting strains of his veena, Narada's divine presence attracted the cobra. Moved by the sage's divine music, the serpent approached Narada humbly, expressing a desire to become his disciple and renounce its violent ways.

However, Narada, wise and discerning, recognized the inherent danger posed by the cobra's natural propensity for violence. He laid forth a condition for acceptance, stipulating that the snake must give up its habit of biting indiscriminately. Committed to its new-found resolve, the serpent decided to embrace non-violence, thereby earning the trust of the surrounding villagers who once feared its venomous bite.

However, no sooner had the snake given up its nature, than it found itself subjected to cruelty and torment at the hands of mischievous children seeking revenge for past frights. Tolerating their endless taunts and assaults, the serpent bore its suffering in silence, unwavering in its commitment to non-violence.

Soon Narada Muni returned, and he found the serpent despondent and distressed. Sensing its pain, the sage imparted a valuable lesson: while non-violence is virtuous, it does not equate to no action in the face of difficulty. Advising the serpent to assert itself by hissing and raising its hood to scare away its tormentors (without biting them), Narada empowered the creature to defend itself without compromising its new-found commitment to non-violence.

Thus, armed with this new-found wisdom, the serpent learned to navigate the delicate balance between non-violence and self-preservation, ensuring its safety while upholding its principles of compassion and peace.

Being non-violent does not mean that we allow others to unnecessarily trouble us.

The stories of Prachinabarhi and the snake teach us valuable lessons about the transformative power of associating with great devotees such as Narada Muni. These stories remind us that no matter what our current state is, we have the potential to cultivate positive attributes and overcome our flaws by associating with evolved souls.

Reflect to Realize

Association with saintly people has profound transformative power. Good association plays a crucial role in our spiritual growth, providing us with the inspiration and guidance needed to develop qualities that are dear to Krishna. Even individuals, steeped in ignorance and cruelty, can become non-violent when guided by enlightened souls. Non-violence is a testament to humanity's capacity for love and empathy. By embracing this virtue, we contribute to a more compassionate and harmonious world, where the inherent dignity and worth of all living beings are honoured and upheld. Let's strive to develop these qualities in the association of great souls.

45

Service to Teachers

Selfless service to spiritually enlightened people converts our theoretical knowledge into practical realization.

Learning any subject, especially spirituality, necessitates the guidance of a teacher. A spiritual teacher or a guru is not merely a disseminator of knowledge but a living embodiment of the divine principles they impart. They possess a deep understanding of the mysteries of existence and generously share their wisdom.

In the following verse, Lord Krishna shares three vital qualities that facilitate effective learning from a guru.

tad viddhi praṇipātena
paripraśnena sevayā
upadekṣyanti te jñānaṁ
jñāninas tattva-darśinaḥ

"To be enlightened by spiritually realized teachers, one needs to (i) approach them with submissiveness (pranipata), (ii) ask relevant

questions to acquire knowledge (pari prashna), and (iii) sincerely serve them (seva)." (4.34)

Lord Krishna stresses in this verse that our inquisitiveness must be preceded by submissiveness and followed by service.

The mood of inquiry significantly affects the process of learning and acquiring knowledge. A spiritual seeker must not be in a challenging spirit while asking questions but be respectful and obedient. Such a mood brings about great blessings upon spiritual seekers, facilitating a deeper understanding of the complex spiritual concepts.

Further, we shouldn't be only on a pursuit of acquiring information from a teacher but must seek transformation by serving them. Our knowledge of scriptures must not be theoretical but must be transformed into practical wisdom. That transformation is facilitated by service to guru. Enthusiastic and loving service fosters a sense of humility and dedication, qualities essential for spiritual growth. By serving selflessly, spiritualists cultivate a mindset of surrender and detachment, overcoming the ego and opening themselves to divine grace.

Serving a spiritual teacher is not an austerity but a sacred privilege that accelerates one's spiritual journey. In this sacred relationship between guru and disciple, the seeker finds guidance, inspiration, and ultimately, connection with the Lord.

Let's explore stories of devoted students who received profound knowledge and abundant blessings by serving their teachers faithfully.

Krishna and Sudama Battle a Storm

In the region of Avantipur, dwelled Sandipani Muni, a revered sage of profound wisdom. It was to his sacred abode that the illustrious sons of Vasudev, Krishna and Balarama, were sent for their tutelage, their hearts brimming with divine radiance and youthful curiosity.

Though Vasudev harboured a reluctance to part with his cherished progeny, he recognized the necessity of education, entrusting their spiritual and intellectual growth to the sage's care. And so, with heads freshly shorn and spirits imbued with reverence, Krishna and Balarama embarked on their educational journey to Sandipani Muni's ashram.

In the serene precincts of the guru's sanctuary, amidst the fragrance of incense and the chanting of sacred hymns, the brothers demonstrated unwavering devotion, serving their revered preceptor with humility and dedication. Enthralled by their exemplary conduct, Sandipani Muni, a repository of timeless wisdom, imparted unto them the sacred scriptures, delving deep into the mysteries of the Vedas and Upanishads.

Their intellects, akin to luminous jewels, absorbed the teachings with unparalleled swiftness, mastering each subject with a brilliance that astounded even the most erudite sages. In but a span of sixty-four days, they delved into sixty-four arts, their minds akin to sages of yore, effortlessly composing sonorous hymns, weaving enchanting melodies, and performing mystic feats that defied earthly bounds.

Amidst the sanctified halls of learning, Krishna forged a bond of friendship with Sudama, a virtuous brahmana youth, his heart attuned to the rhythms of divine grace. Together, they traversed the sacred paths of knowledge, their souls kindred in their quest for spiritual illumination.

One fateful day, tasked with gathering firewood for a sacred offering, Krishna and Sudama ventured into the sylvan depths of the forest, their steps guided by dutiful obedience. Yet, as the heavens unleashed their tempestuous fury, the elements raged, cloaking the world in a shroud of darkness and chaos.

Undaunted by the tumultuous onslaught of nature, they clutched the gathered wood with steadfast resolve, their hands intertwined in a bond forged by shared trials. Through the deluge and the gales, they pressed on, their spirits undimmed by the shadows that engulfed them, their hearts illumined by the flame of devotion.

Meanwhile, within the hallowed confines of Sandipani Muni's ashram, the sage, his heart heavy with concern, awaited the return of his cherished disciples. With bated breath, he prayed for their safe return, his thoughts an unceasing mantra of supplication.

As dawn's gentle rays pierced through the veil of night, Sandipani embarked on a quest to find his beloved wards, his steps guided by paternal concern and unwavering faith. And lo, amidst the tangled labyrinth of the forest, he found them, Krishna and Sudama, their forms battered by the storm, yet their spirits unbroken.

Overwhelmed by a torrent of emotion, Sandipani embraced them, his voice choked with gratitude and affection. "My beloved sons," he exclaimed, "your devotion and selflessness have illumined the path of righteousness. Your unwavering service, even amidst the fiercest tempest, is a testament to the boundless depths of your love and devotion."

With tears of joy streaming down his weathered visage, Sandipani Muni blessed them abundantly, invoking divine grace upon their noble souls. And in that sacred moment, amidst the verdant embrace of the forest, Krishna and Sudama stood as paragons of humility and devotion, their hearts forever intertwined with the eternal teachings of their revered guru.

Despite being the Almighty God, Krishna accepted Sandipani Muni as His guru, emphasizing the importance of mentorship. His actions teach us the value of seeking guidance on the spiritual path.

Knowledge from a guru is attained by submissiveness and selfless service.

Upamanyu's Hunger

In the tranquil embrace of Sage Dhaumya's ashram, nestled amidst the whispering leaves and murmuring brooks, a young disciple named Upamanyu walked a path of simplicity and unwavering devotion. Though mocked by his peers for his lack of scholarly pursuits, Upamanyu's heart remained pure, his spirit tethered to the service of his revered guru.

Assigned the humble task of tending the sacred cows, Upamanyu roamed the verdant pastures with gentle reverence, his days filled with the rhythm of their contented grazing. Yet, his simple existence drew the ire of his peers, who viewed him with disdain, oblivious to the depth of his devotion.

Moved by a desire to test Upamanyu's steadfastness, Sage Dhaumya gently admonished him, instructing that all offerings of food gathered through begging be presented to him first. Undeterred by this decree, Upamanyu obeyed without hesitation, his heart brimming with reverence for his beloved guru.

Yet, as each directive grew more stringent, Upamanyu's resolve remained unshaken, his obedience unwavering even in the face of hardship. Denied even the humblest sustenance, he walked a path of self-denial, his unwavering faith a beacon amidst the trials that beset him.

But fate, in its mysterious design, led Upamanyu down a path fraught with peril, as hunger gnawed at his very being. Desperate and famished, he consumed the leaves of a poisonous plant, unwittingly sealing his fate as darkness descended upon his world, rendering him blind and helpless.

Amidst the anguish of his plight, Sage Dhaumya, his heart heavy with concern, embarked on a quest to find his lost disciple. Guided by the echoes of Upamanyu's voice, he discovered the young boy ensnared in the grip of darkness, his spirit undimmed by the trials that assailed him.

Moved by Upamanyu's unwavering devotion, Sage Dhaumya beseeched the divine Ashwini Kumaras, healers of the celestial realms, to restore his sight. Yet, when the blessed medicine was offered, Upamanyu, bound by his vow of obedience, steadfastly refused.

Impressed by his unwavering commitment to his guru's command, the Ashwini Kumaras, in their boundless grace, bestowed upon Upamanyu a divine blessing, restoring his sight by the power of their mystic arts.

Overwhelmed with gratitude, Sage Dhaumya bestowed his blessings upon Upamanyu, his heart brimming with paternal pride. In the crucible of adversity, Upamanyu had emerged as a beacon of unwavering devotion, his spirit tempered by the fires of his guru's testing, his faith shining bright amidst the darkness that sought to engulf him.

Knowledge is received by submissive service to teachers.

From the above stories of Krishna, Sudama and Upamanyu, we understand the importance of respecting and serving teachers. Although Lord Krishna is the Supreme Almighty, the source of all knowledge, still, while playing the part of a human being, He accepted Sandipani Muni as his guru and served him sincerely. Thus, he taught us the need to accept a guru.

Reflect to Realize

Our theoretical knowledge, when filtered through the channel of seva or selfless service, blossoms into living wisdom. By actively applying our learning through service, we unlock profound realizations. Serving great souls, God, and His devotees becomes indispensable for spiritual growth.

46

Equanimity

When we constantly seek praise from others, we surrender our happiness to their judgement.

In our human experience, the sway of emotions stirred by praise and criticism is a reflection of our vulnerabilities and aspirations. Amid this mixture, the wisdom of the Bhagavad Gita offers a valuable insight. It highlights the path of equanimity in the midst of the turbulent waves of external validation.

Here is a Gita verse where Lord Krishna suggests a mature approach outlook towards praise and criticism.

tulya-nindā-stutir maunī
santuṣṭo yena kenacit
aniketaḥ sthira-matir
bhaktimān me priyo naraḥ

"Wise persons are equipoised towards criticism and praise, for they are always satisfied at heart. They are fixed in knowledge and devotion, and are very dear to Me." (12.19)

To be happy in the warmth of compliments is a natural inclination, offering a temporary sense of affirmation and joy. Yet, the Gita advises us to be cautious, reminding us not to let such praise inflate our egos, for true fulfilment lies beyond the space of external achievements. Instead, it advises anchoring ourself in inner contentment, knowledge, and devotion—the bedrock of lasting fulfilment.

Conversely, criticism usually casts a shadow over our spirits, causing feelings of disheartenment and self-doubt. However, when viewed through the lens of another perspective, constructive criticism becomes a possible catalyst for growth and self-improvement. The Gita teaches us to embrace such feedback with humility and openness, recognizing it as an opportunity to refine our understanding and actions.

Thus, those steadfast in their commitment to inner harmony are undisturbed by both praise and criticism, and remain equipoised towards them. They navigate the tumultuous seas of life with grace and resilience, guided by the timeless wisdom of equanimity imparted in this sacred verse of the Gita.

In short:

- When someone genuinely appreciates us for our good work, we may feel happy and encouraged without becoming proud and overconfident.
- When others criticize us for our mistakes, we should take it as a feedback and try to improve ourselves, without feeling discouraged or disappointed.

Now, let's dive into stories that exemplify this unwavering balance amidst life's ups and downs.

Jada Bharat–The Enlightened Madman

King Rahugan, sovereign of the Sindhu domain, embarked on a journey to Kapilashram, in regal splendour upon a lustrous palanquin. Reaching the river's edge, a need for additional hands arose, and there, amidst the seekers, stood Jada Bharat, sturdy and robust. Compelled into service, Bharat, moved by empathy, sidestepped ants, causing the palanquin's gait to falter.

Baffled by the unsettling sway, King Rahugan demanded an explanation, to which Bharat responded with an account of his meandering steps. Rahugan, dismissing Bharat's maturity and accusing him of frailty, grew increasingly vexed. Yet, Bharat remained calm and unruffled, his composure untouched by the king's ire.

As Rahugan's censure intensified, Jada Bharat, serene and unwavering, explained the transient nature of worldly roles, declaring his identity as an emancipated soul beyond the limitations of the body. Undeterred by threats of punishment, he continued his steady, purposeful pace.

Bharat's profound wisdom struck a chord within Rahugan, sparking a humbling realization of Bharat's elevated state. Setting aside his royal pride, Rahugan fell to the ground before Bharat, seeking enlightenment.

"Who are you?" Rahugan asked, his voice filled with awe. "Are you a learned brahmana, a liberated saint, or perhaps Lord Narayana Himself? Why do you wander like a madman?"

"I was the renowned Emperor Bharat in my previous life," Jada Bharat replied. "Fully absorbed in the Lord's service, I became distracted by an undue attachment to a deer. As a result, I was born as a deer in my next life. However, I retained the memory of my past life and meditated on Lord Hari even in that form. Now, I have been reborn as Jada Bharat, a brahmana, and I wander unnoticed to avoid undesirable associations."

Enlightened by Bharat's teachings, Rahugan expressed deep gratitude and reverence. Unfazed, Jada Bharat resumed his solitary journey, ultimately transcending the confines of mortal existence to attain the eternal kingdom of God.

If we are satisfied, others' comments won't matter.

Vidura–The Wise Minister

Dhritarashtra, the sightless monarch of Hastinapura, fathered a hundred sons, with the eldest among them being the malicious Duryodhana. Coveting the throne of Hastinapura, Duryodhana spared no treachery in his attempts to annihilate the noble Pandavas, his cousins and rightful heirs to the kingdom. Blind Dhritarashtra, further blinded by paternal bias, turned a blind eye to his sons' nefarious deeds.

Duryodhana's transgressions knew no bounds. He conspired to immolate the Pandavas alive by setting ablaze their dwelling. He commanded his brother Duhsasana to publicly shame Draupadi, the chaste wife of the Pandavas. He duplicitously won their kingdom in a rigged game of dice, then exiled them to the wilderness. Even the sage advice of Lord Krishna, who implored peace, fell on deaf ears as Duryodhana adamantly clung to his unjust ways.

In the midst of this moral decay, Vidura, Dhritarashtra's loyal minister and righteous adviser, confronted the king. Urging him to restore the Pandavas' rightful inheritance, Vidura warned of impending doom should Duryodhana persist in his malevolence. He beseeched Dhritarashtra to cast aside his sinful progeny for the greater good of the dynasty.

Duryodhana, consumed by rage, hurled venomous insults at Vidura, dismissing his counsel with contempt. Despite being a venerable elder, a revered uncle, and a stalwart minister, Vidura faced the disdain of his nephew, while Dhritarashtra remained silent, a silent accomplice to his son's insolence.

Undeterred by Duryodhana's scorn, Vidura, with unwavering resolve, laid down his bow and departed from

Hastinapura's halls. His heart unperturbed by the sting of humiliation, he perceived the divine hand guiding his path. Embarking on a sacred pilgrimage, far removed from the tumult of politics, Vidura traversed holy lands, his thoughts perpetually fixed on Lord Krishna in devout reverence.

As fate would have it, the Kurukshetra war erupted in his absence. Banished by an ungrateful Duryodhana, Vidura embraced his exile as an opportunity for spiritual solace, seeking refuge in the divine shelter of the Supreme.

If we remain unaffected by others' bad behaviour, the Lord will show us the way.

Despite King Rahugan's mistreatment, Jada Bharat remained unruffled by his remarks. Similarly, when Duryodhana insulted Vidura, Vidura viewed it as the divine orchestration to liberate him from bad company. If we cultivate resilience towards both praise and criticism, we can navigate life's journey with greater success.

Reflect to Realize

Wise individuals perceive exaggerated praise as potentially stifling, as it often lacks acknowledgement of areas for improvement, while criticism is viewed as an opportunity for growth, providing insight into where one may be faltering. Recognizing the transient nature of both praise and criticism, our focus should prioritize self-improvement over seeking external validation. When we constantly seek praise from others, we surrender our own happiness to their judgement. Therefore, let us foster a mindset of continuous improvement rather than a dependency on accolades. This pursuit will ultimately lead to genuine satisfaction and personal fulfilment.

47

Selflessness

For a selfish person every interaction is a transaction;
for a selfless person interactions are opportunities for service.

Are you aware of the secret to true happiness? Satisfying our own desires is not necessarily the path to joy. Genuine happiness lies in selflessly serving and satisfying others. Real happiness lies in making others happy. Therefore, noble individuals don't just strive for their own benefit; but extend themselves to help others. They are sincere well-wishers of others.

Central to the essence of selflessness is the genuine desire to remove the suffering of others. Driven by empathy and compassion, kind people extend themselves to aid those in need, recognizing the interconnectedness of all beings on the spiritual level. Their actions are not motivated by personal gain or recognition but arise from a deep-seated sense of duty and compassion.

The nature of the soul is to experience love from both others and the Divine. We earn love from others by acting in selfless ways that bring them joy. This doesn't entail forsaking our own desires entirely; rather, it means refraining from selfishness and avoiding actions that cause pain to others. Embracing this mindset not only fosters the happiness of others but also satisfies our own souls.

Lord Krishna describes this quality in the following verse:

labhante brahma-nirvāṇam
ṛṣayaḥ kṣīṇa-kalmaṣāḥ
chinna-dvaidhā yatātmānaḥ
sarva-bhūta-hite ratāḥ

"Those who extend themselves to aid others, who are diligent and liberated from all malice and ignorance, can effortlessly attain the spiritual realm." (5.25)

Furthermore, Krishna highlights that such individuals are characterized by diligence, demonstrating a steadfast dedication to their compassionate endeavours. Their efforts are not half-hearted but are marked by consistent and earnest commitment to serving others, even in the face of challenges. They make systematic plans for the spiritual upliftment of the society in an organized way. Selfless hearts are free from resentment, envy, and prejudice, allowing them to embrace all beings with boundless love. By embodying these noble qualities, we can effortlessly attain the spiritual realm.

Below are accounts of two remarkable individuals who epitomized selflessness. While not all of us may be called upon to make such monumental sacrifices, we can draw inspiration from their noble deeds and strive to emulate their spirit of selflessness in our own lives gradually.

Lord Shiva Drinks Halahal

During the churning of the milk ocean by the devas and asuras, before the emergence of the coveted nectar, various other substances surfaced from the tumultuous waters.

Amidst the vigorous churning, the ocean turned turbulent, causing distress to all its inhabitants. Suddenly, a lethal poison known as *halahal* emerged, spreading its toxic influence far and wide.

Terrified by the venom's potency, the devas sought refuge in Lord Shiva atop Mount Kailasha. Pleading for salvation, they implored the compassionate deity to avert the imminent catastrophe. "O Lord," they prayed, "please save us from this fiery poison. You are powerful enough to counteract this dangerous poison that's spreading everywhere in the universe. Destroying this poison is nothing for you."

Moved by their plight, Lord Shiva conferred with his consort, Parvati, seeking her consent to undertake this noble deed. "O Parvati," he said, "just see how they all have been placed in danger due to the poison. It is a master's duty to protect the suffering dependents. Let me drink this poison to save all the people in this universe."

Recognizing the responsibility incumbent upon a protector, Shiva resolved to ingest the poison to safeguard all beings in the universe. Parvati, fully aware of Shiva's boundless power, readily acquiesced.

With resolute determination, Shiva gathered the poison into his palm and consumed it without hesitation, sparing the universe from impending peril. "Lord Vishnu is pleased when one performs benevolent acts," he remarked.

The selfless act of Lord Shiva earned accolades from Parvati, Vishnu, Brahma, and the entire pantheon of celestial beings, who lauded his boundless compassion and unwavering resolve.

A selfless person takes up hardships to relieve others of their difficulties.

Sage Dadhichi Donates Bones

Once, a fearful demon named Vritrasura launched a ferocious assault on the devas. Despite their valiant efforts, the devas' weapons proved futile against his formidable might as he effortlessly swallowed them whole. Fearing for their lives, the devas sought refuge in Lord Vishnu, beseeching him to intervene and vanquish the relentless demon.

Responding to their prayers, Lord Vishnu graciously appeared before them, assuring them of a solution. "Approach sage Dadhichi," he instructed, "a devout devotee of mine. His spiritually empowered body holds the key to your salvation. Seek his permission to fashion a thunderbolt weapon from his bones, capable of slaying Vritrasura."

Trusting in the Lord's wisdom, the devas approached sage Dadhichi, humbly presenting their request. However, Dadhichi, in a playful tone, expressed his reluctance, emphasizing the profound attachment all beings harbour towards their bodies. "How can one willingly surrender that which is most cherished?" he queried.

Undeterred by Dadhichi's initial refusal, the devas appealed to his innate compassion and wisdom, highlighting the noble purpose behind their plea. Touched by their sincerity, Dadhichi relented, acknowledging the selfless nature of their request. "Though the body is transient," he remarked, "utilizing it for the greater good is its true purpose."

With steadfast resolve, Dadhichi immersed himself in meditation upon Lord Vishnu, transcending the realm of worldly attachment. Unaware of his impending departure, he relinquished his mortal frame, offering it selflessly for the devas' cause.

Gathering Dadhichi's bones, the devas entrusted them to Vishvakarma, the celestial architect, who forged a formidable thunderbolt weapon imbued with Dadhichi's spiritual potency. Armed with this divine weapon, Indra, atop his celestial mount Airavata, led the charge against Vritrasura, ultimately vanquishing the malevolent demon in a fierce battle.

Selfless people readily help others even at their own inconvenience.

Lord Shiva drank deadly poison to save the universe, while Sage Dadhichi willingly gave his bones to create a weapon to defeat a demon. While we may not be capable of such extraordinary sacrifices, we can draw inspiration from these great men, and selflessly help others to the best of our ability.

Reflect to Realize

By extending a helping hand to others, even in small ways, we contribute to the betterment of society and nurture a culture of kindness and compassion. Let us heed the lessons of great beings and endeavour to make a positive impact on the world around us through acts of selflessness and service.

48

Forgiveness

Forgiveness frees our heart from the shackles of grudge and negativity.

Lord Krishna repeatedly delineates the virtues of divine individuals. The following is another such verse where a set of virtues are recommended for us to cultivate.

tejaḥ kṣamā dhṛtiḥ śaucam
adroho nāti-mānitā
bhavanti sampadaṁ daivīm
abhijātasya bhārata

"Those are are noble possesses divine qualities such as strength, forgiveness, resilience, cleanliness, lack of envy, and absence of the desire for recognition." (16.3)

Among all virtues, forgiveness stands out as a crucial attribute for cultivating meaningful relationships. Noble souls possess the ability to pardon even the gravest transgressions, a quality that brings peace to the forgiver and often inspires positive change in the forgiven.

It is natural to feel upset when others wrong us, but holding onto grudges and harbouring bitter feelings for an extended period is harmful. By releasing the burden of past incidents, the forgiver experiences a unique sense of inner peace. Furthermore, forgiveness serves as a catalyst for positive change, encouraging the forgiven individual to reflect on their actions and strive for improvement.

However, it is important to understand that forgiveness does not equate to approving wrongful behaviour. Instead, it involves a conscious decision to release the grip of anger and bitterness, without necessarily absolving the offender of accountability. In some situations, administering appropriate punishment may be necessary to uphold justice and maintain discipline.

Forgiveness embodies the essence of divine love and compassion, transcending ego and division. It is a sacred virtue with the power to heal wounds, mend broken relationships, and pave the way for reconciliation and renewal. As Lord Krishna teaches, forgiveness is not just a virtue to be admired but a transformative force at the heart of spiritual evolution.

Now, let us explore the art of forgiveness through the following narratives, where individuals exemplify this virtue in their actions and attitudes.

The King of Earth Forgives the King of Heaven

King Prithu governed the earth with righteousness, aspiring to perform a hundred sacrifices. He had already completed ninety-nine, and the hundredth was underway in Brahmavarta.

However, Indra, the ruler of heaven, felt threatened by Prithu's impending achievement. Envious of Prithu's success, Indra disguised himself as a sage and deceitfully absconded with the sacrificial horse, a crucial element of the ritual.

Sage Atri discerned Indra's treachery and alerted Prithu's son to apprehend the thief. Indra, in haste, fled through the skies with the stolen horse. Disguised as a mendicant, he was spared from confrontation. "Why do you flee, disguised one?" Prithu's son questioned. "What transgression has compelled you to steal?"

Reluctant to harm a supposed ascetic, Prithu's son refrained from attacking Indra, who then relinquished the horse and his false guise before vanishing. Undeterred by his initial failure, Indra returned in another guise, shrouding the sacrificial site in dense darkness and brazenly stealing the horse once more. "Who dares disrupt this sacred rite?" Prithu's son demanded. "Reveal yourself, thief!"

Despite pursuit, Indra's disguise as a saint forestalled any violent reprisal. His repeated subterfuge sowed confusion among the populace, enticing some to adopt mendicant attire to evade accountability for misdeeds. Provoked by Indra's relentless interference, King Prithu, with bow in hand, prepared to confront him. "Your deception ends now, deceitful one!" Prithu declared.

However, the priests intervened, proposing to offer Indra into the sacrificial fire through their incantations. Lord Brahma, appearing amidst the assembly, cautioned against further aggression, urging Prithu to halt the sacrifice to prevent exacerbating the situation. "Prudence dictates a cessation," Brahma advised. "Indra's folly must not be met with further strife."

Recognizing Brahma's wisdom, Prithu suspended the ritual, demonstrating maturity and deference to divine counsel. "As you command, revered Brahma," Prithu acquiesced. Rather than seeking Indra's demise, Brahma sought his redemption. Thus, when Lord Vishnu materialized, accompanied by Indra seeking forgiveness, Prithu welcomed them warmly.

With humility and remorse, Indra sought Prithu's pardon for his transgressions. "Forgive me, noble king," Indra implored. "I acted out of envy and fear." In a display of magnanimity, Prithu embraced Indra, absolving him of wrongdoing without harbouring resentment. "All is forgiven," Prithu declared. "May you find peace and redemption, Indra."

Prithu's exemplary forgiveness not only restored harmony but also catalysed a positive transformation in Indra. Pleased with Prithu's noble character, Lord Vishnu bestowed abundant blessings upon him. "Your forgiveness is a beacon of light," Lord Vishnu remarked. "May your kingdom prosper, and your heart remain pure."

Being forgiving and obedient attracts the Lord's blessings.

Lord Krishna Forgives Indra

Once, King Nanda arranged for the worship of Indra. At that tender age of seven, Lord Krishna, though appearing as a playful child in Vrindavan, was none other than the Supreme God. Aware of Indra's arrogance, Krishna sought to correct his mindset and impart a valuable lesson by suggesting that they worship Govardhan Hill instead.

Initially hesitant, King Nanda and the villagers agreed to Krishna's proposal, eager to please their beloved child. They performed Govardhan puja with great fervour, circling the hill with cows at the forefront. The new-found festival brought joy to all, except one—Indra.

Infuriated that his worship had been replaced by a simple village child, Indra unleashed the mighty Samvartaka clouds, capable of universal destruction. Relentless rain, accompanied by thunder, lightning, and hail, engulfed Vrindavan, posing a dire threat to its inhabitants.

Responding to the distress of his devotees, Krishna lifted Govardhan Hill effortlessly with his pinky finger, providing shelter for all beneath it. For a week, he held the hill aloft, delighting in the company of his beloved devotees while protecting them from Indra's fury.

Despite Indra's relentless assault, Govardhan Hill remained steadfast, unyielding to the storm's onslaught. Realizing his folly, Indra acknowledged Krishna's supreme authority and ceased the deluge.

Krishna, like a compassionate father guiding an errant child, humbled Indra without punitive measures. His only aim was to rectify Indra's misconceptions. Moved by Krishna's mercy, Indra approached him with humility, seeking forgiveness.

Falling at Krishna's feet, Indra confessed his arrogance and surrendered to him, recognizing Krishna's supreme sovereignty over all. In response, Krishna smiled warmly, advising Indra to remember that all his powers were bestowed by divine grace. With grace, Krishna accepted Indra's worship, forgiving him and reminding him to guard against false pride.

The Lord corrects His devotees' occasional mistakes, and also excuses them.

King Prithu forgave Indra despite Indra's attempts to obstruct his sacrifice. Similarly, Lord Krishna forgave Indra even though he endeavoured to submerge Vrindavan in relentless rains. The forgiving demeanour of Prithu and Krishna led to a transformation in Indra. Drawing inspiration from their actions, let us also strive to forgive others, starting with their minor and unintentional mistakes.

Reflect to Realize

Forgive to be forgiven! Charity means giving to others. But do you know what encompasses one of the greatest charities? The greatest charity is to forgive others without any grudges. But what can inspire us to forgive others? Reflecting on the countless times we've been forgiven by others and by the Lord. Over time immemorial we have committed so many mistakes against God. Still, the Lord has lovingly accepted us and wants us to come back. And apart from God, we might have committed so many mistakes against so many people. If we desire forgiveness from others, shouldn't we extend the same grace to them? Therefore, let's cultivate the habit of forgiveness, to make our life more peaceful and fulfilling.

49

Gentle Speech

Rude speech pains the hearers, while gentle speech wins their hearts.

Speech is indeed a vital means of interaction, isn't it? When we speak with kindness, honesty, and consideration for others, we cultivate an environment of trust and respect, nurturing harmonious relationships. Gentle words have the power to soothe troubled hearts and strengthen the bonds of love and understanding.

Conversely, harsh and hurtful speech can cause wounds that may linger long after the words are spoken. Therefore, mastering the art of speaking kindly is essential for creating a world filled with compassion and empathy.

In the following verse, Lord Krishna imparts wisdom on effective communication:

anudvega-karaṁ vākyaṁ
satyaṁ priya-hitaṁ ca yat
svādhyāyābhyasanaṁ caiva
vāṅ-mayaṁ tapa ucyate

"One's speech should not disturb others. It must be truthful, beneficial, and well-intentioned. Another way to harness the power of speech is by regularly reciting scriptures." (17.15)

There are occasions when firm and assertive communication becomes necessary, particularly in situations where correction or guidance is required for the greater good. Teachers, parents, and mentors may need to adopt a stern tone to instil discipline, impart wisdom, or uphold moral standards. In such cases, the intention behind the speech is rooted in genuine concern.

Barring these exceptional circumstances, Lord Krishna advises us to communicate gently and compassionately in all our ordinary interactions. By doing so, we cultivate a culture of kindness and understanding in which everyone can grow. Thus, the wise use of speech becomes a potent tool for building bridges, fostering harmony, and spreading love and goodwill in the world. Furthermore, immersing ourselves in scriptures like the Bhagavad Gita ensures that we harness the full potential of our speech.

Delve into two stories to get a deeper understanding.

Suniti's Good Advice to Dhruva

King Uttanapada had two queens—Suniti and Suruchi. However, he favoured his younger wife, Suruchi, while neglecting Suniti. Suniti bore a son named Dhruva, while Uttama was Suruchi's son.

Once, Uttanapada sat on his throne with Uttama on his lap. Little Dhruva arrived there, desiring to sit on his father's lap like his stepbrother. However, the King did not welcome him. Suruchi, seeing Dhruva's innocent attempt, spoke harshly to him, "O child, although you are also the son of the king, you cannot sit on his lap or the throne because you are not born of me! If you still wish to sit on the king's lap, then worship Lord Vaasudeva. By His mercy, you may take birth as my son in your next life, qualifying to sit on your father's lap." Uttanapada remained silent.

Suruchi's harsh words shattered Dhruva's heart, and his father's silence deepened his disappointment. Dhruva, breathing heavily, went weeping to his mother Suniti. By the time he reached her, the palace residents had informed her about the incident. Suniti, already heartbroken from being neglected by her husband, was further aggrieved upon hearing how her son was mistreated.

When Dhruva came to her crying, Suniti lifted him onto her lap, feeling the pain caused by her co-wife's harshness. She tried to console Dhruva and instil wisdom in him. Suniti imparted three principles: not to wish harm for others even if they hurt him, to understand that one suffers due to one's own past mistakes, and to worship Lord Vasudeva, as advised by Suruchi, without being envious.

As a noble mother and devotee of Lord Vishnu, Suniti pacified Dhruva with gentle words, aiming to quell his anger and protect his tender heart from hatred. She directed him towards God, emphasizing the importance of devotion to Lord Vasudeva for relief from distress.

She continued, "Dear son, only by worshipping Lord Vasudeva could your great-grandfather Brahma create the universe, and your grandfather Manu achieve happiness and liberation. So, take shelter of Lord Vasudeva. His affection for His devotees surpasses the affection of millions of mothers combined. No one else can relieve your distress like Him."

Inspired by his mother's advice, Dhruva worshipped Lord Vasudeva in the forest for six months and received His darshan, along with several boons.

Our words must aim to motivate and uplift others as much as possible.

Lord Krishna's Message of Peace

"Duryodhana and his cohorts had unlawfully usurped the kingdom of the Pandavas and adamantly refused to restore it even after their exile," Lord Krishna recounted in the assembly. "To avert an inevitable conflict," he continued, "I have come to Hastinapur as a peace envoy on behalf of the Pandavas."

Addressing King Dhritarashtra with solemnity, Krishna implored, "May tranquility prevail between the Kurus and the Pandavas. If the rightful portion of the kingdom is not returned to the Pandavas, war shall ensue, bringing death to many. What shall we gain from such devastation? Your lineage is renowned for its wisdom, virtue, compassion, and honesty. Do not permit your noble heritage to be tarnished. I beseech you to instruct your sons to embrace the path of peace. Spare this world from calamity. The Pandavas regard you as a revered elder. Let the affection you once harboured for them reignite within you. Embrace them as your own sons. These fatherless boys deserve your guardianship."

As the blind monarch sat in silence, Krishna conveyed the Pandavas' message, "After enduring thirteen years of exile, we now seek the restoration of our rightful kingdom. Treat us as a father would his sons, and we shall reciprocate in kind."

Dhritarashtra, visibly unsettled and burdened by guilt for mistreating the Pandavas, shed tears of remorse as Krishna continued, "O king, restrain your sons from their wrongful actions. The Pandavas stands ready to serve you and defend you. Do not engage in conflict with them." Many sages in the assembly echoed Krishna's sentiments.

Responding, Dhritarashtra conceded, "Dear Krishna, I acknowledge the veracity of your words, spoken for the benefit of all. However, my son Duryodhana heeds not my counsel, nor that of Vidura, Bhishma, or any elder. I beseech you to admonish him."

Krishna turned to Duryodhana and beseeched, "I seek your prosperity and happiness as fervently as you do. I implore you to relinquish your obstinate stance and reconcile with your cousins. Such an act would bring joy to your father and all the revered elders of the Kuru lineage. Your father has instructed you to pursue peace. A virtuous man heeds his father's directives. Disregarding the council of elders and well-wishers leads to ruin. Though you have treated the Pandavas harshly from a tender age, they are willing to forgive and embrace you as friends. Do not harbour enmity towards your kin."

Following his discourse on the merits of peace, Krishna expounded on the consequences of war with the Pandavas, "O valiant one, who can withstand the fury of Bhima? Who can engage Arjuna in battle and emerge unscathed? Why do you seek conflict? Let the prosperous Kuru dynasty not be decimated on your account."

Despite Bhishma, Drona, and Vidura urging Duryodhana to heed Krishna's counsel, and Dhritarashtra's entreaty to do the same, the obstinate prince remained impervious to reason.

Furious, Duryodhana rose from his seat and declared, "Krishna, why do you extol the Pandavas and censure me without comprehending the circumstances?"

With unwavering resolve, Krishna interjected, "O fool! You cling to the illusion of your innocence, yet the truth is known to all assembled here. You envied the Pandavas and conspired with Shakuni to defeat them in the game of dice. You subjected virtuous Draupadi to indignity before the entire

Kuru court. Your plea of innocence now reeks of arrogance. If you do not willingly cede their kingdom, you will be compelled to relinquish it in battle. Despite repeated exhortations from your elders to pursue peace, you remain obstinate."

In defiance, Duryodhana stormed out of the assembly, followed by his retinue. Bhishma conceded that war had become inevitable, and Krishna addressed Dhritarashtra, "The responsibility for this lamentable state of affairs lies with all the leaders of the Kuru lineage. You should have forcibly restrained Duryodhana. The time has come for action. Just as I vanquished Kamsa earlier, and brought joy to the Yadavas, one malevolent individual must be sacrificed for the greater good of the entire race. It is imperative that you subdue Duryodhana, Karna, Shakuni, and Duhshasana, and pursue reconciliation with the Pandavas. This is the only path to salvation for the Kshatriya clans."

Dhritarashtra, consumed by fury, rebuked Duryodhana vehemently in a bid to dissuade him from seizing Krishna. Despite Vidura's warning about Krishna's divine prowess, Duryodhana remained obstinate. Pointing accusingly at Krishna, he commanded, "Catch him!" Instantly, his soldiers surged into the hall from all entrances, armed with swords and bows, intent on attacking Krishna.

In response, Lord Krishna began to manifest his colossal form, from which various deities, sages, and celestial beings emerged. Brahma emerged from his forehead, Shiva from his chest, while the celestial beings chanted mantras. The awe-inspiring spectacle overwhelmed most present, who closed their eyes in reverence. Only Bhishma, Drona, Vidura, and Sanjaya were granted the vision to behold Krishna's divine form. With a special dispensation, Dhritarashtra too beheld the magnificence before Krishna resumed his two-armed form and departed the assembly.

Though Krishna had addressed Duryodhana with benevolent intentions, the malevolent prince attempted to arrest him, thereby sealing the fate of war, with victory assured for the Pandavas.

"We should always strive to communicate gently and respectfully with others, but it's important to speak up if we find ourselves being exploited or mistreated."

While there may be moments when speaking up becomes necessary for our own well-being, we should always strive to express ourselves with sweetness and gentleness.

From the story of Dhruva, we learn how harsh words can pierce hearts while soft words can transform hearts. Lord Krishna personally exemplified how one must speak. Sometimes it may become necessary to speak up for one's own good or to correct others, but we must always attempt to speak sweetly and gently. Our speech has to be motivating and encouraging to others in all ways possible.

Reflect to Realize

If using positive words can create a happier world for us and others, why not be happy free of cost? Utilizing uplifting language, devoid of ego and pride, stands as one of the pivotal methods to cultivate a contented life. Yet, our ego often compels us to behave in regrettable ways, leading to subsequent remorse. Thus, rather than inflicting pain through our words, let us seek to tame our ego by recognizing our true identity and nature. Let us learn to be humble and endeavour to communicate positively and observe the transformative impact on our own lives.

50

Humility

Humility is a protective shield that saves us from the attacks of ego.

Humility is often regarded as the cornerstone of noble character. Humility is a virtue that resonates deeply in the hearts of those who strive for inner richness rather than external validation. Those who embody humility are characterized by their simplicity and sincerity. Instead of boasting of their own accomplishments or greatness, they approach life with quiet confidence, grounded in the knowledge of their own limitations, while acknowledging others' greatness.

In the Chapter 13 of the Gita, Lord Krishna presents various aspects of knowledge of which humility is the foremost, as seen in the following verse.

amānitvam adambhitvam
ahiṁsā kṣāntir ārjavam
ācāryopāsanaṁ śaucaṁ
sthairyam ātma-vinigrahaḥ

"Nine virtues inherent in noble souls are humility, pridelessness, non-violence, tolerance, simplicity, service towards the guru, cleanliness, commitment, and self-control." (13.8)

Cultivating these virtues not only fosters harmonious relationships with others but also endears one to the Almighty Lord Krishna.

Humility uplifts the spirits of an individual and society at large. At its core, humility helps us acknowledge the contributions of others, and treat everyone with respect and dignity, instead of being self-obsessed. Thus, humility fosters genuine relationships, by making us more attuned to the experiences and feelings of those around us.

Furthermore, humility serves as a powerful antidote to negative emotions such as envy, arrogance, and pride. By recognizing the inherent worth of every individual and refraining from belittling others, humble people create an atmosphere of inclusivity, acceptance and positivity. They understand that true greatness lies not in the accumulation of power or wealth, but in acts of kindness, compassion, and service to others.

Humility facilitates open-mindedness, acknowledging that there is always room for growth and learning. It involves cultivating a spirit of gratitude, recognizing the contributions of others, and celebrating the successes of those around you. A humble person embraces vulnerability, by his or her willingness to admit mistakes and seek forgiveness when necessary.

A humble person, regardless of his or her fame and accomplishments, respects and expresses gratitude towards everyone, regardless of their social position.

Now, let us delve into tales of illustrious individuals who exemplified the virtues of humility and simplicity.

A Crane, a Hen, and Salt

Parashar Bhatt, a devotee of Lord Vishnu, resided in Srirangam. One day, one of his disciples sought enlightenment, asking, "My revered guru, what are the signs of a true devotee or lover of God?"

Parashar Bhatt directed his disciple to Ananta Acharya, a revered disciple of Ramanuja Acharya, advising him to seek the answer from him at the temple of Lord Venkateswara in Tirupati. Following his guru's counsel, the disciple embarked on the journey from Srirangam to Tirumala to meet Ananta Acharya.

The disciple walked all the way from Srirangam to Tirumala and met Ananta Acharya. Bowing at his feet, he asked, "My dear Sir, Parashar Bhatt has sent me to you. Can you please tell me what the symptoms of a true lover of God are?"

Seeing Ananta Acharya's silence, the disciple thought, "I am not worthy of receiving the answer. I have to become humble and patient. I must serve Ananta Acharya. Thinking so, for the next six months, he served Ananta Acharya. Feeling unqualified, he never attempted to ask his question again.

Then once, during a grand festival at Tirupati, Ananta Acharya arranged a grand feast of Lord Balaji's prasadam. Amidst the crowd, the disciple eagerly awaited his turn to participate in the celebration. However, Ananta Acharya instructed him to serve the guests before honoring the food himself. Humble and obedient, the disciple agreed, serving tirelessly until every guest had been fed.

Only after the feast concluded did Ananta Acharya turn to the disciple, inquiring about the question he had posed six months earlier. With sincerity, the disciple repeated his query, prompting Ananta Acharya to respond cryptically: "A true devotee is like a crane, like a hen, like salt, and like you."

Confused by the unique response, the disciple returned to Srirangam and recounted his encounter with Parashar Bhatt. Intrigued, Parashar Bhatt decoded Ananta Acharya's answer:

- **Crane:** Just as a crane's pristine white body symbolizes purity, a devotee's heart remains free of duplicity or selfishness. Like the crane differentiates between small and large fish, a devotee selectively absorbs wisdom while disregarding trivial chatter. Furthermore, similar to the crane's migration to quieter waters, a devotee seeks solace in the company of the spiritually inclined.
- **Hen:** Much like a hen examines through debris for grains, a devotee finds the essence amid life's distractions, focusing solely on spiritual nourishment.
- **Salt:** It is salt that brings taste to preparation. But salt remains hidden and is not visible in the dish. Those who eat food praise various ingredients in the preparation, but generally not salt. Just as salt relinquishes its identity to enhance the taste of dishes, a devotee selflessly serves without seeking recognition, enriching the lives of others.
- **You:** Your humility and obedience mirrored the selflessness of a devotee, highlighting the willingness to prioritize others' needs above your own.

Through Parashar Bhatt's elucidation, the disciple gained profound insight into the qualities of a true devotee, reflecting on the essence of selflessness and humility in spiritual practice.

Humility attracts the grace of great souls.

Ramanuja Acharya Bows to a Washerman

Once, the revered saint Ramanuja Acharya embarked on a journey to Tirupati, accompanied by his devoted disciples. As they travelled, they encountered a split in the road, unsure of which direction would lead them to their destination. Spotting a washerman nearby, Ramanuja Acharya approached him with respect, seeking guidance to reach the sacred abode of Lord Venkateswara.

The washerman humbly offered directions with a gesture of his hand. Trusting his guidance, Ramanuja Acharya's disciples proceeded along the indicated path. Yet, to their astonishment, they soon realized that their revered guru was not among them. Turning back, they witnessed a sight that left them bewildered and deeply moved.

There, prostrated at the feet of the washerman, lay Ramanuja Acharya, his demeanour, one of utmost humility and reverence. Confused by this unexpected gesture, the washerman stood in disbelief, unsure of how to respond. Hastening to their guru's side, the disciples questioned him with a mix of concern and confusion.

"Why do you, our revered Gurudev, bow before this washerman?" they queried. "You, who are adorned with the titles of Acharya, scholar, and saint, have countless disciples who hold you in the highest regard."

In response, Ramanuja Acharya spoke with humility and sincerity, embodying the values he espoused. "This washerman," he explained, "has guided us on the path to our beloved Lord Venkateswara. Without his assistance, we would have been lost. For his selfless act of kindness, he deserves our worship and gratitude. I am indebted to him."

In witnessing their guru's profound humility and respect for even the humblest of beings, Ramanuja Acharya's disciples gleaned a timeless lesson. His actions spoke volumes, illustrating that true greatness lies not only in words but in deeds and that humility and reverence are virtues to be lived and embodied in every interaction.

Humble people genuinely offer respect to everyone.

Just like the humble student of Parashar Bhatt, if we too approach our teachers with humility, we shall receive their blessings and knowledge. The story of Ramanuja Acharya teaches us that although we may be famous and accomplished, we must be humble, respectful and grateful to every one irrespective of their social position.

Reflect to Realize

Scriptures advise that to cultivate humility, one should continuously chant God's holy names. But how are they interconnected? When we lack humility, we often inflate our own importance, failing to recognize our minuscule existence in the vast cosmic scheme. However, chanting God's name (Krishna, Rama and so on) inspires us to acknowledge our insignificance in comparison to the greatness of the Divine. Through chanting, we come to realize that we are not the center of the universe; rather, it is the Lord who reigns supreme. This realization naturally fosters humility within us. Therefore, let us embrace the practice of chanting God's name and allow our hearts to radiate with humility and grace.

Acknowledgements

Words fall short of expressing my gratitude to Srila Prabhupada, the founder Acharya of the International Society for Krishna Consciousness, who presented the divine literature Bhagavad-Gita with his lucid explanations. It is through the lens of his illuminating purports that I have learnt to understand the depth of the Gita.

I am forever indebted to my beloved guru, His Holiness Radhanath Swami, the founder of Govardhan Ecovillage and an international bestselling author, for enlightening me on the ideal mood of scriptural study and encouraging me with his kind blessings. I learnt profound truths of life by hearing his discourses and by observing his exemplary dealings. I express my earnest gratitude to my dear mentor Gauranga Prabhu, and many other great spiritual teachers and friends who inspired me in various ways in my spiritual journey.

I can't thank Tanay Shah enough for his dedicated efforts in proofreading and editing the manuscript, and improving the quality of the work with his wonderful suggestions. I heartily thank Parth Shah for his thoughtful inputs in refining the manuscript. Without the honest and selfless efforts of these two young brothers, this book wouldn't have taken such a beautiful shape.

My heartfelt gratitude to the Om Books team for making this publication possible for the benefit of all. Finally, I heartily thank all of you, the wonderful readers of this book, for taking part in relishing and reflecting on the profound insights of the Bhagavad Gita.